BASEBALL

◆ ◆ ◆

COLLECTOR'S LIBRARY

BASEBALL

♦ ♦ ♦

Four decades of Sports Illustrated's finest
writing on America's favorite pastime

Copyright ©1993 Time Inc.
All Rights Reserved.

SPORTS ILLUSTRATED is a registered trademark of
Time Inc.

Hardcover ISBN: 0-8487-1147-5
Softcover ISBN: 0-8487-1148-3
Library of Congress Catalog Card Number:
92-85475

Manufactured in the United States of America
First Printing 1993

Published by arrangement with:
Oxmoor House, Inc.
Book Division of Southern Progress Corporation
PO Box 2463
Birmingham, Alabama   35201

SPORTS ILLUSTRATED BASEBALL
was prepared by:
Bishop Books, Inc.
611 Broadway
New York, New York   10012

Cover photograph: Chuck Solomon

The following stories are used by permission:
'A Perfect Day—A Day of Prowess' by Robert Frost,
copyright ©1956, the Estate of Robert Frost;
My Baseball by William Saroyan, permission
granted by the William Saroyan Foundation;
An Old Hand with a Prospect by Pat Jordan;
Yogi by Roy Blount Jr.;
The Curious Case of Sidd Finch by George Plimpton.

Contents

◆ ◆ ◆

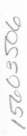

Introduction

♦

When Rod Kanehl, the legendary utility player for the 1962 New York Mets, was asked about a certain play, he would often respond, "You saw it, you write it."

Over the years, *Sports Illustrated* writers have more than met Hot Rod's challenge. Our very first issue, that of August 16, 1954, had Milwaukee Braves third baseman Eddie Mathews on the cover, and since then we have seen a lot of baseball and written it perceptively, movingly, humorously, rhapsodically and just plain well. In fact, I daresay the best writing in SI has usually been about baseball. That's why it's particularly fitting that the first edition of our SI Collector's Library is on the diamond trade. To use a baseball expression, this collection is a natural.

The one problem we had in assembling this book was the overwhelming wealth of material. Which 30 of our countless gems should we include? We necessarily had to leave out many great stories in order to arrive at this lineup, and to the writers of those—you know who you are—we apologize. Now we know how Alvin Dark felt when he managed the 1961 San Francisco Giants: Willie McCovey or Orlando Cepeda at first base?

Despite the limitations of space, we have tried to reflect all of the facets of the game, and our chapters are devoted to the seasons, the men who played, the men who pulled the strings, milestones, the outskirts of baseball and, finally, the game itself. These stories run the gamut from Aaron to Yogi, from ivied Wrigley Field to the retractable SkyDome, from the Cool of Papa Bell to the heat of Nolan Ryan. The writers themselves include such stalwart SI baseball writers as Robert Creamer, William Leggett, Ron Fimrite, Roy Blount Jr., Steve Wulf, Peter Gammons and Steve Rushin, as well as special guest stars Robert Frost, William Saroyan and George Plimpton.

Why does baseball inspire such wonderful writing? Red Smith had a very simple answer to that question. "Today's game," he once wrote, "is always different from yesterday's game." Indeed, though the distance between bases has always been a perfect 90 feet, and home plate has remained 17 inches wide, baseball is forever new: a new season, a new game, a new batter. It is constantly surprising, endlessly fascinating, and alternately enrapturing or heart-breaking.

We trust you'll find those qualities, and more, in this anthology. To employ the brusqueness of Rod Kanehl, We wrote it, you read it. And please enjoy it.

–MARK MULVOY
Managing Editor

SPRING

◆ ◆ ◆

A Time For All Us Children

♦

BY FRANK DEFORD

WHEN FRANK DEFORD VISITED SPRING TRAINING IN 1978, HE
HAD AN OPPORTUNITY TO SEE THE GAME ANEW THROUGH THE
EYES OF HIS SON, CHRISTIAN. FOR THE MOST PART HE FOUND
THE VIEW REASSURING.

"The regulars are on the other diamond," I told him.

He is eight years old, and he nodded, but only blankly, as I
led him in that direction. Then it occurred to me. "You don't
know what *regulars* are, do you?"

"No," he said.

That hurt a little. Regular has always been a classic spring
training term. The regulars have always reported after everyone
else. The regulars have always been given time to get in shape.
Everyone else has to struggle in spring training, bringing their
arms around, scratching to make the squad. The regulars are in
Florida at their leisure.

In the days when I was growing up, a regular anything was
sufficient unto itself. There was no higher compliment than to
be acclaimed a regular guy. A regular fellow! The regular Army
was such a standard that men knew its members simply by initials: "He's R.A."

"Well," I said, "we are going to see Munson, Jackson, Chambliss, Rivers, Nettles—what do you call them?"

"Oh," he said, with instant recognition, "the stars." Verbal inflation is such that regulars have become stars, and mere stars are now superstars. Regular, such a proud, honest word, has been taken from us, appropriated by laxative ads. But never mind. That aside, little else of spring training has been modified. In a world in flux it remains downright immutable; also, pleasant and gracious.

So a couple of weeks ago I took my son, whose name is Christian, with me to visit a few camps. Baseball, more than any other, is a generational game. It speaks best across the years. There are so few things you can show children to illustrate the way it was. But the timelessness of spring training endures and should be shared—can be shared.

Bill Veeck, his good leg crossed over his peg leg, a fresh cigarette in his chops, stared across the sunny fields. To be sure, his White Sox were in sporty new-fangled uniforms, and only a few of them spit tobacco juice upon the greensward. "But it can never change," Veeck allowed. "The same atmosphere must always prevail, because spring training is first and always a time of dreams, of wishful thinking." I introduced my child to Veeck; it is a time for all us children.

Any kid who takes an interest in sports immediately designates a favorite player. The choice is often irrational, as in other affairs of the heart, but it requires neither apology nor explanation. A favorite player holds that estate because ... he's my favorite player.

Bill Russell, the great Boston Celtic center, used to argue with me that children had no business idolizing players; they should reserve such esteem for their own fathers, he said. I contended that it was a healthy sign for a kid to venerate some stranger who excels in the public arena. Somehow this extends a child, providing him with his first attachment to the larger family of the community.

Like most boys, I had a favorite player. His name was Bob Repass, and he played shortstop for the old minor league Baltimore Orioles. While I lived and died with Bob Repass ("Hey, Bob-a-re-pass!" we shouted), I do not recollect that he seriously diminished my devotion to my father. On the other hand, the heritage of Bob Repass still resides with me. He wore No. 6. To this day it is my firm belief that six is my lucky number. Why? Because it is my lucky number, that's why. Because Bob Repass wore it when I was eight years old.

Chris Chambliss of the Yankees is my son's favorite player. Why? Because. And if you are to examine spring training through the eyes of a child, you must begin with the favorite player. Chambliss is an auspicious choice. He is a Navy chaplain's son, guarded, well spoken, a respite from the pinstripe turbulence all about him—"class," in sports parlance.

Chambliss was tired from practice, but he greeted us at his locker and, with time, warmed to the unusual task of addressing a shy child instead of a badgering journalist. "Spring training is always the fun time of the year," he told Christian. "Maybe we should keep that in our minds. Baseball is still a game, whether or not you're making money—and no matter how much. If you're not having fun, you miss the point of everything and it will hurt you, too, because eventually your performance will decline."

It has always been my impression that few top athletes are avid sports fans. These fellows succeed so easily at games—and from such an early age—that they have no need to transfer any of their sporting interest to the performances of others. This is the reason, I think, why so few of them can comprehend the manic affection in which they are held. Chambliss is something of an exception. He collected baseball cards when he was a kid and rooted for his favorites, the Yankees and White Sox.

"Listen, there's nothing wrong with having an idol," he told Christian. "The mistake is trying to copy the idol. That's no good. Try to be as good as your idol, try to be better, but don't ever try to imitate him. That's where an idol is wrong. Be yourself."

Before we spoke to Chambliss, we had watched the regulars (stars) practice. We had come into a piece of luck, because on this morning the regulars worked out on a distant diamond, hidden from all the world by armed security officers and banks of high green Australian pines. Probably on no other day all season would the world champions play together in such glorious seclusion. What might the regulars reveal in their rare privacy?

For the most part, they proceeded with professional dispatch. But there were diversions. Cliff Johnson, the monstrous slugger, was the most engaging presence, ever bantering, razzing his teammates—an amiable figure utterly in contrast to his huge, forbidding form. Otherwise, even a man from outer space would have recognized the two ascendant personalities: 15 and 44, Thurman Munson and Reggie Jackson.

Forty-four had not been on the premises 10 minutes when he informed everyone that he would not be his usual self today because of a sore shoulder. The less his fellows responded with concern to this bulletin, the greater emphasis Jackson placed upon the next recitation. He alone of all the Yankees paid any sort of undue attention to Christian. In a lull, Jackson suddenly bellowed, "We gotta get this — kid outta here so we can talk some —."

The remark was addressed at large, with a smile, and Christian was rather pleased that the great man had paid him notice. Yet, while Jackson's comments were not offensive, they were consistent with the generally insecure posturing that he exhibited. In the end, I came away oddly embarrassed for 44.

By contrast, 15 seemed to move about confidently—tough, almost belligerent. And then came the moment. Jackson was standing behind the third-base side of the batting cage, telling yet another listener about his shoulder. Munson was 15 to 20 feet distant, walking away from Jackson toward the first-base line. I didn't hear precisely what Jackson said to the player next to him, but suddenly Munson tossed a ball in a high hook-shot arc that fell upon the netting in front of where 44 stood. "Some of us gotta work for a living, Jackson," Munson hollered.

The remark was gratuitous—rude, if not mean. Jackson hadn't even said anything to Munson. Jackson looked over at him, more hurt and baffled than angry. Munson smiled back at him, pleased. Christian tugged at me, "Why did he do that?" he whispered, confused.

This July, when I read the latest exclusive about how 15 and 44 really do admire and respect each other deep down inside, I will remember again this uneasy confrontation around the cage ·in Fort Lauderdale early in March. As petty as it was, it was starkly revealing.

Minutes later, Munson was catching batting practice. Johnson was hitting, Jackson was resting against the cage (his shoulder hurt him, he told the fellow next to him). Suddenly, to fill a vacuum, Jackson loudly called Johnson a familiar dirty name. Johnson called Jackson the same thing back. The other Yankees laughed. Christian snickered at the vulgarity, thrilled with being included in this coarse adult male society.

Then Johnson and Jackson started using the dirty word in meaningless ways, topping each other. With every repetition, the players would hoot and holler. Louder and louder, Jackson and Johnson. Saying a dirty word for no reason but to hear it. And the others laughing. Regular knee-slapping. Munson was beside himself. They were just like a bunch of little kids. Whatever these men thought of each other, whatever the travails of last summer, they had been away from one another for five months. They had been with people in suits and ties, with women and children, in the real grown-up world. And now it was spring training, the fun time, and they were children again, teasing and laughing at forbidden words said right out loud. I will remember that in July, too. "If you're not having fun in baseball, you miss the point of everything," Chambliss said.

Of all players, none ended the 1977 season more forlornly than Fred Patek, the shortstop for Kansas City. Because he is only 5' 4", by far the smallest player in baseball, there is a natural disposition to care about Patek, and so it was all the sadder when television showed him slumped alone in his dugout, in pain, beaten, anguished. He had been spiked and then had hit into a double play in the last inning of the last game of the playoffs, when the Royals had the pennant taken from them by the Yankees.

"Oh, it's all behind me now," he said. "The pain was gone after a few hours, the deep involvement after a few days. You have to start again. What hurt was wondering if I had done everything I could possibly do, and when I finally satisfied myself that I had, I was O.K."

It was a hot day in Fort Myers, and Patek sat sweating and shirtless in the clubhouse, sipping a lunch of bean soup and Tab (alternately, that is, though could it really be any worse mixed?). He went on. "The thing that stays with you, though,

14

is wondering whether you ever will get another opportunity to play on a world championship team. Someday, when I'm an old guy, will I look back in dissatisfaction and say, 'Well, I almost made it,' or will I be able to think that for one year I was one of the best players on the best team."

He asked Christian if he would like some Tab or bean soup. Christian declined; he was saving himself for franchise fare on the Tamiami Trail. But then Christian had a question for Patek. When we prepared for this adventure, I urged him to think up some questions he would like to ask, because sportswriters know too much (or think they do) and therefore ask only sportswriter-type questions. I was right. Christian's naive question was to elicit the most original explanation I have ever heard of slumps.

He asked Patek, "Do you ever get scared?"

Patek took a spoonful of bean soup and a swig of Tab and replied, "No, I've never been scared of other players, of spikes, of the ball." Pause. End of answer, it seemed. But then, "I'll tell you something. None of us ever understands why a player goes into a slump. I think that, all of a sudden, the player is scared of the ball. You need a lot of confidence to step up there against a pitcher, and it doesn't take much to shake that. It doesn't necessarily have to have anything to do with baseball. Our lives are too complicated to separate the game from the rest of it. Maybe you're having a fight with your wife. You lose just enough confidence so that you get scared of the ball. You shy away from it. I've found that the best thing you can do in a slump is admit that you're scared."

Patek is the ultimate regular. Because of his size he had more to overcome. To many kids, he is not just a hero but also a patron saint. And that goes not only for short kids, but also for fat kids, skinny kids, nearsighted kids. He has shown what you can do. "When I was a kid your age growing up in Texas," he went on, "I'd listen to all the games I could get on the radio. I was a Yankee fan. I still feel strange about them when we play. But I didn't have an idol. Every player was my hero. I thought baseball players were some kind of superior beings.

"When I finally got a chance to come to a camp, I was so grateful. To get ready, I ran five miles every day. I did sprints, I ran up and down the steps at a stadium. I thought everybody with a chance would do that. I thought, that's the way baseball players are. And then I got there, to the camp, and a lot of these kids with a chance weren't in shape. I couldn't believe these people could actually think they were professional baseball players and be like that. I was really disappointed. I was really hurt ... for baseball."

One of the larger delights of spring training is its informality. In some places, like Sarasota, where the Pale Hose train, it positively resembles a garden party. Bill Veeck sits in the middle, entertaining visitors. Fans wander about, examining unknowns with strange uniform numbers in the 50s, 60s and 70s. Fundamentals are in bloom. On one diamond, the players practice relays from the outfield to third, over and over. On another, pitchers are fielding and firing simulated bunts to third, trying to learn by rote in March how to handle a situation they may not encounter until June or July.

Christian and I drifted over to the batting cages, where sophisticated machines were whirling in hard sliders. The kid was standing there awaiting his turn. His name is Thad Bosley, a tall and thin outfielder with a handsome baby face. Everybody thinks he can be a star, although he might require more seasoning. ("Seasoning" is the best spring training noun. The best verb is "find," always employed by the manager, who declares, "I don't want to go north before we find a centerfielder"—or long reliever, left-handed DH, whatever—as if this desired entity has merely been misplaced over the winter and will be discovered tucked away in the coat closet or the garage.)

Bosley is a thoughtful young man of 21. He had just taught himself to play the piano and was now beginning to master the flute. It was all a matter of regimen, of applying oneself, just like baseball. He referred to spring training, academically, as a time of "refining technique," but he also observed, philosophically, "You are foolish if you don't take the opportunity here to learn a great deal about yourself, too."

Bosley has played professional ball for five years and he has been up to the bigs briefly before, but this spring training is his real start. So, to be perverse, I asked him what he hoped to have at the end. He looked out thoughtfully toward the other players. "When I leave baseball," he said at last, "I would just like people to say, 'Thad Bosley, he could play the game.'"

Oddly enough, Bosley's spring training and the Hall of Fame, the shrine to the players who have completed the most glorious careers—the alpha and omega of major league baseball—share the same tempo and tenor. In between, where the score is kept, it is all big-city hurly-burly, but at Sarasota and the Hall the setting is tranquil. Dust to dust: spring training to Cooperstown, N.Y.

Every year, on a weekday in August, the new members are welcomed into the Hall of Fame in a ceremony conducted on a lawn adjacent to the place. Then, following a hot lunch, two major league clubs play an exhibition at the little stadium down the street. The fans spill over onto the field, which occasions a great many ground-rule doubles. Nobody minds a bit.

Last year the Twins and Phillies played (the Phils blew that one, too), and Ernie Banks led some oldtimers, dead and alive, into the hallowed diamond abbey. A number of the incumbent saints came back, and I directed Christian to them. It is his view that ballplayers are hands that write autographs; only incidentally are those hands attached to a body that plays baseball. "You ought to get that guy," I said, pointing him toward Musial or Feller, Campanella or Marquard. He didn't have the foggiest notion who they were. But what the hell, he didn't know who Ernie Banks was either. "Why are there so many Cub fans here?" he inquired.

The sun came through the clouds just as the mayor of Cooperstown began his welcoming address. There was red, white and blue bunting and the playing of *The Star-Spangled Banner*. On the platform, where the legends-in-their-own-time sat, the only artifacts were a huge plastic baseball and an American flag. That covered just about everything.

The commissioner read off Banks' name, and the place went up for grabs. He was proud and gracious, in a navy blue three-piece suit and a red, white and blue tie, and he concluded his remarks with this thought, "We got the sun out now, we got the fresh air, we got the teams behind us ... so let's play two!"

I remembered all this as I watched the sun cross Thad Bosley's countenance. He had so far to go ... and yet, it was all so much the same. Lay the first two down, Bosley, then take your cuts and run the last one out.

17

The Curious Case
of Sidd Finch

♦

B Y   G E O R G E   P L I M P T O N

WHEN GEORGE PLIMPTON AND THE EDITORS AT SPORTS ILLUS-
TRATED DECIDED TO COOK UP AN APRIL FOOL'S HOAX IN 1985,
NO ONE FORESAW HOW MUCH ATTENTION PLIMPTON'S FANCIFUL
TALE ABOUT A MYSTICAL MET PITCHING PROSPECT WOULD
RECEIVE. MANY READERS WERE DUPED—AMPLE TESTIMONY TO
THE WILD-EYED GULLIBILITY OF SPRING—A FEW WERE OUTRAGED,
BUT BY FAR THE LARGEST NUMBER WERE SIMPLY ENTERTAINED.

The secret cannot be kept much longer. Questions are being asked, and sooner rather than later the New York Mets management will have to produce a statement. It may have started unraveling in St. Petersburg, Fla. two weeks ago, on March 14, to be exact, when Mel Stottlemyre, the Met pitching coach, walked over to the 40-odd Met players doing their morning calisthenics at the Payson Field Complex not far from the Gulf of Mexico, a solitary figure among the pulsation of jumping jacks, and motioned three Mets to step out of the exercise. The three, all good prospects, were John Christensen, a 24-year-old outfielder; Dave Cochrane, a spare but muscular switch-hitting third baseman; and Lenny Dykstra, a swift centerfielder who may be the Mets' leadoff man of the future.

Ordering the three to collect their bats and batting helmets, Stottlemyre led the players to the north end of the complex where a large canvas enclosure had been constructed two weeks before. The rumor was that some irrigation machinery was being installed in an underground pit.

Standing outside the enclosure, Stottlemyre explained what he wanted. "First of all," the coach said, "the club's got kind of a delicate situation here, and it would help if you kept reasonably quiet about it. O.K.?" The three nodded. Stottlemyre said, "We've got a young pitcher we're looking at. We want to see what he'll do with a batter standing in the box. We'll do this alphabetically. John, go on in there, stand at the plate and give the pitcher a target. That's all you have to do."

"Do you want me to take a cut?" Christensen asked.

Stottlemyre produced a dry chuckle. "You can do anything you want."

Christensen pulled aside a canvas flap and found himself inside a rectangular area about 90 feet long and 30 feet wide, open to the sky, with a home plate set in the ground just in front of him, and down at the far end a pitcher's mound, with a small group of Met front-office personnel standing behind it, facing home plate. Christensen recognized Nelson Doubleday, the owner of the Mets, and Frank Cashen, wearing a long-billed fishing cap. He had never seen Doubleday at the training facility before.

Christensen bats righthanded. As he stepped around the plate he nodded to Ronn Reynolds, the stocky reserve catcher who has been with the Met organization since 1980. Reynolds whispered up to him from his crouch, "Kid, you won't believe what you're about to see."

A second flap down by the pitcher's end was drawn open, and a tall, gawky player walked in and stepped up onto the pitcher's mound. He was wearing a small, black fielder's glove on his left hand and was holding a baseball in his right. Christensen had never seen him before. He had blue eyes, Christensen remembers, and a pale, youthful face, with facial muscles that were motionless, like a mask. "You notice it," Christensen explained later, "when a pitcher's jaw *isn't* working on a chaw or a piece of gum." Then to Christensen's astonishment he saw that the pitcher, pawing at the dirt of the mound to get it smoothed out properly and to his liking, was wearing a heavy hiking boot on his right foot.

Christensen has since been persuaded to describe that first confrontation:

"I'm standing in there to give this guy a target, just waving the bat once or twice out over the plate. He starts his windup. He sways way back, like Juan Marichal, this hiking boot comes clomping over—I thought maybe he was wearing it for balance or something—and he suddenly rears upright like a catapult. The ball is launched from an arm completely straight up and *stiff*. Before you can blink, the ball is in the catcher's mitt. You hear it *crack*, and then there's this little bleat from Reynolds."

Christensen said the motion reminded him of the extraordinary contortions that he remembered of Goofy's pitching in one of Walt Disney's cartoon classics.

"I never dreamed a baseball could be thrown that fast. The wrist must have a lot to do with it, and all that leverage. You can hardly see the blur of it as it goes by. As for hitting the thing, frankly, I just don't think it's humanly possible. You could send a blind man up there, and maybe he'd do better hitting at the *sound* of the thing."

Christensen's opinion was echoed by both Cochrane and Dykstra, who followed him into the enclosure. When each had done his stint, he emerged startled and awestruck.

Especially Dykstra. Offering a comparison for SI, he reported that out of curiosity he had once turned up the dials that control the motors of the pitching machine to maximum velocity, thus producing a pitch that went approximately 106 miles per hour. "What I looked at in there," he said, motioning toward the enclosure, "was whistling by another third as fast, I swear."

The phenomenon the three young batters faced, and about whom only Reynolds, Stottlemyre and a few members of the Mets' front office know, is a 28-year-old, somewhat eccentric mystic named Hayden (Sidd) Finch. He may well change the course of baseball history. On St. Patrick's Day, to make sure they were not all victims of a crazy hallucination, the Mets brought in a radar gun to measure the speed of Finch's fastball. The model used was a JUGS Supergun II. It looks like a black space gun with a big snout, weighs about five pounds and is usually pointed at the pitcher from behind the catcher. A glass plate in the back of the gun shows the pitch's velocity—accurate, so the manufacturer claims, to within plus or minus 1 mph. The figure at the top of the gauge is 200 mph. The fastest projectile ever measured by the JUGS (which is named after the oldtimer's descriptive—the "jug-handled" curveball) was a Roscoe Tanner serve that registered 153 mph. The highest number that the JUGS had ever turned for a baseball was 103 mph, which it did, curiously, twice on one day, July 11, at the 1978 All-Star game when both Goose Gossage and Nolan Ryan threw the ball at that speed. On March 17, the gun was handled by Stottlemyre. He heard the pop of the ball in Reynolds's mitt and the little squeak of pain from the catcher. Then the astonishing figure 168 appeared on the glass plate. Stottlemyre remembers whistling in amazement, and then he heard Reynolds say, "Don't tell me, Mel, I don't want to know...."

The Met front office is reluctant to talk about Finch. The fact is, they know very little about him. He has had no baseball career. Most of his life has been spent abroad, except for a short period at Harvard University.

The registrar's office at Harvard will release no information about Finch except that in the spring of 1976 he withdrew from the college in midterm. The alumni records in Harvard's Holyoke Center indicate slightly more. Finch spent his early childhood in an orphanage in Leicester, England and was adopted by a foster parent, the eminent archaeologist Francis Whyte-Finch, who was killed in an airplane crash while on an expedition in the Dhaulagiri mountain area of Nepal. At the time of the tragedy, Finch was in his last year at the Stowe School in Buckingham, England, from which he had been accepted into Harvard. Apparently, though, the boy decided to spend a year in the general area of the plane crash in the Himalayas (the plane was never actually found) before he returned to the West and entered Harvard in 1975, dropping for unknown reasons the "Whyte" from his name. Hayden Finch's picture is not in the freshman yearbook. Nor, of course, did he play baseball at Harvard, having departed before the start of the spring season.

His assigned roommate was Henry W. Peterson, class of 1979, now a stockbroker in New York with Dean Witter, who saw very little of Finch. "He was almost never there," Peterson told SI. "I'd wake up morning after morning and look across at his bed, which had a woven native carpet of some sort on it—I have an idea he told me it was made of yak fur—and never had the sense it had been slept in. Maybe he slept on the floor. Actually, my assumption was that he had a girl in Somerville or something, and stayed out there. He had almost no belongings. A knapsack. A bowl he kept in the corner on the floor. A couple of wool shirts, always very clean, and maybe a pair or so of blue jeans. One pair of hiking boots. I always had the feeling that he was very bright. He had a French horn in an old case. I don't know much about French-horn music, but he played beautifully. Sometimes he'd play it in the bath. He knew any number of languages. He was so adept at them that he'd be talking in English, which he spoke in this distinctive singsong way, quite Oriental, and he'd use a phrase like "pied-à-terre" and without knowing it he'd sail along in French for a while until he'd drop in a German word like "angst" and he'd shift to that language. For any kind of sustained conversation you had to hope he wasn't going to use a foreign buzz word—especially out of the Eastern languages he knew, like Sanskrit—because that was the end of it as far as I was concerned."

When Peterson was asked why he felt Finch had left Harvard, he shrugged his shoulders. "I came back one afternoon, and everything was gone—the little rug, the horn, the staff.... Did I tell you that he had this long kind of shepherd's crook standing in the corner? Actually, there was so little stuff to begin with that it was hard to tell he wasn't there anymore. He left a curious note on the floor. It turned out to be a Zen koan, which is one of those puzzles which cannot be solved by the intellect. It's the famous one about the live goose in the bottle. How do you get the goose out of the bottle without hurting it or breaking the glass? The answer is, 'There, it's out!' I heard from him once, from Egypt. He sent pictures. He was on his way to Tibet to study."

Finch's entry into the world of baseball occurred last July in Old Orchard Beach, Maine, where the Mets' AAA farm club, the Tidewater Tides, was in town playing the Guides. After the first game of the series, Bob Schaefer, the Tides' manager, was strolling back to the hotel. He has very distinct memories of his first meeting with Finch: "I was walking by a park when suddenly this guy—nice-looking kid, clean-shaven, blue jeans, big boots—appears alongside. At first, I think maybe he wants an autograph or to chat about the game, but no, he scrabbles around in a kind of knapsack, gets out a scuffed-up baseball and a small, black leather fielder's mitt that looks like it came out of the back of some Little League kid's closet. This guy says to me, 'I have learned the art of the pitch...' Some odd phrase like that, delivered in a singsong voice, like a chant, kind of what you hear in a Chinese restaurant if there are some Chinese in there.

"I am about to hurry on to the hotel when this kid points out a soda bottle on top of a fence post about the same distance home plate is from the pitcher's rubber. He rears way back, comes around and pops the ball at it. Out there on that fence post the soda bottle *explodes*. It disintegrates like a rifle bullet hit it—just little specks of vaporized glass in a *puff*. Beyond the post I could see the ball bouncing across the grass of the park until it stopped about as far away as I can hit a three-wood on a good day.

"I said, very calm, 'Son, would you mind showing me that again?'

"And he did. He disappeared across the park to find the ball—it had gone so far, he was after it for what seemed 15 minutes. In the meantime I found a tin can from a trash container and set it up for him. He did it again—just kicked that can off the fence like it was hit with a baseball bat. It wasn't the accuracy of the pitch so much that got to me but the *speed*. It was like the tin can got belted as soon as the ball left the guy's fingertips. Instantaneous. I thought to myself, 'My god, that kid's thrown the ball about 150 mph. Nolan Ryan's fastball is a change-up compared to what this kid just threw.

"Well, what happens next is that we sit and talk, this kid and I, out there on the grass of the park. He sits with the big boots tucked under his legs, like one of those yoga guys, and he tells me he's not sure he wants to play big league baseball, but he'd like to give it a try. He's never played before, but he knows the rules, even the infield-fly rule, he tells me with a smile, and he knows he can throw a ball with complete accuracy and enormous velocity. He won't tell me how he's done this except that he 'learned it in the mountains, in a place called Po, in Tibet.' That is where he said he had learned to pitch ... up in the

mountains, flinging rocks and meditating. He told me his name
was Hayden Finch, but he wanted to be called Sidd Finch. I
said that most of the Sids we had in baseball came from Brooklyn. Or the Bronx. He said his Sidd came from 'Siddhartha,'
which means 'Aim Attained' or 'The Perfect Pitch.' That's what
he had learned, how to throw the perfect pitch. O.K. by me, I
told him, and that's what I put on the scouting report, 'Sidd
Finch.' And I mailed it in to the front office."

The reaction in New York once the report arrived was one
of complete disbelief. The assumption was that Schaefer was
either playing a joke on his superiors or was sending in the fig-
ment of a very powerful wish-fulfillment dream. But Schaefer is
one of the most respected men in the Met organization. Over
the past seven years, the clubs he has managed have won six
championships. Dave Johnson, the Met manager, phoned him.
Schaefer verified what he had seen in Old Orchard Beach. He
told Johnson that sometimes he, too, thought he'd had a
dream, but he hoped the Mets would send Finch an invitation
so that, at the very least, his *own* mind would be put at rest.

When a rookie is invited to training camp, he gets a packet
of instructions in late January. The Mets sent off the usual liter-
ature to Finch at the address Schaefer had supplied them. To
their surprise, Finch wrote back with a number of stipulations.
He insisted he would report to the Mets camp in St. Petersburg
only with the understanding that: 1) there were no contractual
commitments; 2) during off-hours he be allowed to keep completely to himself; 3) he did not wish to be involved in any of
the team drills or activities; 4) he would show the Mets his
pitching prowess in privacy; 5) the whole operation in St.
Petersburg was to be kept as secret as possible, with no press or
photographs.

The reason for these requirements—he stated in a letter written (according to a source in the Met front office) in slightly
stilted, formal and very polite terminology—was that he had not
decided whether he actually wanted to play baseball. He wrote
apologetically that there were mental adjustments to be made.
He did not want to raise the Mets' expectations, much less
those of the fans, and then dash them. Therefore it was best if
everything were carried on in secret or, as he put it in his letter, "in camera."

At first, the inclination of the Met front office was to disregard this nonsense out of hand and tell Finch either to apply, himself, through normal procedures or forget it. But the extraordinary statistics in the scouting report and Schaefer's verification of them were too intriguing to ignore. On Feb. 2, Finch's terms were agreed to by letter. Mick McFadyen, the Mets' groundskeeper in St. Petersburg, was ordered to build the canvas enclosure in a far corner of the Payson complex, complete with a pitcher's mound and plate. Reynolds's ordeal was about to start.

Reynolds is a sturdy, hardworking catcher (he has been described as looking like a high school football tackle). He has tried to be close-lipped about Finch, but his experiences inside the canvas enclosure have made it difficult for him to resist answering a few questions. He first heard about Finch from the Mets' general manager. "Mr. Cashen called me into his office one day in early March," Reynolds disclosed. "I was nervous because I thought I'd been traded. He was wearing a blue bow tie. He leaned across the desk and whispered to me that it was very likely I was going to be a part of baseball history. Big doings! The Mets had this rookie coming to camp and I was going to be his special catcher. All very hush-hush.

"Well, I hope nothing like that guy ever comes down the pike again. The first time I see him is inside the canvas coop, out there on the pitcher's mound, a thin kid getting ready to throw, and I'm thinking he'll want to toss a couple of warmup pitches. So I'm standing behind the plate without a mask, chest protector, pads or anything, holding my glove up, sort of half-assed, to give him a target to throw at ... and suddenly I see this windup like a pretzel gone loony, and the next thing, I've been blown two or three feet back, and I'm sitting on the ground with the ball in my glove. My catching hand feels like it's been hit with a sledgehammer."

He was asked: "Does he throw a curveball? A slider? Or a sinker?"

Reynolds grinned and shook his head. "Good questions! Don't ask me."

"Does it make a sound?"

"Yeah, a little *pft, pft-boom!*"

Stottlemyre has been in direct charge of Finch's pitching

regimen. His own playing career ended in the spring of 1975 with a rotator-cuff injury, which makes him especially sensitive to the strain that a pitching motion can put on the arm. Although as close-lipped as the rest of the staff, Stottlemyre does admit that Finch has developed a completely revolutionary pitching style. He told SI: "I don't understand the mechanics of it. Anyone who tries to throw the ball that way should fall flat on his back. But I've seen it. I've seen it a hundred times. It's the most awesome thing that has ever happened in baseball."

Asked what influences might have contributed to Finch's style and speed, Stottlemyre said, "Well, *cricket* may have something to do with it. Finch has taken the power and speed of the running throw of the cricket bowler and has somehow harnessed all that energy to the pitching rubber. The wrist snap off that stiff arm is incredible. I haven't talked to him but once or twice. I asked him if he ever thought of snapping the *arm*, like baseball pitchers, rather than the wrist: It would increase the velocity.

"He replied, very polite, you know, with a little bob of the head: 'I undertake as a rule of training to refrain from injury to living things.'

"He's right, of course. It's Ronn Reynolds I feel sorry for. Every time that ball comes in, first you hear this *smack* sound of the ball driving into the pocket of the mitt, and then you hear this little gasp, this *ai yee!*—the catcher, poor guy, his whole body shakin' like an angina's hit it. It's the most piteous thing I've ever heard, short of a trapped rabbit."

Hayden (Sidd) Finch arrived in St. Petersburg on Feb. 7. Most of the rookies and minor-leaguers stay at the Edgewater Beach Inn. Assuming that Finch would check in with the rest of the early arrivals, the Mets were surprised when he telephoned and announced that he had leased a room in a small boarding-house just off Florida Avenue near a body of water on the bay side called Big Bayou. Because his private pitching compound had been constructed across the city and Finch does not drive, the Mets assigned him a driver, a young Tampa Bay resident, Eliot Posner, who picks him up in the morning and returns him to Florida Avenue or, more often, to a beach on the Gulf where, Posner reports, Finch, still in his baseball outfit and carrying his decrepit glove, walks down to the water's edge and, motionless, stares out at the windsurfers. Inevitably, he dismisses

Posner and gets back to his boardinghouse on his own.

The Met management has found out very little about his life in St. Petersburg. Mrs. Roy Butterfield, his landlady, reports (as one might expect) that "he lives very simply. Sometimes he comes in the front door, sometimes the back. Sometimes I'm not even sure he spends the night. I think he sleeps on the floor—his bed is always neat as a pin. He has his own rug, a small little thing. I never have had a boarder who brought his own rug. He has a soup bowl. Not *much*, is what I say. Of course, he plays the French horn. He plays it very beautifully and, thank goodness, softly. The notes fill the house. Sometimes I think the notes are coming out of my television set."

Probably the member of the Met staff who has gotten the closest to Finch is Posner. When Posner returns to the Payson complex, inevitably someone rushes out from the Mets' offices asking, "Did he say anything? What did he say?"

Posner takes out a notebook.

"Today he said, 'When your mind is empty like a canyon you will know the power of the Way.'"

"Anything else?"

"No."

While somewhat taxed by Finch's obvious eccentricities, and with the exception of the obvious burden on the catchers, the Mets, it seems, have an extraordinary property in their camp. But the problem is that no one is sure if Finch really wants to play. He has yet to make up his mind; his only appearances are in the canvas enclosure. Reynolds moans in despair when he is told Finch has arrived. Sometimes his ordeal is short-lived. After Finch nods politely at Reynolds and calls down *"Namas-te!"* (which means "greetings" is Sanskrit), he throws only four or five of the terrifying pitches before, with a gentle smile, he announces *"Namas-te!"* (it also means "farewell") and gets into the car to be driven away.

One curious manifestation of Finch's reluctance to commit himself entirely to baseball has been his refusal to wear a complete baseball uniform. Because he changes in his rooming house, no one is quite sure what he will be wearing when he steps through the canvas flap into the enclosure. One afternoon he turned up sporting a tie hanging down over the logo on his jersey, and occasionally—as Christensen noticed—he wears a hiking boot on his right foot. Always, he wears his baseball cap back to front—the conjecture among the Met officials is that this sartorial behavior is an indication of his ambivalence about baseball.

In hopes of understanding more about him, in early March the Mets called in a specialist in Eastern religions. Dr. Timothy Burns, the author of, among other treatises, *Satori, or Four Years in a Tibetan Lamasery*. Not allowed to speak personally with Finch for fear of "spooking him," Burns was able only to speculate about the Mets' newest player.

According to sources from within the Met organization, Burns told a meeting of the club's top brass that the strange ballplayer in their midst was very likely a *trapas*, or aspirant monk.

A groan is said to have gone up from Nelson Doubleday. Burns said that Finch was almost surely a disciple of Tibet's great poet-saint Lama Milaraspa, who was born in the 11th century and died in the shadow of Mount Everest. Burns told them that Milaraspa was a great yogi who could manifest an astonishing phenomenon: He could produce "internal heat," which allowed him to survive snowstorms and intense cold, wearing only a thin robe of white cotton. Finch does something similar—an apparent deflection of the huge forces of the universe into throwing a baseball with bewildering accuracy and speed through the process of *siddhi*, namely the yogic mastery of mind-body. He mentioned that *The Book of Changes*, the *I Ching*, suggests that all acts (even throwing a baseball) are connected with the highest spiritual yearnings. Utilizing the Tantric principle of body and mind, Finch has decided to pitch baseballs—at least for a while.

The Mets pressed Burns. Was there any chance that Finch would come to his senses and *commit* himself to baseball?

"There's a chance," Burns told them. "You will remember that the Buddha himself, after what is called the Great Renunciation, finally realized that even in the most severe austerities— though he conquered lust and fear and acquired a great deal of self-knowledge—truth itself could not necessarily be found. So after fasting for six years he decided to eat again."

Reached by SI at the University of Maryland, where he was lecturing last week, Burns was less sanguine. "The biggest problem Finch has with baseball," he said over the phone, "is that *nirvana*, which is the state all Buddhists wish to reach, means literally 'the blowing out'—specifically the purifying of oneself of greed, hatred and delusion. Baseball," Burns went on, "is symbolized to a remarkable degree by those very three aspects: *greed* (huge money contracts, stealing second base, robbing a guy of a base hit, charging for a seat behind an iron pillar, etc.), *hatred* (players despising management, pitchers hating hitters, the Cubs detesting the Mets, etc.) and *delusion* (the slider, the pitchout, the hidden-ball trick and so forth). So you can see why it is not easy for Finch to give himself up to a way of life so opposite to what he has been led to cherish."

Burns is more puzzled by Finch's absorption with the French horn. He suspects that in Tibet Finch may have learned to play the *rkang-gling*, a Tibetan horn made of human thighbones, or perhaps even the Tibetan long trumpet, the *dung-chen*, whose sonorous bellowing in those vast Himalayan defiles is somewhat echoed in the lower registers of the French horn.

The Met inner circle believes that Finch's problem may be that he cannot decide between baseball and a career as a horn player. In early March the club contacted Bob Johnson, who plays the horn and is the artistic director of the distinguished New York Philomusica ensemble, and asked him to come to St. Petersburg. Johnson was asked to make a clandestine assessment of Finch's ability as a horn player and, even more important, to make contact with him. The idea was that, while praising him for the quality of his horn playing, Johnson should try to persuade him that the lot of a French-horn player (even a very fine one) was not an especially gainful one. Perhaps *that* would tip the scales in favor of baseball.

Johnson came down to St. Petersburg and hung around Florida Avenue for a week. He reported later to SI: "I was being paid for it, so it wasn't bad. I spent a lot of time looking up, so I'd get a nice suntan. Every once in a while I saw Finch coming in and out of the rooming house, dressed to play baseball and carrying a funny-looking black glove. Then one night I heard the French horn. He was playing it in his room. I have heard many great horn players in my career—Bruno Jaenicke, who played for Toscanini; Dennis Brain, the great British virtuoso; Anton Horner of the Philadelphia Orchestra—and I would say Finch was on a par with them. He was playing Benjamin Britten's *Serenade*, for tenor horn and strings—a haunting, tender

29

piece that provides great space for the player—when suddenly he produced a big, evocative *bwong* sound that seemed to shiver the leaves of the trees. Then he shifted to the rondo theme from the trio for violin, piano and horn by Brahms—just sensational. It may have had something to do with the Florida evening and a mild wind coming in over Big Bayou and tree frogs, but it was *remarkable*. I told this to the Mets, and they immediately sent me home—presuming, I guess, that I was going to hire the guy. That's not so farfetched. He can play for the Philomusica anytime."

Meanwhile, the Mets are trying other ways to get Finch into a more positive frame of mind about baseball. Inquiries among American lamaseries (there are more than 100 Buddhist societies in the U.S.) have been quietly initiated in the hope of finding monks or priests who are serious baseball fans and who might persuade Finch that the two religions (Buddhism and baseball) are compatible. One plan is to get him into a movie theater to see *The Natural*, the mystical film about baseball, starring Robert Redford. Another film suggested is the baseball classic *It Happens Every Spring*, starring Ray Milland as a chemist who, by chance, discovers a compound that avoids wood; when applied to a baseball in the film, it makes Milland as effective a pitcher as Finch is in real life.

Conversations with Finch himself have apparently been exercises in futility. All conventional inducements—huge contracts, advertising tie-ins, the banquet circuit, ticker-tape parades, having his picture on a Topps bubble-gum card, chatting on *Kiner's Korner* (the Mets' postgame TV show) and so forth—mean little to him. As do the perks ("You are very kind to offer me a Suzuki motorcycle, but I cannot drive"). He has very politely declined whatever overtures the Mets have offered. The struggle is an absolutely internal one. He will resolve it. Last week he announced that he would let the management know what he was going to do on or around April 1.

Met manager Davey Johnson has seen Finch throw about half a dozen pitches. He was impressed ("If he didn't have this great control, he'd be like the Terminator out there. Hell, that fastball, if off-target on the inside, would carry a batter's kneecap back into the catcher's mitt"), but he is leaving the situation to the front office. "I can handle the pitching rotation; let them

handle the monk." He has had one meeting with Finch. "I was
going to ask him if we could at least give him a decent fielder's
mitt. I asked him why he was so attached to the piece of rag
he was using. 'It is,' the guy told me, 'the only one I have.'
Actually, I don't see why he needs a better one. All he will
ever need it for is to catch the ball for the next pitch. So then I
said to him, 'There's only one thing I can offer you, Finch, and
that's a fair shake.' "

According to Jay Horwitz, the Mets' public-relations man,
Finch smiled at the offer of the fair shake and nodded his head
politely—perhaps because it was the only nonmaterial offer
made. It did not encroach on Finch's ideas about the renunciation of worldly goods. It was an ingenious, if perhaps uninten-
tional, move on the manager's part.

Nelson Doubleday is especially hopeful about Finch's ultimate
decision. "I think we'll bring him around," he said a few days
ago. "After all, the guy's not a nut, he's a Harvard man."

In the meantime, the Mets can only wait. Finch periodically
turns up at the enclosure. Reynolds is summoned. There are no
drills. Sometimes Finch throws for five minutes, instantly at top
speed, often for half an hour. Then he leaves. Security around
the enclosure has been tight. Since Finch has not signed with
the Mets, he is technically a free agent and a potential find for
another club. The curious, even Met players, are politely
shooed away from the Payson Field enclosure. So far Finch's
only association with Met players (other than Reynolds) has
been the brief confrontation with Christensen, Cochrane and
Dykstra when the front office nervously decided to test his
control with a batter standing in the box. If he decides to play
baseball, he will leave his private world of the canvas enclosure
and join manager Johnson and the rest of the squad. For the
first time Gary Carter, the Mets' regular catcher, will face the
smoke of the Finch pitch, and the other pitchers will stand
around and gawk. The press will have a field day ("How do
you spell Siddhartha? How do you grip the ball? How do you
keep your balance on the mound?"). The Mets will try to protect him from the glare and help him through the most traumatic of culture shocks, praying that in the process he will not
revert and one day disappear.

Actually, the presence of Hayden (Sidd) Finch in the Mets'

training camp raises a number of interesting questions. Suppose the Mets (and Finch himself) can assuage and resolve his mental reservations about playing baseball; suppose he is signed to a contract (one wonders what an ascetic whose major possessions are a bowl, a small rug, a long stick and a French horn might demand); and suppose he comes to New York's Shea Stadium to open the season against the St. Louis Cardinals on April 9. It does not matter that he has never taken a fielding drill with his teammates. Presumably he will mow down the opposition in a perfect game. Perhaps Willie McGee will get a foul tip. Suppose Johnson discovers that the extraordinary symbiotic relationship of mind and matter is indefatigable—that Finch can pitch day after day at this blinding, unhittable speed. What will happen to Dwight Gooden? Will Carter and the backup catchers last the season? What will it do to major league baseball as it is known today?

Peter Ueberroth, baseball's new commissioner, was contacted by SI in his New York office. He was asked if he had heard anything about the Mets' new phenomenon.

No, he had not. He had heard some *rumors* about the Mets' camp this spring, but nothing specific.

Did the name Hayden (Sidd) Finch mean anything to him?

Nope.

The commissioner was told that the Mets had a kid who could throw the ball over 150 mph. Unhittable.

Ueberroth took a minute before he asked, "Roll that by me again?"

He was told in as much detail as could be provided about what was going on within the canvas enclosure of the Payson compound. It was possible that an absolute superpitcher was coming into baseball—so remarkable that the delicate balance between pitcher and batter could be turned into disarray. What was baseball going to do about it?

"Well, before any decisions, I'll tell you something," the commissioner finally said, echoing what may very well be a nationwide sentiment this coming season. "I'll have to see it to believe it!"

SUMMER

...

Casey Puts It
On Ice

♦

BY   ROBERT   CREAMER

IN JULY 1956, WHEN BOB CREAMER CHECKED IN ON THE NEW
YORK YANKEES, HE FOUND THEM AT THE HEIGHT OF THEIR
POWERS, WELL ON THEIR WAY TO WINNING THEIR SIXTH WORLD
CHAMPIONSHIP AND SEVENTH PENNANT IN EIGHT YEARS.

Sometimes pennants are not won in July. Sometimes baseball
teams labor and sweat on into late September, and muscles tire
and stomachs hurt and the shadows grow long and cold over
the grandstand before *the* game is won, *the* game that means it's
all over, it's in the bag, the pennant's on ice.

The New York Yankees, however, won this year's American
League pennant last week under a hot sun and a sultry sky in
midsummer. There still remained almost a half season of play
for the Yankees and for their only serious challengers, and you
could hear the hoary warnings that the old ball game isn't over
till the last out in the ninth, and, "I'll believe they've won the
pennant the day they clinch it, and not before." But do not be
misled. The false modesty of the victors and the false hopes of
the vanquished won't alter a thing. Barring a miracle (and who
ever heard of 1951?) the pennant race is over, no sudden losing
streak or winning splurge from now through that last Sunday in

34

September is going to change the American League entry in the 1956 World Series.

It may seem dull, a little later on, to have the pennant race over so early, but now, in July, it's vastly exciting. There are few teams in the history of major league competition who won a pennant more dramatically than this year's Yankees. Consider.

In June everyone was saying that New York was running away with first place. As the Yankees headed west on June 15 they had a drab two weeks behind them—five victories and seven defeats—but they had lost only a game and a half of their lead and they were still five full games in front. In the west they swept three straight games from Cleveland and three straight from Detroit. They bowled into Chicago in style, like an American Army Corps in World War II moving into an undefended occupied town, all-conquering, cheerful, supremely confident.

But in Chicago were the White Sox, who refused to believe the Yankees had the pennant sewed up. They had been playing good ball. Their pitchers had been doing beautifully all season, and their hitters had shrugged off a disabling early slump. Now, with the addition of Pitcher Jim Wilson and Outfielder-First Baseman Dave Philley, the Sox knew they were a good, solid ball club. Other teams might grow pale when the Yankees came to town, but the White Sox waited in confident ambush in Comiskey Park.

They beat the Yankees four straight times. They walloped them Friday and Saturday and twice Sunday and turned the pennant race inside out in the most stunning upheaval of the season. They moved to within one game and only four small percentage points of first place, and they dragged third-place Cleveland to within 4½ games and fourth-place Boston to 7½. Baseball fans everywhere were thrilled: here was a brand-new pennant race. Excitement spread with electric speed through the baseball-loving element in the population. It's a farfetched picture, admittedly, but it was something like the reaction to the Poznan riots in Poland: someone had rebelled against the galling Yankee yoke, and perhaps now a new day was at hand.

But, like Poznan, it wasn't. It was magnificent, this Chicago uprising, but it was only a gesture. And it backfired. It turned the cheerful, confident Yankees into a grim, ruthless, retaliatory band of marauders. A sour Yogi Berra looked up at a reporter after the fourth straight Chicago triumph and grunted, "So what? They ain't gonna win the pennant."

The Yankees, agreeing to a man with Berra, went looking for every victory they could find. They leveled Kansas City three nights running; they shelled Washington three times in four games; they raced through Baltimore; they steam-rollered Boston twice in three games; they swung back to Washington and mopped up the Senators again, three straight times. They rested three days at All-Star time, and then they returned to the wars.

The Cleveland Indians, who had won 16 of the 20 games they played after the Yankees had beaten them three straight that time in mid-June, came into Yankee Stadium still mired in third place but still hoping, still fighting. They were to be followed into the stadium by the Chicago White Sox, who, too, were still hoping, still fighting. Successive sweeps in New York by the Indians and the White Sox could snarl the race beautifully, but it turned out the sweeping was to be done by the Stengel broom.

The Yankees spotted the Indians a 3–1 lead on the first day and then battered their way back to win 9–5.

The next night in Yankee Stadium, before the second Cleveland-New York game, Broadcaster Red Barber asked a Cleveland sportswriter about the Indians' chances. "They're all through," the writer said flatly. "They haven't a chance. All they'll do from here on in is play out the schedule."

That night the Indians lost again, 10–0.

On Saturday the Indians tried a third time. They took a 3–0 lead, lost it, fell behind by a run and then tied the score in the ninth. But in the 10th, with the bases loaded, the Yankees' Billy Martin hit a sharp single into left for the winning run. On the scoreboard in center field the White Sox-Red Sox final score was outlined in lights: Boston had four runs, eight hits, one error; Chicago had no hits, no runs, no errors. It was more than a beating the veteran Mel Parnell had given them. The White Sox were the first club to be at the wrong end of a no-hitter at Fenway Park in 30 years. It was Chicago's sixth successive defeat. Coming at this particular point, it spelled humiliation and heralded the crash of pennant hopes.

The next day, Sunday, was the last gasp. Cleveland limped out of Yankee Stadium and up to Fenway Park, only to split two games with the Red Sox, causing both teams to lose ground. In New York the White Sox met the Yankees in a double-header. Chicago lost the first game 2–1. In the second they opened up a 3–0 lead, but the Yankees, as always, scrambled back to tie it up. The White Sox held on, fought back, even as the Indians had a day earlier, and in the top of the 10th went ahead 5–4. But in the last of the 10th Jim Wilson walked Mickey Mantle, walked Yogi Berra and, after a sacrifice, walked Joe Collins, to load the bases. He struck out Andy Carey, but then, off the endless Yankee bench, came Hank Bauer to pinch-hit. It was a strange situation, because no one seemed to doubt the outcome. If Wilson managed to get Bauer out and save the game it would be an upset, pure and simple.

He didn't. Bauer chopped a grounder into left, two runs scored, the Yankees won the game and the double-header, and for all practical purposes the pennant race was over.

The Yankees, after losing those four games in Chicago three weeks earlier, had won 17 of their next 19 games. They had extended their lead from four percentage points to 124, and their lead in games from a puny one to an overwhelming 10½.

What is the magic that explains this Yankee surge? Is it simply that the American League is so poorly stocked with player talent that one well-balanced club can tear it apart? And that in the National League the Yankees would be just another team?

One of the Yankee-chasing American League managers laughed at that. "I don't really know the National League at all," he said, "but I can tell you this. If the Yankees were in it, they'd be in first place there too."

The reason? "Talent!" the American Leaguer yelled. "The players. They got 'em and they get 'em. Stengel's got players on his bench who'd make a better team than some of the teams we have in the majors right now. How do they get them? They have good people and they work hard. And they have prestige: that Yankee name, those World Series' checks. You take a boy has a chance to sign—for the same deal—with two or three different clubs and one of them's the Yankees. Who's he going to sign with? Us? You're darn right he isn't! It's the Yankees! Damn, no wonder they're so tough to beat."

Specifically, the Yankees have such as Mickey Mantle and Yogi Berra. There was a story around last week that other Yankee players were beginning to resent the publicity that Mantle has attracted this year. A veteran Yankee player hooted. "Listen," he said. "He's DiMaggio. He's the big man. Everybody on this club roots for him. Mantle and Berra, they're making money for all of us."

Specifically, the Yankees have surprisingly competent pitching, not so good perhaps as Cleveland's historic staff, but better, the knowing say, than Chicago's and probably better than Boston's. The magic here, again, is depth.

Specifically, the Yankees have a museum collection of superb fielding infielders: Gil McDougald, Andy Carey, Billy Martin, Jerry Coleman, Phil Rizzuto and Billy Hunter. Specifically, the Yankees have, after Mantle and Berra and the infielders, an in-the-game-and-out squad of fine power hitters who are neither regulars nor substitutes: Elston Howard, Hank Bauer, Irv Noren, Bob Cerv, Norm Siebern, Joe Collins, Bill Skowron. They, more than anything else, are the hallmark of Casey Stengel's Yankees, the backbone of his platoon system.

Stengel has revolutionized baseball since he took over as manager of the Yankees in 1949 by using the players on his bench not as replacements in an emergency but as extra troops to be held in reserve in each game until the proper time comes to commit them. Most of the other clubs in major league baseball have begun to recognize the advantages of this system, but many of them still can't seem to get shed of the old idea that if you have two good third basemen (or whatever) you keep one and trade the other for a pitcher. Stengel hangs on to both. If he gets a third he may put *him* into a trade for the pitcher, but, on the other hand, he may hang on to all three.

The result is that Stengel right now has 13 topflight major league infielders and outfielders to juggle in and out around Mantle and Berra. Each feels he is good enough to be a rightful regular, and when he finds himself in the lineup, he plays his skillful, daring, opportunistic heart out to prove his real worth to Stengel. Casey observes the man's abilities and how he utilizes them, makes a few mental notes and several thousand oral ones. Then, when he wants a player who can hit a ground ball to the right side with one out and a man on third base, he knows whether to use, say, Noren or Collins against a pitcher who tends to keep the ball low, say, or high.

Last week's pennant-cinching games were sharp evidence of this. Martin, Collins and Noren were among those on the bench in Saturday's game against Cleveland. In the eighth inning, after Bob Lemon had relieved Herb Score, the Yankees received an unexpected break when Al Rosen errored on what should have been a third-out grounder. Stengel, when he finds his foot in the door, wastes no time in exploiting his advantage. He threw in Collins and Noren to bat for Bauer and Carey. Both worked bases on balls on the 3 and 2 count, to force across the run that gave the Yankees the lead. The Indians tied the score in the ninth, but Martin, who went into the game as a fielding replacement for Carey, won it in the 10th. The next day, in the first game of the double-header with Chicago, Carey and Bauer were back in the lineup, and Carey drove in the winning runs. In the second game Bauer was on the bench again, but in the 10th inning, called on to pinch-hit, he delivered the game-winning hit.

"Depth!" American Leaguers insist whenever they discuss the Yankees. "Depth. Bench strength. Reserves."

Whatever it's called, the magic in it has wrapped up for Casey Stengel his seventh pennant in eight seasons, even though the victory-greedy old fellow will have to wait till September to take formal possession.

A Wild Finale—
And It's Boston!

♦

B Y   W I L L I A M   L E G G E T T

ALL THROUGH AUGUST AND SEPTEMBER THEY BATTLED IN THE
AMERICAN LEAGUE AND IT WASN'T UNTIL THE SEASON'S FINAL
DAY THAT THE BOSTON RED SOX, LED BY THE MIRACULOUS PLAY
OF TRIPLE-CROWN WINNER CARL YASTRZEMSKI, EMERGED TRI-
UMPHANT. IN OCTOBER, WHEN THE SMOKE HAD CLEARED, BILL
LEGGETT LOOKED BACK AT ONE OF HISTORY'S MOST DRAMATIC
PENNANT RACES.

Cal Ermer, the gray-haired manager of the Minnesota Twins,
stood behind the batting cage at Boston's Fenway Park early
last Sunday afternoon, watching his team take batting practice
in preparation for what turned out to be the vital game of the
longest, daffiest and most desperate American League pennant
race in history. "In bullfighting," Ermer said, "I understand that
the moment of truth usually comes sometime around 4 in the
afternoon. I have a feeling that it will come a lot earlier today."
    Not really. It was 3:21 p.m. when the truth came out about
Ermer's Twins. In the ensuing 24 minutes the city of Boston
went wild as the Red Sox scored five runs to beat Minnesota
5–3 to win their first pennant since 1946. Of course, in keeping
with the nature of the race, Boston's victory could not be fully

savored until nearly four hours later when Bobby Knoop of the California Angels picked up a ground ball 700 miles west at Tiger Stadium in Detroit and turned it into a double play. That ended the game there and knocked the Tigers, who up to then had a chance to tie, into oblivion.

In retrospect, this season's American League race seemed destined from the start to be won by the Red Sox, who now take their place with the 1914 Braves and the 1951 Giants as the most improbable pennant winners in baseball's long and wonderfully colored history. Since July, people in New England—and almost everywhere else in the U.S., except Detroit, Chicago and Minnesota—had been talking about the Red Sox and their chances of winning as "the impossible dream." They kept dying in August and September—do you remember that they lost five out of seven games to Baltimore as summer turned to fall two weeks ago?—and, like a fighter who is either punch-drunk or gallant, kept getting up and swinging. Before those last two decisive games against Minnesota, a wire was pinned upon a bulletin board hung in Boston's clubhouse. It read: "We ask nothing, but our hopes are high. Godspeed." And when the Red Sox trotted out on the field for their final game of the season, the swollen crowd of 35,770 in Fenway Park (2,246 beyond official capacity) stood and cheered. The crowd in Boston wanted the Red Sox to win, sure, but the salute the team received was more a thank-you for bringing back the thrill of winning baseball to one of the great baseball cities.

The man who had made the Red Sox win all season long was Carl Yastrzemski, the brown-eyed, 28-year-old left fielder who in the last two dramatic games against the Twins did more than it seems possible for one man to do in a baseball game. Yastrzemski made breathtaking running catches and at least one utterly extraordinary throw, and he hit—oh, how he hit! Eight times he came to the plate in the two games, and seven times he got hits; two infield hits, a double, three solid singles and a dramatic three-run homer.

The most important thing that Yastrzemski did, however, was take charge of a pennant race that during the final two weeks of the season threatened to disintegrate into farce. Just because four teams are locked in a fight for a championship does not mean that the race is automatically majestic—not if the teams involved play poor baseball, fumble away opportunity after opportunity and lose as many games as they win. That was what was happening, except for Yastrzemski.

The White Sox, the scramblers, had found themselves in the perfect spot, half a game out, five games to play against Kansas City and Washington, their nonpareil pitching staff rested and ready. But the White Sox were shut out three times in these last five games, lost them all and fell clammily out of the race.

The Tigers kept lurching into contention and then, as though aghast at finding themselves in the spotlight, scurrying into shadow. They beat the White Sox twice, once with a spellbinding seven-run rally in the ninth, then dropped a doubleheader the next day. They rallied to win four straight and the lead, then bowed 5–0 to the Washington Senators and blew two seemingly sure wins to Boston. They rallied again to win three straight, then threw away a 4–2 lead to Washington in the ninth. On the final weekend of the season, confronted with successive doubleheaders, they won the big first game each day and then died in the second.

Minnesota held onto first place, either in whole or in part, from September 2 to the end of the season, except for two days in midmonth and on the fateful 1st of October. The Twins, though they did not know it for certain at the time, abandoned the pennant in Chicago when they were beaten once, twice, three times by the White Sox, the middle game falling through their hands like quicksilver when the Sox scored four times in the last of the ninth to win 5–4.

Yet by last Saturday afternoon Boston's chances for a pennant required a sweep of the Twins, and Minnesota had its two best pitchers, Jim Kaat and Dean Chance, ready to pitch. The Twins had always played well in Fenway Park; in their pennant-winning year, 1965, they had beaten the Red Sox in 17 of 18 games and had won eight of nine played in Fenway.

But bad luck and bad morale dogged this year's Twins. Not long before the crucial meeting with the Red Sox, the team divided even further on the question of who would get World Series shares and why. Many veteran members of the Twins felt that Sam Mele, the deposed manager, should be cut in. He had handled the club from late 1962 until Owner Cal Griffith relieved him of his post in early June this year and replaced him with Ermer. The players argued violently, and the wishes of the veterans were rejected. As one of them said, "I was never so ashamed of anything in my life. And we had enough problems even before that came up."

When they went against Boston in the showdown series last weekend, the Twins played their absolute worst. An elbow injury forced Minnesota's best September pitcher, Jim Kaat, out of the first game in the third inning. But even so, the Red Sox seemed always to be the attacking team. In the Saturday game Minnesota carried a 1–0 lead into the fifth inning, and then Boston got two runs. The Twins tied the game in the sixth, but when Ron Kline came on in relief George Scott launched his first pitch into the center-field stands for a homer that put the Sox ahead. In the seventh Boston put two runners on base, one on a grievous error by Shortstop Zoilo Versalles, and Yastrzemski came to bat. Carl instantly homered into the bullpen, and one Vice-President, six governors, two Senators and all of Boston stood up and cheered, though the Vice-President was just being polite.

That homer eventually proved to be the hit that won Yastrzemski baseball's Triple Crown and Boston the pennant. When Yastrzemski went out to left field the next inning, with the crowd still cheering, he scraped for a moment at the grass with his spikes and hollered over his shoulder to the man in the left-field scoreboard to ask about the progress of the Detroit-California game. Then, when the crowd finally quieted down he looked up into the stands and raised his cap just slightly. Later he said, "I knew the dream was no longer impossible."

In Sunday's game Yastrzemski had trouble picking up a base hit by Harmon Killebrew, and it went through his legs for an error that let Minnesota go ahead 2–0. "I felt awful," he said afterward, "like I goofed the whole world up." But in the sixth inning Yaz's hit was the key one that rocketed Boston to the championship. With the bases loaded, the Red Sox losing 2–0, he deftly pounded a single to center to tie the game. That was the inning that Pitcher Jim Lonborg launched with a startling safe bunt, and when it was over Boston led 5-2. But Yastrzemski was not through. With Minnesota threatening in the seventh inning, one run in, Killebrew chugging to third and Bob Allison digging for second with the tying run after dumping a double, seemingly, into the left-field corner, Yastrzemski came up with the ball, threw strongly and perfectly to second and cut Allison down. "I looked for an exacting second," Yastrzemski said later. And then he threw, to the right base at the right time.

When the game was over Yastrzemski was pounded on the back by Tom Yawkey, who has been the owner of the Red Sox for more than three decades. Later, after Detroit had lost to California, Yawkey walked over to Yastrzemski and said, "Carl, I don't know what to say to thank you. In my 33 years of baseball nothing has ever had me more excited." Yastrzemski looked at Yawkey and said, "Do we finally get a chance to drink the champagne?"

Dick Williams, the 38-year-old manager, raised a glass and said to Yawkey, "Here's to the pennant." Yawkey said, "I haven't had a drink in four years, but I'll drink to that." The impossible dream had come true.

On the Lam with the Three Rivers Gang

♦

BY   ROY   BLOUNT   JR.

IN THE SUMMER OF 1971 ROY BLOUNT PAID A CALL ON A LOOSE
CONFEDERATION OF BALLPLAYERS CALLED THE PITTSBURGH
PIRATES. IN THE MONTHS THAT FOLLOWED, THEY WOULD WIN
THE NATIONAL LEAGUE EAST, DEFEAT THE SAN FRANCISCO
GIANTS IN THE NL PLAYOFFS AND FINALLY OVERCOME THE BALTI-
MORE ORIOLES IN A STIRRING SEVEN-GAME WORLD SERIES.

In their locker room in picturesque new Three Rivers (that is,
the Allegheny, the Ohio and the Monongahela) Stadium, the
Pittsburgh Pirates were enjoying themselves. Manny Sanguillen,
the hottest-hitting long-armed Panamanian catcher in baseball,
yelled at Dave Giusti, perhaps the best reliever in baseball,
"Hey, you too old to throw a fassball inside," and then he
roared with laughter.

Dock Ellis, the hottest-talking, hottest winning pitcher in the
National League, explained that his one-year-old daughter's
name, Shangaleza Talwanga, meant "everything black is beautiful" in Swahili. Manager Danny Murtaugh, who looks like a
cross between a bulldog and Barry Fitzgerald, sat in his office
rocking chair, quietly rocking and chewing. Reserve Infielder
Jose Pagan walked up to All-Star Leftfielder Willie Stargell and

hit him five or six good solid blows to the chest.

"O.K.," Pagan announced. "I'm ready. I feel good."

Stargell looked down on his little teammate and agreed. "You do," he said. And not just Pagan. Almost all the Pirates were feeling good and going good. As they loosened up last week for the Dodgers, the Bucs had grounds for team euphoria. They had won 11 in a row and were leading the National League East by 11½ games, with a winning percentage of .667, best in the majors.

They were at home at Three Rivers (that is, at the Mononga-hela, the Allegheny and the Ohio) where their record for the year was a cozy 36–13. They were batting .284—14 points high-er than the fabled 1970 Big Red Machine had—and they were leading both leagues in home runs.

Their ace pitcher, Ellis (the only Pirate who wears a fuzzy—or as he prefers to call it, a "velvetized"—batting helmet) was riding a personal winning streak of 13.

Their batting bulwark, Stargell (the only Pirate whose num-ber is marked on everything—even his shower shoes—in a Roman numeral) was leading baseball with 31 home runs and 88 RBIs, and their bullpen bulwark, Giusti, had a similarly stag-gering total of 19 saves.

Their Hall of Fame rightfielder, Roberto Clemente, was hit-ting around .340, as usual, and a couple of weeks before in Houston he had made a catch about which Astro Manager Harry Walker declared, "He took it full flight and hit the wall wide open. It was the best I've ever seen."

They owned an offensive depth that would bring honor to a nuclear submarine. The Pirates' fourth outfielder, Gene Clines, had exactly the same lifetime batting average (covering 31 games in '70 and 52 in '71) as Ty Cobb, and their fill-in second baseman was old Bill Mazeroski—hitting for a better average than when he was a perennial All-Star. Due back soon from Marine camp was Dave Cash, batting .322 and already estab-lished, at age 23, as Mazeroski's worthy successor. Altogether, with seven American blacks, six Latins and a white minority which included at least one Polish American, one Texas Ameri-can and two redheads, the Pirates had perhaps the richest assortment of ethnic strains ever to heap threats, obloquy and even full nelsons upon one another, day after day, in active harmony at Three Rivers—that is, at the Ohio, the Monongahela and the Allegheny.

Then, that night against the Dodgers, the Pirates lost a baseball game.

Afterward the clubhouse lay silent as a tomb. "Either you do," intoned Stargell at his locker, "or you don't." After a long moment, he added, "The bitter with the sweet."

It seemed an extreme reaction to one defeat in 12 games, but as Starter Steve Blass (now 11–4)—who hadn't even played in the loss—explained the next day when some sparkle had returned to the atmosphere, "Well, we lost. We didn't know how to react. I didn't know what to say to my wife."

Then the Pirates dropped two out of three to the Giants, their probable opponents in the National League playoffs in October. After the first of those defeats Stargell sat with his 4-year-old son Wilver Jr., called Son-Son, in his lap and asked him if he was ready for the forthcoming father-and-son game.

"Yes," smiled Son-Son.

"Kin you pole it?" asked Stargell.

"Yes," smiled Son-Son.

Stargell wasn't smiling. He had struck out three times and his knees were very bad. Sitting disconsolately next to him was Giusti. After striking out Willie Mays with the bases loaded the night before, Giusti had suggested that Mays couldn't hit a good fastball anymore. Then, this night he had walked Mays in the ninth with the bases loaded on an overly discreet fastball, and followed that by giving up a grand-slam homer to Willie McCovey. Sanguillen wasn't reviling Giusti now. Nobody was saying anything to him, or to anybody—except Stargell to Son-Son. It was awful.

Even at such a moment it was hard to feel sorry for the Pirates. And, as a matter of fact, they promptly rebounded from the Giant series by taking two straight and getting a weekend split in San Diego to maintain an overpowering division lead over Chicago and St. Louis. Stargell brought his home-run total to 32. The Pirates' don'ts and their bitters look pale in comparison with their dos and their sweets.

Take the prime case of Stargell. His knees are puffy, pitted and dumpy looking, and the ravaged cartilages in them apparently make it an ordeal for him to play. He does not like to talk about the problem because, as he says, "I didn't make any excuses when I was having a terrible season and I'm not going to make any now."

Stargell has always had trouble with his knees. One was operated on after the 1964 season, when he was only 23, and the other the next year. At least one of them may have to be cut into again this winter. The other day, Stargell glanced across at Clines and said: "I wish I had just one of his legs." But since Clines is a slim sprinter some five inches shorter than the 6' 2½" Stargell, such an arrangement would require Stargell to play left field at a 45-degree angle. And however ruefully he may regard his pins, Stargell should not trade the rest of himself for anything.

He has an enormous trunk that seems to swell visibly in the batting box as he paws in the dirt with his front foot in a pent-up way, like a man getting ready to lift something tremendous or stop a charge. As he waits, Stargell swings his bat around and around in a plane perpendicular to the plate, so that it looks like a propeller taking its first few spins. Then : Woomp!

Stargell is one of two men in memory to hit a ball over the right-center field wall in old Forbes Field at the 436-foot mark. Stargell's went an estimated 542 feet. In the 61½ years big-league ball was played in Forbes Field, 18 home runs were hit over its right-field roof; Stargell hit seven of them. Four balls have been hit into the upper deck of Three Rivers since the Pirates moved in last July, three of these to right field and all three by Stargell.

The matter of ball parks—which ones to hit in or out of—is of considerable significance. In Stargell's 10-year career he has never hit more than 33 home runs. That is primarily because of Forbes Field.

Forbes Field represented the thinking of Barney Dreyfuss, the Pirates' first president, who hated, even in the deadball era, anything resembling a cheap homer. Forbes Field had a small homer pocket in the right-field corner, but a ball hit directly over the head of a base runner with a modest lead off first had to travel 375 feet to reach the fence; the right-center power alley was 408 feet; the left-center alley was 457 feet. Accordingly, no Pittsburgh team has led the league in home runs since 1903, which was before Forbes Field. Occasionally some observer would wonder why, since Forbes was such a bad place to hit home runs in, no one ever pitched a no-hitter there. But the more spacious the park, the more room there is for singles, doubles and triples to fall in between fielders—and the single-double-and-triple hitter is what Pittsburgh has specialized in, from Honus Wagner through Paul and Lloyd Waner and Kiki Cuyler to Dick Groat, Matty Alou and Clemente.

The main difference between the Pirates who eked out a division title last year and the Pirates who are outmuscling all of baseball now is that not only are the line-drive hitters like Clemente, Cash, Sanguillen, Al Oliver and Clines still flourishing, but Stargell is heading toward 50-plus homers, Third Baseman Richie Hebner and First Baseman Bob Robertson (who reached Three Rivers' left-field upper deck) have good shots at 30 and almost anyone in the lineup is a feasible threat to hit one out. Three Rivers' fences are at nice, standard 340-, 385- and 410-foot distances.

In 1969 Stargell's wife Dolores kept track of her husband's long drives at Forbes Field and figured out that in the new stadium (then under construction) he would have hit 52 instead of 29 for the year. Last year Stargell had four in Forbes Field, nine in Three Rivers and 18 on the road. This year he already has 18 at home.

Three Rivers isn't purely sweet for Stargell, however, because the artificial turf is hard on his legs. The harder outfield surface is more tiring to stand and run around on, and balls take quick, skidding bounces on the Tartan Turf that require knee-wrenching quick cuts of Stargell, who is a conscientious defensive craftsman.

The bitter with the sweet. Even at Stargell's All-Pro fried chicken parlor, in Pittsburgh's ghetto Hill section, a Stargell homer does not necessarily trigger the fountain of free chicken and merrymaking of popular belief. Stargell's place is attractive and serves good food, and it makes good its promise to serve free to anyone present when the radio announces a Stargell blast, but a counterman on duty recently said, "Last time there was one guy in here drinking an orange Slush, and so many junkies outside in the street that it looked like a parade, and junkies aren't buying any chicken. Then Stargell hits one, word gets out and then they all want to come piling in. Uh-uh. I paid for that Slush and put it down for promotion, and that's all. Another time there was a drunk in here ordered $1.48 worth of chicken, and I gave him his change, and Stargell hit one. I told the guy to give me the two cents back and the chicken was free, and he didn't want to do it. He didn't know what was going on. I told him, 'Listen, just gimme the two cents back, I'm trying to do you a favor.' Finally he did and I gave him his $1.50 back and he said, 'Well, good. That was my last money. Now I can go buy a drink.'"

Meanwhile, the Pirates are keeping things in perspective, too. Asked what the difference is between his pitching this year and last, Dock Ellis says only, "Runs. Runs." Then he also offers a complaint: "Whenever I say something, it comes out in the papers that I made a complaint." Ellis' most famous assertion—which turned out to be mistaken—was that he would not start in the All-Star Game against Vida Blue because they were both black. More recently he made headlines by observing that the National League was using two different kinds of baseballs, one of which is "too fat" for his hand.

Asked what he is doing differently this year, Steve Blass, says, "I find it hard to take it all too seriously. I'm not a heart surgeon. If I'm not throwing well I keep on throwing, and if I am throwing well, I enjoy it. This year I'm throwing well. And we're scoring a lot of runs. Our trainer, Tony Bartirome, is having a great year although he finished sixth in the All-Star balloting...."

"This ball club," says Manny Sanguillen, "it makes no difference whether we're in third place or first, we the same. We keep each other happy. Me—I'm happy all the time. I think I was happy when I was born. Hey Robertson—I hate to tell you, but you don't have power."

Ellis is listening to some loud music whose lyrics, sung along by Ellis, consist largely of "funky ... oh yeah." Suddenly the volume goes down. Ellis complains, and asks whose idea that was. Someone points to Clemente. Clemente, the ranking superstar of the club. Clemente, who declares that official scorers do not want him to win a batting championship. Clemente, whom no one used to be able to kid.

"Do you notice how the room went silent?" whoops Ellis. And he breaks into his Clemente imitation. Hobbling, twitching his neck and saying in a Latin accent, "Oh, I not like I used to be. I a little bit of an old man now."

"Did you see Clemente slide lass night?" yells Sanguillen, flying halfway across the room in an imitation of that slide, and then freezing on the floor. "I want to go help him up, the old man!" Clemente pretends not to notice; at least, he doesn't appear outraged.

So, the Pirates are keeping their heads up remarkably well for a team of walking wounded that is only 11 games out in front. Some of them, after all, even remain healthy—though Sanguillen says he used to be a much more robust man before he took up baseball.

"I used to be big in the chest, big in the arms. Baseball take it off. The sweat run down.... I used to box and swim, I used to be *big*. But still, you don't see many guys that can do *this*." He flexes and produces a biceps the size of a grapefruit. He tweaks it with his fingers. Nothing happens. He tweaks it a little harder, and—bo-ing, there springs up a small muscle on top of a muscle. "That's muscle," says Sanguillen.

Stargell, too, still has life in him. He is in the dressing room after a Pirate victory over the Giants, in which he stroked an RBI single and tried to acquire another run by stealth. When the Giants left home plate unattended, he stole in from third. But the home-plate umpire, perhaps because Stargell sneaked up on him and made him jump as he was bending over brushing off the plate, had maintained that time was called. Now Stargell is automatically responding to the same tired old questions—about why he is hitting so many more home runs and how many more he expects to hit.

At last he arises to take his shower, takes two flip-flop steps in his number VIII shower shoes, and stops.

"Just one thing," he says. He pauses for emphasis. "I stole home."

And then he struts—not broadly, but subtly, the way a 215-pound man with bad knees and more than 30 home runs in July who knows in his heart that he really did steal home would strut—off to the shower.

51

Into a
Golden State

♦

B Y   S T E V E   R U S H I N

NOT TOO LONG AFTER SPORTS ILLUSTRATED'S INCEPTION IN 1954, THE DODGERS AND GIANTS SHOCKED THE BASEBALL WORLD BY DESERTING NEW YORK FOR THE FAIR CLIMES OF CALIFORNIA. IN THE SUMMER OF 1992, THE MAGAZINE DISPATCHED STEVE RUSHIN TO DISCOVER JUST HOW THE GAME WAS FARING ON THE LEFT COAST—PARTICULARLY DURING THE SEASON MOST ASSOCIATED WITH THAT SUNNY STATE: SUMMER.

Evian vendors. Baseball in California means Evian vendors. And clubouse haircuts by Bruce of Laguna. Ballpark cappuccino. Dodger-blue skies in sun-Orange County. Early exits. No socks, just stirrups. Umps working the breakfast plate at Belisle's near Disneyland. Bleacher beach balls. Lou Rawls. Riot makeup games. Hotel wake-up quakes. Ballpark ... *sushi*?

This is how I spent my summer vacation: Photographer V.J. Lovero, his assistant, Bob Binder, and I were assigned to commune with California baseball. So we rented a sedan with a sunroof and a cellular phone, took a Pasadena on the optional car-fax and set out to discover the Golden State's baseball ethos, or at least to locate its best fish-taco stand. Over seven games in seven days last week, we bagged rays in all five of California's big league ballparks and traveled light the length of the state. You have to travel light. As a sign outside Candlestick Park says: No cans, no bottles, no weapons.

It has been 35 years since Horace Stoneham pulled a Horace Greeley and went west. Stoneham moved his New York Giants to San Francisco after the 1957 season, the same year the Brooklyn Dodgers fled Flatbush for El Lay, and major league baseball had realized its manifest destiny. The Athletics are now in their 25th year at the Oakland Coliseum. Dodger Stadium just turned 30. Jack Murphy Stadium in San Diego will host the All-Star Game next week.

This is a celebratory summer for California baseball, to be sure, but that is hardly the reason for our road trip, despite what I may have told my editors. No, for the real reason, I quote actor Tom Hanks, who once contentedly snatched and deflated a beach ball that violated his airspace during an Angel game at Anaheim Stadium, saying afterward, "I've always want-ed to do that." Well, *I've* always wanted to do that, too, and here would be a week's worth of opportunities.

Oakland, San Francisco, Anaheim, San Diego, Los Angeles. That would be our itinerary. What should we expect? I asked Montreal Expo catcher Gary Carter, a Culver City, Calif., native and former Dodger and Giant who has played in each of the parks on our list. The Kid graciously offered this scouting report on California fans: Oakland—"Kind of laid-back." Ana-heim—"Pretty laid-back." San Diego—"Somewhat laid-back."

I'll pick up the rest of Carter's candid observations later on, but for now, let's hit the road. Or Shall I say, *Let's get busy?* That's the phrase with which Arsenio Hall begins most of his shows. Later I will meet a Dodger Stadium peanut vendor who has guested—it's a verb in California—on every major television talk show except *The Arsenio Hall Show.* "I'll wait until my book comes out before I see about his show," Roger (The Peanut Man) Owens will tell me while producing a business card from his wallet. "It is called *Working for Peanuts—and Loving It!*"

That same vendor also ... I'm sorry. I've digressed. I inad-vertently veered off on a mental exit ramp there, which is easy to do in California. We were about to begin the trip. But first a precaution: In case any of you become lost during this travelogue, we should arrange a place to meet later on in the story. How about the Rubio's fish-taco stand by the press gate at Jack Murphy Stadium? After all, it is there that I would overhear a man standing in line say to the group of kids he was chaperoning, "Let's all meet back here after the sixth-inning stretch, O.K.?"

O.K. by me.

Here, then, is my diary of the week. I'm, calling it *Seven Days That Shook the San Diego Marriott Hotel and Marina*. See you after the sixth-inning stretch.

Sunday, June 28, Oakland
This morning, I slept through California's most powerful earthquake in four decades, though a hotel housekeeper later woke me while taking her new eight-cylinder riding Hoover for a test drive in the hallway outside my room.

A Channel 4 newsman says of the quake that struck Southern California at 4:58 a.m., leaving a 7.4 on the Richter scale, "Once again, Californians are being told to prepare for the Big One." William Randolph Hearst's sometimes sensationalist San Francisco *Examiner* reports that at the Anaheim Marriott, where I will be staying later during this trip, a woman was suddenly "pitched from her bed."

I also have a reservation at the San Diego Marriott, where the Giants were sleeping when the quake hit. Pitcher Francisco Oliveras woke to plaster falling on his face. Third baseman Matt Williams and catcher Kirt Manwaring checked out of the hotel. "I didn't like the sound the building was making," Pitcher Bryan Hickerson tells the *Examiner*. "Too much popping and snapping." *Popping and snapping?* Take a baseball tour of most states, and those are the sounds of fastballs and catchers' mitts.

Because downtown San Francisco, where I am staying, is hosting 20,000 convention-going librarians, and 400,000 parading gays and lesbians (and a statistically inevitable number of overlapping lesbian librarians), it takes forever to get through traffic and across the Bay Bridge to the Oakland Coliseum for the A's–Minnesota Twins matinee.

In fact, we will spend so much time in transit this week that I will be able to fill out a solid lineup card of license plates when the trip is over, including the likes of PWR HTR, I TRN 2, STRIK 3. To whom would I hand this lineup card? To the guy with the plates that read 3X YROUT. Who am I? I'm a native of Minnesota, a TWIN FAN, you could say, though I enjoy an occasional DODGR DOG when I'm in my guise as a SPTWRTR. These are actual California plates. I will see them all on this trip.

The Coliseum turns out to be the least rich of our five venues. Aside from partaking of the state's finest tailgating, and watching the Twins hang an ungodly 10-spot on the scoreboard in the fourth inning, and having my Polaroid picture taken with a cardboard cutout of Jose Canseco, and dropping bogus missives into the Fan Feedback Boxes—*feedback*, man; is that California, or what?—and invading the carnival-like Family Entertainment Center, where fans are screening a pre-Olympic basketball game on TV ... besides that, there isn't anything to *do* here. Nothing to do but watch baseball, I mean.

So the crowd is dust by the seventh-inning stretch. (That's right: They stretch in the *seventh* inning here. Interesting.) In the sixth the Coliseum bleachers are full and the nearby BART train-station platform is empty. Then suddenly, in the seventh, the bleachers are empty and the platform is full. It happens that quickly.

Coliseum, Coli-don't.

Monday, June 29, San Francisco
Rainy days and Mondays always get me down. So imagine what today, a rainy Monday, is doing to me. We arrive at Candlestick at 4 p.m. for the Giants' 6:35 p.m. tilt with the Atlanta Braves, only to learn that the game has already been called. It is the Giants' first June rainout in 20 years.

To recap the trip thus far: Day One, biggest earthquake in 40 years. Day Two, first rainout in 20 years.

The evening is not a complete washout. We repair to dinner at Kincaid's Bay House, a bar and restaurant in Burlingame. Giants first baseman Will (the Thrill) Clark soon appears at a table in the lounge. Above the bar there is a bottle of something, capped by miniature antlers, that goes for $245 *a shot.* We opt to send a light beer to Clark instead. He then sends us a Coors Light. The three of us ask our waitress if the Thrill could maybe, you know, send over three straws.

Tuesday, June 30, San Francisco
"Candlestick," says Carter, continuing his scouting report. "The

people who can brave that weather—you get some real fans
there." The Stick is said to be like the Rock (nearby Alcatraz
Island), only less hospitable. But today all is blue skies and
beachwear in the bleachers.

We meet 12 guys out here who are also visiting each of the
California ballparks. Candlestick is the final stop for their red
Econoline van. I ask them for their favorite part of the trip.
Here are their replies:

"Five grass fields."

"No fights. I'm from Boston, so it took me a while to
adjust."

"Sushi in Anaheim."

"Well drinks in Anaheim."

"Dodger Stadium the day of the earthquake: 12,000 no-
shows."

"Tijuana on our night off. Tijuana better be awarded the next
expansion franchise."

"The way each park reflects each city—from the friendliness of
San Diego to the arrogance of Orange County."

"Yes. Fascism is alive in Orange County. It's alive in the ush-
ers at Anaheim Stadium."

Tab Taber— *Tab Taber*, man; is that California, or what?—is a
26-year-old high school teacher from nearby Sunnyvale who
organized this trip for his friends. They range in age from 25 to
36 and have come from as far as Jamaica. Just how do they
know each other? "Basically," says Taber, "we all formed quality friendships through baseball."

There is one other thing Taber would like to say. He says it
in much the same way a Marine might say "Semper Fi." It is
very important to him, as a Californian, to make this point.
"We never came late," he says. "And we never left early."

We watch the Giants lose 4–3 to the Braves. But Clark, perhaps buoyed by the barley we sent him last night, goes 2 for 4
in his first game after missing three with a rib injury, a fact that
makes our six-hour, 380-mile postgame drive down I-5 to
Greater Los Angeles fairly fly by.

Our inland route is no U.S. 1—the majestic coastal highway
that snakes past Big Sur and Hearst's San Simeon manse—but it
does afford views of sprawling vineyards, land the color of
wheat, skies like a bad starving-artist painting, the garlic capital

of the world (Gilroy), NASA's Jet Propulsion Lab and Magic Mountain's hideous Viper roller coaster, which is so nasty that an L.A. traffic-helicopter pilot once got nauseated on it. Otherwise it's just pretty much San Dimas, where *Bill & Ted's Excellent Adventure* was set, and the Richard Nixon Library, in Yorba Linda, before we roll past Disneyland and into the Anaheim Marriott, where I fear that I may be pitched from my bed.

Wednesday, July 1, Anaheim
The pancakes are the size of an on-deck circle. "You order an eclair there, and it weighs, like, seven pounds," Roseanne Arnold has said. It isn't on the menu, but I am fairly certain they will give you a side order of pure cholesterol, if you ask. I am talking about Belisle's in Garden Grove, five minutes from Anaheim Stadium. It is where American League umpires meet to eat red meat.

The Texas-Style Breakfast comes with, among other things, a dozen eggs (any style) and a 26-ounce sirloin steak. It retails—I'm not making this up—for $49.95. "The last time I ordered the meatloaf at Belisle's," says Angel trainer Rick Smith, "my family ate for a week afterwards. We had meat loaf burritos, meat loaf chili. I'm serious."

We go to the umpires' room at the Big A before today's game between the Angels and Twins, but the crew tells me I'd have to talk to their colleagues Ken Kaiser, Durwood Merrill or Rocky Roe for the best Belisle's stories. I'm serious. I swing by the Angel clubhouse, where several players are having their hair cut by two barbers who deliver. The entire bullpen had its hair done in the trainers' room yesterday. I know I said up above that the stylist was Bruce of Laguna, but I had been misinformed. They're actually Jamie and Rick of Anaheim Hills.

What really sets Anaheim apart is sushi. Oakland has vegeterian burgers with blue cheese dressing. San Francisco slipped something called the Rib-B-Que past the FDA. But sushi? "We always sell a lot of it, yes," one of the smiling sushi saleswomen tells me. "We sell more when Boston and New York are in town." The *yakisoba* doesn't sell so well when, say, Milwaukee plays here.

Given the proximity of Disneyland, it's no surprise that fans of the visiting team tend to people Anaheim Stadium, as evidenced by the cheers that go up every time the Twins score in their 2–1 win. Is there such a thing as an Angel fan? I wore an Angel cap to each ballpark I visited and was showered with indifference at every turn. The cap elicited only one comment, from a drunken fan in San Diego who asked me why I was wearing it. If I wore a Red Sox cap in Yankee Stadium, on the other hand, it would likely be thrown from the second deck, with my head in it. You know, I think I like Anaheim better.

Thursday, July 2, San Diego
To get to San Diego from Anaheim, you simply merge onto the San Diego Freeway, pass Nixon's old digs at San Clemente, pass Camp Pendleton, the Marine base, and pass the nearby immigration checkpoint. In between, we pull off at San Onofre State Beach—"Old Man's," as we surfers call it. We gape for a moment at the beauty of it all, then pile back in the car and tune to Lee (Hacksaw) Hamilton on all-sports radio station XTRA, transmitting out of Tijuana. Hacksaw is asking California manager Buck Rodgers about his thoughts during the Angels' bus crash in New Jersey six weeks ago.

"To be honest," says Rodgers, "I thought we were going to eat the salad right there." *Eat the salad?* What a health-conscious, California-vegeterian, life-affirming euphemism for death. Or so I am thinking as I disembark at the antihistoric green cathedral on Friars Road—the unstoried Jack Murphy Stadium. How unstoried? I forthwith reproduce the entire contents of the notebook that I carried with me this evening:

Jack Murphy Stadium is named for Jack Murphy. Jack Murphy was a beloved San Diego SPTWRTR. There is a bronze bust of Murphy outside the stadium, next to a bronze bust of former Padres owner and McDonald's founder Ray Kroc. This is not exactly Monument Park or Yankee Stadium. Especially when you consider the half dollar-sized dollop of pigeon pudding on Kroc's forehead. More than one fan notes that Kroc looks alarmingly like Mikhail Grobachev. Memo to the stadium cleanup crew: Buff the man's noggin before the All-Star Game, for God's sake.

Sure, an eclair-fueled Roseanne once sang the national anthem quite badly here. And yes, former Padres leftfielder Jerry Turner once threw the ball backward here, to the outfield wall, while trying to throw a runner out at the plate. "And no doubt if the

Padres' "Mr. Indispensable," Whitey Wietelmann, 73, weren't off tonight, he could tell some stories, especially about the time he was batboy for a team Jim Thorpe played on. But Whitey isn't here. So all we have to show for San Diego is another home team loss, 3–2 to the Expos, running the California teams' record to 0–4 on this trip. We leave with only that. That, and a gutful of fish tacos. *Mmmmmmmmmmmm.* All is not lost.

Friday and Saturday, July 3 and 4, Los Angeles
Dodger Stadium is California in a nutshell, so to speak. Where else could you find The Peanut Man, who has been throwing his wares to customers for as long as the Dodgers have played here? The Peanut Man did *The Tonight Show* twice. "But only once with Johnny," he notes. "The second time, George Carlin was guest-hosting."

"You get the biggest crowds in Dodger Stadium," says Gary Carter, "because you have all the glitz and all the glamour." Where else could The Peanut Man be a celebrity, collecting $2,000 in prepaid orders from wealthy "season-peanut holders," who then needn't fish for a dollar every time they call for nuts at the ballpark?

Where else could you find Mike Brito? Brito, the dapper, panama-hatted Dodger scout, who stands behind the screen with a radar gun each game, is signing autographs during batting practice.

Where else could a player, during *a game*, wear stirrups without any socks underneath? Dodger reliever Roger McDowell is doing just that. Where else could a vendor call, "Hey! Evvv-iii-ian waaaaater, heah! Hey! Evvv-iiiian waaaaaater, heah!" as if he were hawking cold Buds? Where else could there be a double-header, as there is here on Friday, to make up for a game against the Philadelphia Phillies that was called on account of rioting? Where else could Lou Rawls—Lou Rawls?—be found schmoozing in the manager's office?

Only in L.A. On the Fourth of July, a man behind me at a Dodger Dogs stand drops a quarter that bounces off my sneaker. It is L.A. Kings owner Bruce McNall. (A rare-coin collector, McNall retrieves his two bits from the concrete.) The guy who played Starsky is sitting in the Club Level seats. And isn't that Richard Mulligan at the yogurt stand?

Everyone beats the Dodgers this season, and everyone tries to beat the Dodger traffic. But after L.A. loses 3–2 to the Phillies on Saturday—the Dodgers had swept Friday's doubleheader—virtually the entire sellout crowd of 44,418 stays for what the P.A. announcer calls "a pyrotechnical tribute to this great nation."

Before the lights go out, fans are ushered onto the immaculate outfield sod to better view the fireworks. Can you see this at Shea Stadium?

After seven days spent in sun-saturated, baize-covered ballparks, I have 60 feet six inches of sausage products in me. My body carries a processed nacho-cheese-like substance like most bodies carry blood plasma. I am in blue heaven, even if I never did get to deflate a beach ball. And then the pyrotechnical tribute to this great nation begins, and suddenly the sky is alight with the colors of the flag. All at once, the crowd breaks into *God Bless America*. All of us.

To be honest, I thought I was going to eat the salad right there. And if I had, I would have gone happy.

FALL

◆ ◆ ◆

Never Pumpkins Again

♦

BY WILLIAM LEGGETT

IN 1969 BASEBALL PLAYED WITNESS TO THE MIRACLE OF THE
METS, WHO STUNNED THE WORLD BY BECOMING CHAMPIONS
ONE SEASON AFTER FINISHING 24 GAMES BEHIND THE PENNANT-
WINNING ST. LOUIS CARDINALS. BILL LEGGETT FILED THIS REPORT
IN THE AFTERMATH OF NEW YORK'S WORLD SERIES TRIUMPH
OVER THE HEAVILY FAVORED BALTIMORE ORIOLES.

It was nearing midnight in the Diamond Club four stories above
what remained of the playing field at Shea Stadium, and the
New York Mets, the most improbable champions in 100 years of
professional baseball, gathered in a circle around the bandstand.
Swaying back and forth with their arms wrapped around each
other, they sang *Heart* from the musical *Damn Yankees*. ("When
your luck is battin' zero/Get your chin up off the floor;/Mister
you can be a hero/You can open any door, there's nothin' to it
but to do it./You gotta have heart/Miles 'n miles 'n miles 'n miles 'n miles 'n
heart....") Next they sang *God Bless America*. And then, as the
clock struck midnight, they all turned back into pumpkins.

No, they didn't, not really, for somewhere in the delirious
weeks leading up to their victory over Baltimore, the Mets had
been touched with permanent magic. Of course, no world

championship will ever be the same again, either, as Cecilia
Swoboda pointed out to her husband the next morning in their
home on Long Island. Ron Swoboda was talking—and talking
and talking—about what had been one of the biggest upsets in
World Series history when Cecilia smiled. "Ron," she said,
"you can only win it for the first time once."

About the same time Al Weis, a man who hits a home run
about as often as Gil Hodges smiles during a World Series
game, thought again about the homer that had tied Baltimore
in the seventh inning of the fifth and final game. During eight
years in the major leagues, both with the Chicago White Sox
and New York, Weis had gone to bat more than 600 times
before home crowds without hitting a homer. But he got hold
of a fastball from the Orioles' Dave McNally and began to run
as fast as he could. "When I got near second base," he said, "I
started hearing the crowd roar and thought something must
have happened. I guess I don't know how to react to a home
run. I only know how to react to singles and doubles."

Also that day, as he cleared out his locker in Shea, Ken
Boswell looked at the stack of mail before him. The hard-hit-
ting second baseman had batted .422 through the Mets'
stretch drive and had led the team with five runs batted in
against the Atlanta Braves during the National League playoffs. As a bachelor from Austin, Texas he receives a lot of
mail. "The girls from Brooklyn," Boswell said, "keep writing
and inviting me to go over and try their spaghetti, but they'd
have a better chance if they tried spareribs. After I woke up
this morning I went down into the street and some people
were saying, 'There goes Ken Boswell.' When I get home to
Austin they are going to have a Welcome Home Ken
Boswell Parade. I hope they mean me and not some other
Ken Boswell."

Despite all the things said by the Mets about their inspired
victory, it remained for Earl Weaver, the manager of the Orioles, to put his finger on the heart of the matter. After thinking over his team's defeat for two days, Weaver said, "We hit
the ball right where they could show off their defensive ability." Almost unbelievably, after the first game nearly half of the
balls hit by the Orioles for outs went toward either Shortstop
Bud Harrelson or Centerfielder Tommie Agee, the two

strongest gloves in the New York defense. Harrelson had a spectacular Series, going into the hole between third and short time and again to turn a hit into an out, and it will be a long time before anybody forgets Agee's play in center.

But the 66th World Series will be remembered for many things. Those were not really angels in the Met outfield: they were the Flying Wallendas. Donn Clendenon set a record for a five-game World Series by hitting three home runs and he only got into four of the games. For the first time in 35 years a manager, Baltimore's Weaver, got bounced from a Series game. When the Mets finally clinched the championship, a blizzard of ticker tape settled over Manhattan and at Shea Stadium fans pulled up chunks of turf, festooning themselves with the magic sod as if its new-established healing qualities could cure all their fears and ills as merely walking upon it had cured those of their heroes.

The reason for the emotional binge, of course, was that just a short while before the Mets really had been pumpkins. Five days before the Series started, Casey Stengel, who alone made the Mets something to talk about eight years ago, stood in the victorious clubhouse after the playoff series against Atlanta. "Yes, yes, yes," said Stengel, "it's taken eight years but now the people are beginning to know their names!" Tom Seaver and Jerry Koosman and Cleon Jones, of course; but now Weis, Harrelson, Swoboda, Jerry Grote, Art Shamsky, Gary Gentry and Nolan Ryan, too. They were being talked about, admittedly as the urchins who threw the snowballs that knocked the stovepipe hats off the autocrats' heads.

In their first bungling year as a baseball team the Mets lost 120 games, and a saying developed around New York that went, "I've been a Met fan all my life." By 1967 New York had done all to baseball that could be done to it, and the natives were growing restless. During that year the Mets put uniforms on 54 different players with results that are still frightening. Players sent their laundry out and had to have friends pick it up for them and mail it on to their next destination. The fans couldn't tell the players *with* a scorecard.

In spring training this year Manager Gil Hodges explained how he felt about the constant shifting of personnel. "It doesn't do anything but breed unrest among the players," he said.

"There's no feeling of security knowing you may be the next to go. Those days are over."

This year the Mets got to the World Series by using only 29 men, and their followers knew who they were watching. Even the banners improved. Gone were the derogatory signs, as Shea Stadium's peculiar art form assumed a positive note that made the place more fun than ever before. As the Mets drove toward the division championship a large sign made of reflecting tape appeared high above home plate. LET'S GLOW METS! During the Series a sign greeted Baltimore's huge slugger, Boog Powell, with A 500 POUND BIRD. And in the victory crush on the field after the Orioles had been defeated for the fourth straight time, a youngster held a placard that said, TWEET TWEET.

The Mets seemed to have a unique rapport with their fans and talked about them frequently. They didn't resent it even when they were booed. Ed Kranepool won a game in July and got a tremendous ovation. Often the brunt of jokes, he said, "The last time they cheered me was when I signed." Swoboda, after striking out five times in one game, said, "They booed the hell out of me and if I was them I would have followed me home and booed me there, too."

Swoboda obviously learned something that day. In the Series he batted .400, drove in the winning run of the final game and made two magnificent catches. All the Mets, in fact, showed in the Series that they had come a long, long way. Following their defeat in the first Series game, their pitching settled down— something it was unable to do in the playoffs. After Don Buford's first-inning homer, when it seemed that Baltimore was about to decimate the Mets, only one Oriole leadoff man reached base in the next 26 innings. Only four times in all did an Oriole start an inning with a hit.

Baltimore's failure to handle New York pitching was most evident when Buford, Paul Blair, Brooks Robinson and Dave Johnson were at bat. These four hit a composite .080 for the Series and did not produce one extra base hit after Buford's fourth-inning double in the first game. Of the skimpy total of 23 hits that the Orioles collected, five came out of the ninth spot in the order. And of the nine runs batted in by Baltimore three were accounted for by Pitchers McNally and Mike Cuellar.

If there was a turning point in the Series it came in the second inning of the third game, with the Mets leading 1–0 on Agee's leadoff homer. With two out, Grote, who caught all five games, walked and was moved to second by Harrelson's single. Jim Palmer threw a terrible pitch to Gentry, who promptly drove it into right center for a double to score Grote and Harrelson. In 74 at bats during the regular season and the playoffs, Gentry, one player who has never been accused of being a "pretty good hitter for a pitcher," batted home only a single run and hit but a solitary double. He was sweating out an 0-for-28 slump when he jumped on Palmer's bad pitch.

The third game may well turn out to be the best that Tommie Agee will ever play; it probably is the most spectacular World Series game that any centerfielder has ever enjoyed. Agee is easily the best example of Gil Hodges' patience. Twenty-seven different players had worked in center field for New York before Agee arrived in 1968 from the Chicago White Sox. On the first pitch of spring training that year he was hit in the head by Bob Gibson of the Cardinals, and early in the regular season he went through an 0-for-34 slump. He hit only .171 in Shea Stadium and seemed to take the Great Circle Route under fly balls. He was pressing. But, although he could not seem to do anything right, Hodges kept playing him, telling Agee not to quit on himself.

At first, 1969 was not an easy year for Agee, either. He encountered slumps and Hodges benched him but, as the Mets played good ball, Agee became a vital man in the attack. He started rallies on offense and stopped the opposition with fine catches in the outfield.

But nothing he did in the regular season approached his third-game performance. Behind 3–0, Baltimore started what looked like a big rally in the fourth inning by putting two runners on with two out and Elrod Hendricks at bat. Normally a pull hitter, Hendricks hit a pitch to deep left center, and Agee, shaded toward right, went galloping after the ball. He caught it two steps from the wall with a spectacular backhand catch to end the inning. Three innings later, after an even longer run, he dove to rescue a potential triple with the bases loaded. Agee had made a difference of five runs on defense with his fielding and one on offense with his homer as New York won 5–0. The crowd of 56,335 at Shea Stadium sensed for the first time that the Orioles, doubtless a very fine team, could be had by the Mets.

66

New York's drive to the division championship, the National League pennant and finally the World Championship was surrounded by such hysteria and commercialized sentimentality that certain hard statistics were all but overlooked. The foremost of these shows how well New York played in Shea Stadium. From the middle of August through their final victory in the Series, the Mets won 26 of 31 games there—a percentage of .839. Before their final playoff victory over the Braves, New York pitchers gave up only six home runs in their last 253 innings played at Shea, a remarkable accomplishment since Shea Stadium is considered by home-run hitters as a hitting successor to the Mets' ancestral home, the Polo Grounds. Little wonder Baltimore had trouble.

The Orioles must now suffer through a long winter after what had been, until they met the Mets, a superior season. When Bowie Kuhn, the imposing new Commissioner of Baseball, shook hands with Weaver after the Series he said, "I've just congratulated the Mets and told them they'd beaten the best damn team in sight." The Orioles certainly were, and had it not been for an amazing catch here, a miraculous stab there they might have reversed the whole course of what, mystically, the whole country had begun to regard as inevitable—the triumph of the rankest underdogs. Instead, they return to Baltimore, where only a million watched them this year and perhaps fewer will care to view them the next.

Probably no man has suffered through a more frustrating Series than Frank Robinson. When he wasn't being walked by the careful Met pitchers, Robinson hit the ball hard—once for a home run, in the fifth and last game. But four of his smashes ended in nothing but beautiful outs. As Baltimore packed for its return home, Robinson said, "I'm awfully disappointed it all had to end this way for us. It would be silly to try and take anything away from the Mets because they just played great ball. But don't forget about us. We'll be back."

Now the Mets feel that they will be back, too, but search and you will not find a man in the entire organization who thought that 1969 would be a year in which the team would win its division championship, let alone a World Series. This was to be a season in which the club became respectable and might even finish as high as third in the East. Just the year before they had wound up 16 games below .500 and in ninth place, 24 games behind pennant-winning St. Louis.

It was absurd to think that New York could win 100 games. But the Mets did. It is equally absurd to believe that those 100 games were won with luck. If one holds to the baseball cliché that the breaks tend to equal out, then maybe the Mets were repaid all in one season for seven long years of bad breaks.

But, more important, the Mets were a hungry club and gave of themselves as teams do only in novels. Only four of them had been regulars for as long as three years. It was a smart team. Of the 27 men who contributed to New York's rise, 22 had been to college—a remarkable percentage for a baseball club. And it was a team that was being prodded from underneath. This year the Met farm system produced four pennants in the minor leagues, twice as many as any other organization, which means that more good new Mets are on their way up.

Looking them over last week, Ted Williams said that he saw the possibility of the Mets becoming a dynasty, and it is pretty hard to doubt anything Teddy Ballgame says these days. Although dynasties have a way of lasting for about a year in the National League, the Mets, bless 'em, always seem to defy established principles. With their victory justly acclaimed as a triumph for baseball, it may be hoped that any residual tarnish from the hyperbole of Madison Avenue and New York politicians will soon wear off, leaving only the warm success that is likely to endure and honor the sport.

Anyone who drove away from Shea Stadium last week, past candy stores, playgrounds and lots in Queens and Nassau County, had to notice youngsters by the thousands throwing phantom baseballs and diving to make catches that really could not be made. The kids were dreaming that they were Agee, Jones and Swoboda; Seaver, Koosman and Gentry; Harrelson, Weis and Clendenon. And older people dreamed, too, and wondered if during any five days in their entire lives they had tried as hard as the Mets did.

Triple Crown
to the Clowns

♦

BY   RON   FIMRITE

AFTER THE OAKLAND A'S WON THEIR THIRD CONSECUTIVE
WORLD SERIES, RON FIMRITE EXAMINED THEIR IMAGE AND THEIR
PLACE IN BASEBALL HISTORY.

Must the Oakland A's forever endure the melancholy fate of
the clown who longs to be taken seriously? Or is it time now
to look beyond the harlequin pose and see the A's for what
they have become—one of the finest baseball teams of the past
half century?

By demolishing the Los Angeles Dodgers in five games, the
A's last week become only the third team in history and the
first not wearing New York Yankee uniforms to win as many
as three consecutive World Series. The Yankees won five
straight from 1949 to 1953 and four straight from 1936 to 1939,
but if the A's can avoid tearing themselves asunder in civil war-
fare, even these extraordinary achievements are within reach.

And yet, for reasons not entirely of their own device, the A's
are seen by many fans as career funnymen who, in the manner
of The Three Stooges, are mainly intent upon rapping pates.
The A's do have truculent moments. This past season they led
the major leagues in clubhouse punchups and they seem

constantly to be wrangling either among themselves or with their owner, the megalomaniacal Charles O. Finley, whose toy the team is. The A's also wear funny clothes and they play in a city about which a former resident, Gertrude Stein, once said, "There is no there there."

There was a there there last week, though, and the A's were responsible for filling the void. Pouncing on every Dodger mistake, they won all three games in the Oakland Coliseum and saved themselves the inconvenience of traveling south for the weekend. The Dodgers, who hit .272 during the season, hit .228 against the A's superior pitching and only once scored more than twice—in their sole victory, the Series' second game. The loser in each of the games scored only two runs, and four of the five scores were 3–2, which is a measure of the sort of pitching that characterized this World Series.

The teams were closely matched, save for the A's almost uncanny ability to convert an opponent's slightest error, mental or physical, to their advantage. This, ultimately, separates champions from almost-champions.

Dodger Manager Walter Alston had said before the Series began that if his fine young team had one flaw it was defense. The Dodgers were capable of making the difficult plays, but they were also capable of botching the easy ones. A team with the A's instinct for the jugular could ask for no more. Indeed, in each of the climactic games in the East Bay, a Dodger botch, though seemingly trivial at the time, led to disaster. The A's, meanwhile, were converting base hits into double plays, which is *their* style.

The final three games of the California Series were played in some sort of weather inversion. October, with rare exception, is a balmy, clear-skied month in the San Francisco Bay area. Last week was not balmy, it was hot—in the 90s in some communities. It was not clear, it was smoggy. This was August in Los Angeles, not October in Oakland. The brownish air, the windless skies, the stifling heat should have made the Dodgers feel right at home, whereas the A's should have choked on the strange vapors.

"I wish the damn Dodgers would leave," a San Franciscan muttered one day over his beer in the Templebar, "so we can get our weather back."

But not even Mother Nature can repress the A's. They played in these conditions as skillfully as if their natural habitat had been Chavez Ravine, not the flatlands alongside the Nimitz Freeway.

With game-time temperatures in the 80s—game time being 5:30 p.m. as a convenience for Eastern television audiences—the A's quickly applied the heat to their Southern neighbors. What finally brought the Dodgers down, though, was the heat they inadvertently applied to themselves through errors.

In the first of the three games, an error by Dodger Catcher Joe Ferguson on a third-inning fumble of a hopper in front of the plate led directly to the A's first two runs. Ferguson made another error in the fourth, missing a throw from center field, after the A's had scored their third run. The irony is that Ferguson had been a defensive hero playing right field in the first two Series games. For their part, the A's choked off Dodger rallies with double plays in the fourth, eighth and ninth, the last one ending the game. Dick Green, the fielding star of the Series, participated in all three, tying a record for second basemen. The Dodgers' runs came on homers by Bill Buckner and Willie Crawford off Starter Jim (Catfish) Hunter and Reliever Rollie Fingers.

The only big inning of the entire Series was set in motion by yet another Dodger miscue. In the sixth inning of the penultimate game Oakland's Bill North led off with a walk. North stole 54 bases during the regular season, so Dodger Pitcher Andy Messersmith, protecting a 2–1 lead, was anxious—too anxious, it developed—to make certain that he did not advance into scoring position through further thievery. After a number of uneventful tosses to First Baseman Steve Garvey, Messersmith finally threw the ball away and North hurried to second. He scored from there when Sal Bando blooped a single to right field. Suddenly the A's were off to a four-run inning and a 5–2 victory. This game also ended with a double play, the result of a sensational diving catch and hasty feed to second by the acrobatic Green.

It was 81° when the fifth and final game of the Series started, but the skies were returning to their traditional blue and the clouds were pinkened by the late-afternoon sun, not browned by impurities. The weather seemed to be on its way home, taking the Dodgers with it.

71

In the first inning, North, on base after forcing leadoff hitter Bert Campaneris, attempted to steal. Steve Yeager, catching this night for Los Angeles, threw hard to intercept him. The ball sailed untouched into center field and North pressed on to third. He scored from there when Bando, patiently fouling off pitches he could not hit solidly, finally found one he could and sent a long sacrifice fly to left.

In the second inning, Ray Fosse, a .196 hitter in the regular season, stroked a line-drive homer to left for a 2–0 A's lead. But the Dodgers tied the score in the sixth on a sacrifice fly by Jim Wynn and a single by Garvey, the noblest Dodger of them all and the leading hitter (.381) among Series regulars. The A's now had to wait for another mistake or two. It was not a long wait.

As Dodger Leftfielder Buckner assumed his position for the bottom of the seventh inning, he became a target for debris-throwing rowdies in the Coliseum's left-field bleachers. Buckner had annoyed Oakland fans earlier in the week by comparing the A's unfavorably with such National League also-rans as the Pirates and the Reds. Now in retaliation, if it can be assumed that Buckner's assailants were sufficiently literate to read his remarks, the fans were pelting him from on high with garbage, Frisbees, even whiskey bottles. The start of the inning was therefore delayed while the field was cleared. Ordinarily when such a delay occurs, a pitcher will continue warming up. But the Dodger pitcher on this occasion was the academician, Mike Marshall, and nothing Marshall does is ordinary. Instead of tossing a few warm-up pitches, Marshall devoted these leisure moments to declaiming on the vulgarity of Oakland spectators to Buckner and the umpires.

Joe Rudi, a thinking man's hitter, observed all this and, reasoning that Marshall's arm would not be warm, concluded that the pitcher would eschew a breaking pitch in the hope of sneaking a fastball past him. Rudi was ready. He belted Marshall's first pitch, a not-so-sneaky fastball, into those riotous bleachers, and the 1974 baseball season was, for all practical purposes, over.

Buckner was an even more direct participant in the final Dodger boo-boo of the year. Leading off the eighth he singled to center and when the ball skipped past the lunging North for an error, he tried to advance all the way to third. It proved a foolish gamble as Reggie Jackson, backing up North, threw to Green, who relayed the ball perfectly to Bando for the out. Instead of a man on second with nobody out and sluggers Wynn, Garvey and Ferguson coming up, the Dodgers now had no one on with one out. That finished them. They are a young, relatively inexperienced but powerful and aggressive team, and they will be back. But in this Series they played directly into the hands of the opportunistic A's.

"We wait for the door to open," said Jackson in the clubhouse afterward. "And when it does, we go through."

Any of a number of A's could have been named the Most Valuable Player, but the honor finally fell to the industrious Fingers, who pitched in all four Oakland victories and saved the final one for winning Pitcher John (Blue Moon) Odom, his opponent in a clubhouse scrap only six days before.

If for no other reason, the Series was memorable in that the A's players finally upstaged their boss. Not that Finley went unobserved. He was sued by Mike Andrews, the martyr of the 1973 Series, charged with contractual violations by Hunter and accused by First Baseman Gene Tenace of using Manager Alvin Dark as a puppet—not an entirely unfamiliar indictment.

Still, Finley did his best to dance his way into our hearts. He welcomed as a Series seatmate Lucianne Buchanan, the incumbent Miss California. During the first game in Oakland it was solemnly announced to the multitudes over the Coliseum public-address system that Charlie O. would shortly be telephoning President Ford to ask him to throw out the first ball at either of the next two games. The phone was clearly visible resting in front of Finley on the roof of the Oakland dugout. The white-maned, green-jacketed owner seemed puffed up with importance. Newsmen were later advised that because of the press of business, the President had asked for a rain check.

But Charlie O.'s quest for a first-ball-tosser was not that easily sidetracked. Minutes later, the reporters were told over the press speaker system that Finley had urged Richard M. Nixon to come out of retirement and handle the first-ball chores. Nixon, as is his wont lately, "regretfully declined because of health reasons." Finley had managed to develop ordinary tastelessness into something transcendental.

He also called a melodramatic team meeting before the fourth game, at which nothing more consequential than Buckner's unkind appraisal of the A's was on the agenda. Snapped Jackson, "I don't need no pre-game dump to rev me up."

True, the A's are self-starters. They were under tough Dick Williams and they are under God-fearing Alvin Dark, who herded them through the playoffs and World Series quicker than the more renowned Williams ever did. When asked what the essence of the team is, Bando replied without hesitation, "Character. We have a nucleus of guys who give 100% 100% of the time. These are people who are not just satisfied with making a big salary. They want more than that. They want to win."

It is a pity that such stalwarts should so continually be subjected to embarrassment, either by their owner's actions or their own. As true champions, they deserve better, although it is difficult to perceive where they will get it. They seem destined to wear the cap and bells.

Rumors have persisted almost since Finley's arrival in Oakland six years ago that he would soon leave the Bay Area baseball market to the San Francisco Giants and transfer his franchise to a more receptive community—New Orleans, perhaps, or Toronto, Seattle or Washington, D.C. The rumors were revived virtually on the eve of the Series, prompting a familiar denial by Robert T. Nahas, president of Oakland-Alameda County Coliseum, Inc., the nonprofit corporation that manages the ball park.

"In order to assure the fans and press of the stability of the franchise in Oakland," said Nahas, "we want to repeat that our long-term lease with Mr. Finley started on the first day of April 1968 and continues through the last day of the 1987 baseball season."

Jackson, Bando, Rudi, North, Campaneris, Hunter, Blue, Holtzman, Fingers and the rest may be a bit long in the tooth by 1987 and their manager might well be Tatum O'Neal. So figure on a seven-game Series that year.

Game 6

♦

B Y   P E T E R   G A M M O N S

SIX MONTHS AFTER THE METS' DRAMATIC COMEBACK AGAINST THE BOSTON RED SOX IN THE 1986 WORLD SERIES, PETER GAMMONS OFFERED THIS ANALYSIS OF GAME 6, THE MOST REMARKABLE GAME IN A REMARKABLE SERIES.

It was time for a new season, but the question under discussion was from the old: Do you send Don Baylor up to bat for Bill Buckner?

Philadelphia manager John Felske and scout Ray (Snacks) Shore were standing behind a batting cage in Clearwater, Fla., early in spring training, reliving the night of Oct. 25, 1986. "I was sitting there in my den with two outs in the bottom of the 10th," said Felske, "and I turned to my wife and said, 'This is where I want to be someday.'

"Ten minutes later, I said to my wife, 'God, I hope I'm never *there.*' "

"I'm a John McNamara man," said Shore, who worked closely with McNamara when they were both with the Reds from 1979 to 1982. "But the one thing I'll never understand is letting Buckner hit against [Jesse] Orosco in the eighth."

"That's because you've never been a manager," Felske said.

"Buckner had knocked in 102 runs. He helped get them there. A manager has to live with his players. As a manager, I understand. Why does McNamara have to listen to this crap after he took a team that was picked for fifth place all the way to Game 7 of the World Series?"

Felske paused, composing himself. Then, faster than you could say, "Greg Luzinski, 1977," he said, "But I will agree that he's got to get Buckner out of there for defense...."

The next morning, in Winter Haven, Fla., the manager in question, John McNamara, greeted the arrival of the full Red Sox squad with a closed-door, stern speech imploring them to forget what happened last October. Said one player afterward, "We became the first team in history to be told before the first workout of the spring not to think or talk about making it to the seventh game of the World Series."

"Last year should be remembered not for one inning or one game," said veteran relief pitcher Joe Sambito, "but what for most of us was the best of times."

The worst of times, of course, came in the bottom of the 10th inning of Game 6 of the World Series, when the Boston Red Sox turned a 5–3, two-out, bases-empty lead into a 6–5 loss to the New York Mets. In order, Gary Carter singled, Kevin Mitchell singled, Ray Knight singled to score Carter and send Mitchell to third, Mitchell scored on a wild pitch as Knight went to second, and Knight scored the winning run when Mookie Wilson's grounder went through Buckner's legs. Though it has been used many times before, the first paragraph of Charles Dickens's *A Tale of Two Cities* truly does describe Game 6: "It was the best of times, it was the worst of times, it was the age of wisdom, it was the age of foolishness, it was the epoch of belief, it was the epoch of incredulity, it was the season of Light, it was the season of Darkness, it was the spring of hope, it was the winter of despair, we had everything before us, we had nothing before us, we were all going direct to Heaven, we were all going direct the other way...."

Game 6 has now taken its place with the other great World Series contests: Game 8 in 1912, Game 4 in 1947, Game 7 in 1960 and Game 6 in 1975. But in a way it stands alone as the greatest "bad" game in Series history. The Mets, who in 1986 won more games (116) than all but two teams ever, were facing the Red Sox, who hadn't won a World Series since Babe Ruth pitched for them. For much of the Series the two teams bumbled around like a couple of September cellar dwellers. And managers McNamara and Davey Johnson, otherwise sound strategists, often seemed to be off in other worlds.

"Answering questions about that game is something I'll always have to deal with," says McNamara. More incredibly, Johnson will always have to answer questions about screwing up a World Series he *won*. A month after the game, Larry Bowa, a friend who played with and for Johnson, called him and asked, "What in the world were you thinking?"

Regardless of the managing, there was still very little art to this game. Aside from a sinking Marty Barrett liner that Lenny Dykstra stabbed in the first, a long fly by the star-crossed Buckner that Darryl Strawberry ran down on the warning track in the second and Wade Boggs's dive into the stands in the fourth to catch a Keith Hernandez pop-up, there was small cause, defensively, for Vin Scully to raise his voice. The Red Sox' go-ahead run in the seventh inning and the Mets' tying run in the eighth came after wild throws, and the Mets' tying and winning runs in the 10th came on a wild pitch and the croquet shot through Buckner's wicket. The winning pitcher, Rick Aguilera, had a 12.00 ERA for the Series. And when you look at the box score, your eye immediately falls on the line that reads, "Stanley pitched to one batter in the 10th."

"We *lost* that game," said Barrett, the Sox' second baseman. "They won the seventh game, but we *lost* on Saturday night." That's why the game's legitimate heroes, players like Wilson and Orosco, seem to have played only supporting roles. And that's why you wonder if Buckner, McNamara, Bob Stanley and Calvin Schiraldi will forever be scarred, like Fred Merkle, Mickey Owen and Ralph Branca before them.

"Shots," Buckner calls media reminders of what happened. Ten days before spring training he told *The Boston Globe*, "I'm not going to talk about what happened anymore." But Buckner did point out that Stanley wasn't covering first when Wilson's grounder went through his legs. For his part, Stanley took some off-season shots at McNamara's decision-making process, and the pitcher's wife, Joan, was quoted as saying that Rich Gedman "blew it" because he had failed to stop Stanley's inside pitch to Wilson. Roger Clemens, the Boston starter, publicly wondered why McNamara took him out of the game with a 3–2 lead after seven innings, and Baylor privately seethed at not being used. "All season long we won as a team, and as soon as we lost, some of the guys started pointing fingers," says Baylor

And the Mets? "We had accomplished so much and had come from behind in such dramatic fashion in the playoffs that the sixth game just seemed like a good bounce that gave us the chance to win what we believed we should win," says Wilson. But even Hernandez, who went to the manager's office and popped open a beer after he made the second out in the 10th inning, admitted, "I couldn't believe what I was watching on TV." Says Bobby Ojeda, who was traded from the Red Sox to the Mets the winter before, "Even though we knew we deserved it, we know we won because of Stanley's wild pitch and Buckner's error."

Unlike Game 6 of the '75 World Series, which was about as lively as a Lennon Sisters Special until Bernardo Carbo's eighth-inning, three-run home run tied the game for the Red Sox, this game was filled with might-have-beens from the outset. Especially in the first inning. Ojeda was working on three days' rest—a problem because he is an emotional, combative sort whose best pitch, a changeup, is even more of a strain on the arm than a fastball. "I was working on adrenaline," he says. He also did not have his usual control. After the game began, appropriately enough, with a one-hopper by Boggs that slapped off the glove of Knight at third, Ojeda survived two shots to the outfield, the second by Buckner, whose at bat was interrupted by the arrival of a parachutist. Ojeda walked Jim Rice. Dwight Evans then hit a towering drive off the fence in left center, and Boggs scored easily. True, Dykstra did make a fine play on the carom and rifled a quick, accurate throw to cutoff man Rafael Santana, but....

How could Rice not have scored from first with two out? "I couldn't believe it," admits Ojeda. Recalls Red Sox third base coach Rene Lachemann, now a coach for Oakland, "I had to watch Dykstra and the relay, and when I turned to pick up Jimmy, he was barely around second." Rice to this day claims, "The ball was hit too hard to score on." But there were *two* outs. Did he get fooled, assume the ball was out of the park and go into a trot, as he did in the third inning of the seventh game when he hit the ball off the wall and was thrown out at second on what should have been a double? Despite a knee operation in the fall of '85, Rice is not *that* slow. But the Red Sox run the bases as if they're guiding golf carts around a retirement community, and Rice—of whom Charles Scoggins of *The Lowell Sun* once wrote, "He stops at each base to scrape the gum off his shoes"—is particularly cautious. So four singles, a walk and a double in the first two innings produced only two runs.

Through four innings Clemens had a no-hitter and that 2–0 lead. To his credit, Ojeda battled for his life, and his survival is particularly amazing considering that—as he found out later—the Red Sox knew practically everything he was throwing at them. "I was tipping my changeup," Ojeda says. "Since I'm primarily a fastball-changeup pitcher, it didn't take much to figure what was coming if it wasn't going to be my changeup."

Clemens, finally recovered from the flu that had so weakened him in the playoffs and the second game of the Series, struck out six Mets the first time through the order and had retired eight straight entering the fifth. Neither Clemens nor any succeeding Boston pitcher noticed the big woman in red behind home plate who was trying to distract him by continually rolling her arms, much like one of Gladys Knight's Pips. Whoever she was, she was persistent, because she kept it up until the baseball went through Buckner's legs.

Despite his impressive numbers, it hadn't been an easy game for Clemens. Carter, Strawberry and Santana had fouled so many pitches that his four innings seemed more like seven; he had already thrown 73 pitches. "I was throwing hard," says Clemens, "but I wasn't putting the ball where I wanted." Clemens walked Strawberry to lead off the fifth, and Strawberry did for the second time in the game what the Red Sox did only once in their 14 postseason contests: He stole second. Knight fouled off three pitches, then Clemens threw a "bad" slider that Knight hit through the middle for an RBI single.

Then came a Wilson at bat that would have nearly as much importance as the one five innings later. After Clemens threw two fastballs past him and the count reached 2 and 2, Mookie fouled off two pitches. Clemens then tried to get a slider in. The slider to Knight had hurt Clemens, but this one hurt him twice as much. Not only was the pitch out over the plate, but Clemens also released it in such a way that it popped a blister that had been developing on his index finger. Wilson pulled a ground-ball single into right. The ball took a final, fidgety hop in front of Evans and bounced off his chest. Knight, a slow runner who never would have challenged Evans's rifle arm, dashed to third base.

The Mets still trailed 2–1, but they had runners at the corners with none out. Santana, a .218 hitter during the season, was due up, followed by Ojeda. Here came the first of Johnson's second-guessed maneuvers. He had Danny Heep bat for Santana, who had had two hits off Clemens in Game 2. That meant Johnson's only remaining shortstops were Kevin Elster, a nervous rookie with 22 games of big league experience, and Howard Johnson, a utilityman who is considered a defensive liability.

"How could you be pinch-hitting that early?" Bowa asked.

"I thought it might be our one shot to get Clemens out of there," Johnson replied.

Johnson was subscribing to the strategy Earl Weaver had taught him: Use your guns whenever you think your time has come, no matter what inning. But as another manager puts it, "He was only going to use Ojeda one more inning, so why not keep Santana in the game and bat for the pitcher?" Heep hit into a double play that tied the score at 2–2, and Ojeda grounded out. He pitched one more inning, keeping the Sox at bay in the sixth.

Clemens's blister prevented him from throwing his slider, and because he didn't have a particularly good curveball in the late season, he decided simply to move his fastball around and change speeds. Wally Backman and Hernandez singled with one out in the sixth, but Clemens struck out Carter with a perfect pitch on the outside corner. He then held his breath as Barrett snapped up Strawberry's sharp grounder.

In the top of the seventh Roger McDowell walked leadoff hitter Barrett. Rather than sacrifice him over—the Red Sox were 1 for 4 trying to bunt in the game—McNamara removed the bunt sign for Buckner and sent Barrett. Buckner grounded out, moving Barrett into scoring position. When Knight fielded Rice's routine grounder and threw the ball over Hernandez's head, Boston had runners at first and third with one out and Evans up. On a 3-and-2 count, McNamara sent Rice. Sure enough, Evans hit a perfect double-play ball to Backman. However, Rice beat Backman's flip to Elster, and though Elster's throw got Evans at first, Barrett had scored to give the Red Sox a 3–2 lead.

The Red Sox had a chance to make it 4–2 when Gedman punched a two-out single through the shortstop hole into left-field. With two outs in a big ballpark, and considering Wilson's weak arm, Lachemann naturally waved Rice around third. However, Rice cut the bag like a 16-wheeler turning into a McDonald's, while Wilson charged the ball and released it quickly. The ball arrived in Carter's mitt on a fly, and Rice was out. "How we didn't score and put the game away in the first eight innings is just as much the story as what happened in the 10th," Barrett said later.

Clemens held the lead in the bottom of the seventh, retiring the side on 17 pitches—giving him 135 for the game. But while pitching to Wilson—naturally—he tore the fingernail on his middle finger, and when he got back to the dugout, he was bleeding from two fingers. McNamara and pitching coach Bill Fischer approached him.

"Does it sting?" McNamara asked.

"Sure, it stings," said Clemens.

"I told them I couldn't throw any sliders, but I could get them out with fastballs and forkballs," Clemens now says. "They told me that if the first couple of hitters got on, they might hit for me."

At the postgame press conference, McNamara clearly implied that Clemens asked out of the game because of the blister. "My pitcher told me he couldn't go any further," said McNamara. When George Grande of ESPN later asked Clemens off-camera what McNamara had said, Clemens got upset and started off to confront McNamara.

"Fischer stopped me and told me it was a misunderstanding, that Mac didn't mean it," recalls Clemens. "I wanted to pitch the eighth inning, then turn it over to Calvin with three outs to go."

Despite that minor imbroglio and the other questions that besieged McNamara over the winter, this fact remains: Through seven innings that October night the manager had looked like a genius. By starting Al Nipper in the fourth game, on a night no Boston pitcher could have beaten Ron Darling, McNamara had given his ace—Clemens—a full five days of rest. And Clemens had given the Red Sox the lead with just six outs to go.

In the top of the eighth, Dave Henderson reached base courtesy of the first of two boots by Elster. Spike Owen sacrificed Henderson to second, then McNamara had rookie Mike Greenwell bat for Clemens. Interestingly enough, McNamara's defense for not sending Baylor up to hit for Buckner three batters later was: "We wouldn't pinch-hit with a lead."

Greenwell struck out, and Johnson had McDowell walk Boggs intentionally. But then McDowell also walked Barrett to load the bases. Johnson had little choice but to bring in Orosco, who would retire 16 of the 18 batters he faced in the Series and should have been the MVP instead of Knight. Here is where Johnson committed his primary strategical boo-boo. The pitcher was scheduled to lead off the bottom of the inning, so with his best reliever in the game and the Red Sox one inning away from a world championship, Johnson should have made a double switch in order to keep Orosco in the game for at least the ninth inning. He could have put Lee Mazzilli or Mitchell in left and put Orosco in Wilson's spot, thus letting the new leftfielder lead off the bottom of the eighth. "Davey forgot," says one manager. "This wasn't one of my better games," Johnson admitted later.

It's far too easy to criticize managers, and very often the critics can't see the forest for the trees. While Johnson can sometimes be an unorthodox strategist, he is usually borne out in the long run by his players' performances. But in this case, he did forget. An inning later he would compound the situation by double-switching Strawberry out of the game, which led to Strawberry's pouting, which led to Strawberry's hotdogging it around the bases in Game 7 to show his manager up, which led to Nipper—who gave up the home run—hitting Strawberry in the back in spring training.

So this was the situation: bases loaded, two outs in the eighth and the lefty Orosco on the mound. The scheduled batter was Buckner, who showed great fortitude—some said folly—by playing on his battered legs. But he was also 10 for 55 in postseason play and 1 for 11 with runners in scoring position for the

Series. A lefthanded swinger, Buckner had hit .218 in the regular season against lefty pitchers. And Orosco is, in the words of Dodger scout Jerry Stephenson, "the toughest pitcher in the league on lefties," an opinion supported by the fact that lefthanded hitters batted .187 against him during the season.

Clearly, McNamara had a decision to make. He thought about using Baylor, who was on the bench because the Red Sox couldn't use a DH in the National League park. McNamara and Buckner later denied it, but other players sitting on the bench claim the manager approached Buckner to tell him he was taking him out. But before McNamara could say anything, Buckner talked him out of any move. "When Johnson came out of the dugout, Mac started to tell Buck, 'If they go to the lefthander....,' " says one of the players. "Buck argued, 'I can hit the guy.' He said something else and that was that. It wasn't like a bullying thing. It was as if Mac thought to himself and said, 'Hey, the guy's done this much with all those problems....' "

"I was in the clubhouse swinging a bat and was never told that I was going to bat," says Baylor. "Although I did hear that [McNamara was talked out of the move] from another player."

McNamara contends that he didn't want to pinch-hit for Buckner with a lead and that previously he replaced Buckner with Dave Stapleton at first only after Buckner had been removed for a pinch runner. But, in fact, Stapleton had gone in for defense in several postseason games. "We didn't hit for Buckner during the season," said McNamara. "Why then?"

But he also didn't have Baylor on the bench all season. While Baylor had batted only .230 against lefthanders, he was a major reason the Red Sox were there. His homer preceding Henderson's in the fifth game of the playoffs against the California Angels was the biggest hit of the season, and he had transformed the "me" mood of the clubhouse to a "we." Baylor certainly believed he should have batted. When a reporter said after the game, "I guess Buckner doesn't get hit for there," Baylor replied, "Why?"

"It's stupid to even debate about my hitting there," insists Buckner. "I hit the ball pretty hard, too." He did, and Dykstra ran it down in left center. It was still 3–2. Orosco was done, and so was Clemens. And Buckner was still in the game to play defense.

For all of Boston's weeping and teeth-gnashing over the 10th, the Red Sox were fortunate to get that far. In the bottom of the eighth, Mazzilli batted for Orosco and pulled Schiraldi's pitch into right for a single. Then the black flies—Dykstra and Wally Backman—went to work. Dykstra laid down a perfect bunt, and Schiraldi picked it up and bounced a throw to second in the dirt. Backman laid one down, too, and Schiraldi fielded it again, cautiously throwing to first for the out. But the tying run was on third and the go-ahead run on second. Schiraldi walked Hernandez intentionally to load the bases.

Schiraldi went to 3 and 0 on Carter, and as the NBC camera homed in on his face, Calvin looked exactly like a 24-year-old rookie who has suddenly realized that half the nation is watching him. "It just so happened that when I screwed up, it was the World Series," he said.

Johnson gave Schiraldi a break. He flashed Carter the green light to swing, and Carter, ever the hero, swung at a waist-high fastball, hitting it hard to Rice in leftfield. Mazzilli scored easily from third, and the game was tied 3–3. With two outs and Dykstra on third, Strawberry flied out to end the inning.

Then Johnson pulled the double-switch, putting Aguilera in Strawberry's spot and keeping Mazzilli in the game in right. Afterward, while the rest of the Mets rejoiced, Strawberry blasted the manager. "I didn't notice him doing anything spectacular," Johnson said.

The Met manager wasn't off the strategic hook yet. The Mets had runners on first and second with no outs in the ninth after Schiraldi walked Knight and Gedman misplayed Wilson's bunt. The next hitter was Elster. "That's a tough place to ask a rookie to get down a bunt against a guy like Schiraldi," explains Johnson. "A .167-hitting backup shortstop had better be able to bunt," says another manager. But Johnson wasn't taking any chances, especially after Elster had already messed up two balls at shortstop. So he sent up Howard Johnson to bunt. HoJo's stab at the first pitch looked like a pelican diving for a fish. "I didn't like the looks of that," says the manager, "so I took off the bunt. I did the same thing with Orosco in the eighth inning of the seventh game; he singled up the middle for the final run and no one said anything." When Johnson tipped strike three into Gedman's glove for the first out, the second-guessers howled. Mazzilli lined out, Dykstra flied out—and it was on to the 10th.

At precisely 11:59 p.m. Henderson, leading off, rifled an Aguilera pitch off the leftfield scoreboard. "Hendu" might have achieved cult status in Boston, what with his home run in the fifth game of the ALCS, and now this one. With two outs Boggs doubled to left center and the redoubtable Barrett singled him home to give the Red Sox a 5–3 lead. All the Red Sox needed were three outs. Schiraldi may be considered a once-around-the-order short reliever, but he had closed out two of the last three playoff wins, as well as the Series opener, and the Red Sox were going to stick with him.

In the Boston clubhouse, the champagne was laid out. Backman flied out to left. The NBC roadies set up the post-game riser as Peter Ueberroth, announcer Bob Costas and Red Sox owners Haywood Sullivan and Jean Yawkey began to get in position. The MVP trophy was going to Bruce Hurst. Hernandez lined out to center. As the last newspaper deadlines in the East approached, journalists typed out flash leads. Fred McMane of United Press International was about to send: "Dave Henderson, playing the hero Boston has sought for 68 years, homered in the top of the 10th inning Saturday night to give the Red Sox a 5–3 victory over the New York Mets and their first World Series title since 1918."

Hernandez disgustedly walked back down the runway to the clubhouse and joined Met scout Darrell Johnson—yes, the very same Darrell Johnson who had managed the Red Sox in the '75 World Series—in the manager's office for a beer.

Carter drilled a 2–1 fastball into leftfield. Next up, Mitchell. When Hernandez was at the plate, Mitchell was up in the clubhouse; he had taken his uniform pants off and was on the phone making a reservation for his flight home to San Diego. "I didn't think I'd be hitting," he told Dave Anderson of *The New York Times* this spring. "I hadn't hit against a righthanded pitcher all season in that situation. Heep was still on the bench. I figured he'd hit for me, so I went up to the clubhouse." That shows how closely some players follow the game, because Heep had pinch-hit for Santana in the fifth—and was out of the game. When Johnson read Mitchell's quote, he said, "Now I'm even happier about the deal [for Kevin McReynolds]."

Howard Johnson came running into the clubhouse. "Get out there, you're hitting," he hollered at Mitchell. "I hung up the phone, then I slipped my pants back on," said Mitchell, "but I'd taken off everything under them. My jock, my underwear." Mitchell wasn't totally disconcerted. He remembered that when he and Schiraldi had played together in Jackson, Miss., in 1983, the pitcher had told him that if he ever faced him, he would start him out with a fastball inside, then try to get him with a slider away. That's exactly what Schiraldi did, and Mitchell hit the slider for a single to center.

Schiraldi then got two strikes on Knight. "He was so excited," says McNamara, "that he just forgot how to pitch Knight. No big deal. He's human. He was a rookie." McNamara, who managed Knight in Cincinnati, had told his pitchers that when Knight gets behind in the count, he looks for the inside fastball and fights it off, so they should put the ball on the outside corner. But Schiraldi came up and in. Knight fought it off, dumping a quail into right center, and Mitchell raced around to third. McNamara then decided he'd better go to the veteran Stanley, who had struck Wilson out in Game 3.

Stanley, a $1 million-per-year pitcher, had been unhappy about his bullpen role since McNamara had made Schiraldi the closer in early August. He felt the manager had lost nearly as much faith in him as the Fenway Park fans, whom he blamed for his 6.00 ERA at home. This was what Stanley had foreseen in April, when he vowed, "They may boo me now, but they'll love me when I'm standing on the mound when we win the World Series."

Wilson fouled Stanley's first pitch to the screen, took two balls, then fouled another into the dirt to even the count at 2 and 2. For the second time that morning, the Red Sox were one strike away. Met third base coach Bud Harrelson told Mitchell to be ready to go on a wild pitch.

Wilson fouled off the next pitch, and the next one. What happened next is subject to debate. Stanley told friends that Gedman called for a fastball up and in, then set a target down and out. Gedman has refused any comment except to say: "I should have stopped any pitch." An infielder claims that Stanley misread the sign and that Gedman was in position for Stanley's best pitch—a sinker—out over the plate. Instead, the pitch took off, sailing low and inside. Wilson spun out of the way. The weary Gedman, who was so intense in the playoffs that he chipped three teeth by grinding them, couldn't get his glove on the ball. As it squirted to the screen, Mitchell danced across the plate. Knight went to second.

The score was tied, 5–5. For the third time the Mets had come from behind; the Red Sox, it should be noted, did not come from behind in the entire Series. With "eerie efficiency," as Costas describes it, the visiting clubhouse was cleared of the riser, the trophy, the champagne and the Red Sox owners in less than one minute.

Stanley then missed a chance to end the inning without another pitch, which would have left the Mets with a pitching choice of Doug Sisk or Randy Niemann. As Stanley took his stretch, Barrett signaled for a pickoff, sneaked over to second and waited for Stanley to whirl and throw. "We had Knight dead," says Barrett. While Barrett screamed from the second base bag, the oblivious Stanley delivered to Wilson, who fouled the pitch off.

On the 10th pitch of his at bat, Wilson topped a ground ball toward the first base bag. Buckner was playing deep behind the base. He hustled over to the line, but there was no way he could have made the play himself. Stanley was racing to the bag, but to this day Buckner believes Wilson would have beaten Stanley on the play. "I would have been there," insists Stanley. As Buckner reached down to corner the ball, it skittered between his legs. McNamara has a ready answer for those who felt Stapleton would have made the play. "If the question had been range, that would have been justified criticism," McNamara argues. "But the one thing Buckner has is a soft pair of hands. He catches what he gets to."

As the ball trickled onto the outfield grass, Knight raced home with the winning run—and the Mets had miraculously survived. "When you get within one strike and don't win, you don't deserve to win," Red Sox pitcher Tom Seaver said later.

After a day of rain they played Game 7, and at first it seemed that the Red Sox had suffered no ill effects from the disaster. They jumped off to a 3–0 lead over Darling in the second inning on back-to-back homers by Evans and Gedman and a run-scoring single by Boggs. Hurst, meanwhile, was pitching so well that he allowed only a single base runner in the first five innings. But then the Mets tied the score at 3–all on three singles, a walk and a fielder's choice. Schiraldi replaced Hurst in the seventh, and Knight greeted him with a home run to give the Mets a 4–3 lead. Two more runs scored on an RBI single by Santana and a sacrifice fly by Hernandez. Although the Red Sox closed the gap to 6–5 in the eighth, the Mets came right back with two more runs, on Strawberry's in-your-face homer off Nipper's and Orosco's fake bunt. Orosco set the Red Sox down in order in the ninth. It was a game that was fairly exciting unto itself, but following Game 6, it was an anticlimax.

McNamara, Buckner, Stanley and Schiraldi will try to put Game 6 back in the closet, but it will be no easy task. McNamara acknowledged that by holding his little spring training meeting.

"The Mets were a great team," Buckner insists, and he is right. "We had a great year. Last March, was there anyone in this country who thought we'd make it to the seventh game of the World Series? Remember the fifth game of the playoffs, Clemens's 24 wins, all the teams that made runs at us during the season. Forget one game."

Forget it? New Englanders haven't let .307 lifetime hitter Johnny Pesky forget he held the ball in the '46 Series—and he wasn't even at fault. Forget it? When the *Today* show observed Fred Merkle Day a while back, it wasn't because "Bonehead" had a good rookie year in 1908. Forget it? At the New York Baseball Writers Dinner last January, Ralph Branca was introduced to Clemens as "the guy who gave up Bobby Thomson's homer." That happened only 36 years ago.

There are just some things you never forget.

A Series
To Savor

♦

BY STEVE RUSHIN

IN 1991, THE MINNESOTA TWINS AND THE ATLANTA BRAVES,
TWO UNDERDOGS SUDDENLY ON TOP, BATTLED THROUGH
WHAT WILL SURELY BE REMEMBERED AS ONE OF THE GREATEST
WORLD SERIES IN BASEBALL HISTORY. STEVE RUSHIN WROTE THE
STORY TO MATCH.

The truth is inelastic when it comes to the 88th World Series.
It is impossible to stretch. It isn't necessary to appraise the nine
days just past from some distant horizon of historical perspective. Let us call this Series what it is, now, while its seven
games still ring in our ears: the greatest that was ever played.

Both the Minnesota Twins and the Atlanta Braves enlarged
the game of baseball, while reducing individual members of
both teams to humble participants in a Series with drama too
huge to be hyperbolized. There were five one-run duels, four
of them won on the game's final play, three extended to
extra innings—all categories that apply to the ultimate, unfath-
omable game played on Sunday night in Minneapolis, in
which a 36-year-old man threw 10 innings of shutout baseball
in the seventh game of the World Series. Grown men were
reduced to tears and professional athletes to ill health in the

aftermath of the Twins' winning their second world championship in five seasons.

This was the *winners'* clubhouse: An hour after Jack Morris beat the Braves 1–0 for the title, Twins pitcher Kevin Tapani broke out in a red rash. "I'm surprised if I don't have ulcers," said infielder Al Newman, slouched lifelessly on a stool. "I think I'll get checked out."

Across the room, Morris lay propped against a television platform, pondering the events of the previous days. "I don't know if it will happen tomorrow or the next day," he said, "but somewhere down the road, they're going to look back on this Series and say...."

Say what, exactly? Morris, like the scribes spread out before him, was overwhelmed by the thought of describing all that had transpired, and he allowed his words to trail off into a champagne bottle. The bubbly had been broken out by clubhouse attendants shortly after 11:00 p.m., when pinch hitter Gene Larkin slapped the first pitch he got from Alejandro Pena to left center, over the head of Brian Hunter, who, like the rest of the Atlanta outfield, was playing only 30 yards in back of the infield in an effort to prevent Minnesota's Dan Gladden from doing precisely what he did: bound home from third base in the bottom of the 10th, through a cross-current of crazed, dazed teammates, who were leaping from the third base dugout and onto the field.

Even Atlanta second baseman Mark Lemke, whose name had become familiar to the nation earlier in the week, was moved, in defeat, by the momentous nature of the game. "The only thing better," he said, "would have been if we stopped after nine innings and cut the trophy in half."

Impossibly, both the Braves and the Twins had loaded the bases with less than two outs in the eighth inning and failed to score. Improbably, both threats had been snuffed with mind-boggling suddenness by double plays. Atlanta was done in by a slick 3–2–3 job courtesy of Minnesota first baseman Kent Hrbek and catcher Brian Harper. The Twins were stymied by a crowd-jolting unassisted DP by Lemke, who grabbed a soft liner off the bat of Hrbek and stepped on second. So by the bottom of the 10th, when Harper, seeing Larkin make contact, threw his batting helmet high into the air in the on-deck circle and Gladden jumped onto home plate with both feet, the switch was thrown on a 30-minute burst of emotion in the Metrodome stands, an energy that, if somehow harnessed, would have lit the Twin Cities through a second consecutive sleepless night.

For it was only 24 hours earlier that Minnesota centerfielder Kirby Puckett had virtually single-handedly forced a seventh game by assembling what has to rank among the most outrageous all-around performances the World Series has ever seen. Puckett punctuated his night by hitting a home run in the bottom of the 11th inning off Atlanta's Charlie Leibrandt. The solo shot gave the Twins a 4–3 win and gave Puckett's teammates the same "chill-bump feeling" Braves manager Bobby Cox confessed to having had in Atlanta, where the Braves had swept Games 3, 4 and 5 earlier in the week to take a three game to two lead into Minneapolis.

Hrbek was reduced to a 10-year-old when the Series was tied last Saturday night; Sunday morning would be Christmas Day. "Guys will be staring at the ceiling tonight," he said following Game 6. "They won't even know if their wives are next to 'em. I know I won't. She won't want to hear that, but...."

Minnesota hitting coach Terry Crowley was reduced to a doddering man in long underwear that same evening, pacing a small circle in the clubhouse, head down and muttering to no one, "It's unbelievable. Unbelievable."

And Twins manager Tom Kelly fairly shed his skin in the aftermath of that game, wriggling from the hard exterior he has worn throughout his career and revealing himself to be, like the rest of us, both awed and addled by all he had witnessed. "This is storybook," Kelly said. "Who's got the script? Who is *writing* this? Can you *imagine* this?"

Understand what Kelly and 55,155 paying customers had just seen Puckett do beneath the dome. In addition to his game-winning home run, he had singled, tripled, driven in a run on a sacrifice fly, stolen a base and scored a run of his own. In the third inning he had leapt high against a Plexiglas panel in centerfield, hanging there momentarily like one of those suction-cup Garfield dolls in a car window, to rob Ron Gant of extra bases and Atlanta of an almost certain run.

After the game had remained tied at three through the eighth, ninth and 10th innings, Cox brought in lefthander Leibrandt to face the righthanded-hitting Puckett, who was leading off in the bottom of the 11th. Why Leibrandt? He had won 15 games in the regular season, Cox pointed out later. But Cox may as well have said what was on everybody's mind—that it didn't matter whom he put on the mound to face Puckett. The man was going to hit a home run no matter what. That was the only logical conclusion to his Saturday in the park. Puckett did just that, and the tortured Leibrandt walked off the field, his face buried in the crook of his right arm.

Afterward, teammates filed almost sheepishly past Puckett's locker, some shaking his hand, others embracing him, most of them without any words to say. This 5' 8" escapee of one of North America's worst slums—Who *is* writing this, anyway? Who *did* imagine this?—acknowledged he was having difficulty grasping the enormity of the evening. "Ten, 30, 50 years from now, when I look at it, it might be different," he said. "Right now? Unbelievable, man. Unbelievable."

Yes, this Series was baseball's most epic tale. It included twin props—the Minnesota fans' fluttering hankie and the Atlanta fans' chopping tomahawk—that grew equally tiresome as the Series grew increasingly enervating. And it was a tale that engaged two teams that, preposterously, had finished last in their divisions a year ago. Yet, similar as they were, the teams had two distinct followings for the Series: The nationally cabled Braves were America's Team, while the Twins became Native America's Team.

After the Twins put a stranglehold on the first two games of the Series, which had opened on Oct. 19 in Minneapolis, by producing game-winning dingers from two bottom-feeders in their batting order—Greg Gagne and Scott Leius? Who *is* writing this?—the Series went south in geography only. Before Game 3, Native Americans picketed Atlanta–Fulton County Stadium, protesting from behind police lines that the Braves' nickname and the team's tomahawk-chopping fans were disrespectful to their people. Ticket holders approaching turnstiles were implored by placard-bearers to, among other things, "Repatriate remains to ancestral burial grounds!"—which is a difficult thing to do between pitches. "No one," said Atlanta pitcher John Smoltz, "is going to stop this city from having fun right now."

Likewise, no gun-toting yahoo was going to stop Hrbek from having his usual hellacious good time in the ball yard. His mother, Tina, was telephoned at 3:30 a.m. on the eve of Game 3 by an anonymous moron, who told her that her son would "get one between the eyes" in Atlanta. Yet Hrbek, who in Game 2 had leg-wrestled Gant from first base to tag him out and kill a rally, came to Georgia wary of nothing more than ... gingivitis. He tipped his cap to the bloodlusting crowd that booed him during introductions, tomahawk-chopped the fans from the top step of the Minnesota dugout and blithely flossed his teeth during live TV interviews. All the while he went one-for-Dixie and found the time to reconcile the joy of playing in the Series with the anguish of a death threat. "This game sucks," he said, "but it's a lot of fun."

Their villain already cast, 50,878 Braves fans showed up for Game 3, the first World Series game ever played within 500 miles of Atlanta. When it finally came time to play ball, y'all, and the first pitch was thrown by 21-year-old Braves starter Steve Avery at 8:38 p.m., flashbulbs popped throughout the park like bursts of white lightning. "I feel sorry for Dan Gladden," said Braves first baseman Sid Bream later of the Twins' leadoff hitter. "He was probably seeing 5,000 baseballs thrown at him."

For each flashbulb, there was photographic evidence for a fan that he or she was present the night the largest cast ever to appear in a World Series game put on the longest-running night show in Series history. When the curtain dropped four hours and four minutes later at 12:42 a.m. after a record 42 players had traversed the stage, Atlanta reserve catcher Jerry Willard would pronounce himself "exhausted." And he was one of two position players on either roster who *didn't* play.

When Chili Davis, pinch-hitting against Pena, squeezed off a two-run tracer bullet to leftfield in the eighth inning, the game was tied at four. It would go to extra frames and send scorekeepers into a hopelessly dizzying spiral of pinch hitters, double switches and defensive replacements, thus birthing the biggest box score the World Series has ever known.

Before the bottom of the 12th, Braves catcher Greg Olson told Lemke, a career .225 hitter with a dwarflike presence at the plate, that Lemke—a.k.a. Lumpy, a.k.a. the Lemmer—would get the game-winning hit that inning. Olson is a Minnesota native who spent 13 days with the Twins in 1989, during which time he was given the T-shirt, emblazoned with a caricature of Puckett, that Olson wears beneath his uniform to this day. Lemke, having no such talisman to draw upon for strength, pretended not to hear his teammate's prediction. "But I said to myself, 'Ehhhh, I don't *think* so,' " said the Lemmer later. This recollection came, of course, shortly after Lemke had singled to drive in rightfielder David Justice, who scored inches ahead of Gladden's throw and Harper's tag.

With Lemke's late game-winner, bedlam and then bedtime ensued in Atlanta. The Braves were 5–4 victors, and Lemke, at his locker, looked longingly at a bottle of Rolaids the size of a sweepstakes drum. "I get big-time heartburn," he said as just one of several cardiologically concerned members of the Braves. As Justice put it: "If we win the World Series now, I think you're going to see some guys have heart attacks in here. I really do."

Eighteen hours later, as baseball commissioner Fay Vincent settled into his special overstuffed, faux-leather easy chair along the first base line and prepared to take in Game 4, he needed only a reading lamp and a stand-up globe to look completely at home. And that was all an observer needed to do on this night: Look at home, to the thick and transfixing traffic at the plate. It was there, in the fifth inning, that Harper tagged out Lonnie Smith in a bone-rattling collision and, moments later, put the touch on Terry Pendleton as Pendleton tried to score on a not-wild-enough pitch that bounded in front of home plate.

In the top of the seventh, Minnesota's Mike Pagliarulo hit a solo homer to break a 1–1 tie. In the bottom of the seventh, Smith did the same to retie things. Stomach linings could be heard eroding throughout the stadium before Lemke, who wears a PROPERTY OF UTICA COLLEGE INTRAMURALS T-shirt under *his* uniform, slugged a one-out triple in the bottom of the ninth. One batter later, Willard emerged from the dugout to pinch-hit.

Willard's parents, Faye and Jerry Sr., had arrived two days earlier from Port Hueneme, Calif. They had driven three straight days to Atlanta, only to see their son sit on the bench during the most populous World Series game ever played. *Coach Cox, why don't you play my son? You play all the other kids.* On this night, however, Willard would heroically fly out to shallow rightfield, just deep enough to allow Lemke to tag up from third and slide past Harper, who appeared to tag him out as the two made contact. In fact, Harper never laid the leather on the Lemmer, and another page in the epic was turned. "Same two teams here tomorrow," Skip Caray dryly told his radio audience as he signed off following Atlanta's 3–2 win.

Game 5 was a godsend for both teams, though Minnesota wouldn't acknowledge it at the time. The Braves' 14–5 tom-tom drumming of the Twins at last broke the skein of hyper-tense games that had endangered the central nervous systems of all those who had been watching them. On the Atlanta side, Smith tied a Series record by homering for the third consecutive game. On the Minnesota side, Kelly removed oh-fer right-fielder Shane Mack from his lineup and rendered him Mack the Knifeless as well. "We hit the razor blades," Kelly said of Mack, who was so disconsolate after the benching that "he was ready to cut his throat."

After the Twins had taken their Game 5 punishment, Atlanta fans stayed at the stadium to send off their team, and the play-ers enthusiastically embraced the crowd in this love-in. The Braves were fully expected to return from Minneapolis with a world championship, what with Avery pitching on Saturday against Minnesota starter Scott Erickson. The former was so cool that when former President Jimmy Carter introduced him-self in the Atlanta clubhouse following Game 5, Avery respond-ed, "Howyadoin'." The latter, meanwhile, had posted a luke-warm 5.19 ERA in the postseason. And yet....

Erickson allowed only five hits in six innings in Game 6, though various Braves scorched balls right at Twins infielders or launched missiles that landed millimeters foul. But give the Twins credit. "If you got any pride at all, and your back's against the wall, you're going to fight your way out," said Puckett, who was raised in the crime-infected Robert Taylor Homes on Chicago's South Side and who fought his way out of Game 6 with two fists. Said the man afterward, "I'll get my rest when I'm dead."

Twins reliever Rick Aguilera picked up the win, just as he had in the dramatic sixth game of the 1986 Series as a member of the New York Mets, cannibalizing the Red Sox and Bill Buckner. What is it about Game 6? Boston's Carlton Fisk hit his unforgettable body-English home run off Cincinnati's Pat Darcy in the 12th inning of Game 6 in '75. And while the Red Sox went on to lose Game 7, they are as inextricably linked to that Series as are the Reds. The same unforgotten status would be bestowed upon Sunday's loser, no doubt. "Whatever happens tomorrow," Puckett said haltingly on Saturday, "it's been a great Series. I mean, I want to win. But if we don't, I'm just honored to be a part of this."

Morris would concede no such thing. "In the immortal words of the late, great Marvin Gaye," he said on the eve of Game 7, " 'Let's get it on.' " And that they did, the Braves and the Twins. Morris outlasted the 24-year-old Smoltz. On this night it appeared he would have outlasted Methuselah.

When the seventh game and the Series had finally been bled from the bodies on both sides, when the two teams had stopped their cartoon brawl, raising ridiculous lumps by alternately slugging each other over the head with a sledgehammer, when all of 60 minutes had passed after the last game, Pagliarulo stood wearily at his locker. "This was the greatest game," he said. "How could the TV guys describe it? They had a chance to win—but they didn't. We had a chance to win—but we didn't. Then we did. I kept thinking of the '75 Series tonight. This is why baseball is the greatest game there is."

The greatest game there is. The greatest games that ever were.

PLAYERS

◆ ◆ ◆

The Mantle
of the Babe

♦

B Y   R O B E R T   C R E A M E R

IN SPRING OF 1956, BOB CREAMER PAID A CALL ON MICKEY
MANTLE, WHO WAS LEADING THE NEW YORK YANKEES TOWARD
YET ANOTHER PENNANT. MANTLE WAS ALSO HAVING A FINE
YEAR PERSONALLY—INDEED, HE WOULD FINISH THE SEASON WITH
52 HOME RUNS, 130 RUNS BATTED IN AND A .353 BATTING
AVERAGE—MAKING HIM ONE OF ONLY FOUR PLAYERS SINCE
WORLD WAR II TO WIN BASEBALL'S TRIPLE CROWN.

A thick-bodied, pleasant-faced young man, carrying a bat,
stood at home plate in Yankee Stadium, turned the blond bullet head on his bull's neck toward Pedro Ramos, a pitcher in
the employ of the Washington Senators, watched intently the
flight of the baseball thrown toward him, bent his knees,
dropped his right shoulder slightly toward the ball, clenched
his bat and raised it to a near-perfect perpendicular. Twisting
his massive torso under the guidance of a magnificently tuned
set of reflexes, Mickey Mantle so controlled the exorbitant
strength generated by his legs, back, shoulders and arms that
he brought his bat through the plane of the flight of the pitch
with a precision which propelled the ball immensely high and
far toward the right-field roof, so high and far that oldtimers in

98

the crowd—thinking perhaps of Babe Ruth—watched in awe and held their breath.

For no one had ever hit a fair ball over the majestic height of the gray-green façade that looms above the three tiers of grandstand seats in this, the greatest of ball parks.

Indeed, in the 33 years since the Stadium was opened not one of the great company of home run hitters who have batted there—the list includes Babe Ruth, Lou Gehrig, Joe DiMaggio, Jimmy Foxx, Hank Greenberg and about everyone else you can think of—had even come close to hitting a fair ball over the giant-sized filigree hanging from the lip of the stands which in both right and left field hook far into fair territory toward the bleachers.

Mantle hit the filigree. He came so close to making history that he made it.

The ball struck high on the façade, barely a foot or two below the edge of the roof. Ever since, as people come into the stadium and find their seats, almost invariably their eyes wander to The Spot. Arms point and people stare in admiration. Then they turn to the field and seek out Mantle.

On that same day that he hit the façade Mantle hit a second homer. This one was his 20th of the season and it put him at that date (May 30) 12 games ahead of the pace Babe Ruth followed when he established his quasi-sacred record of 60 in 1927. Other players in other years had excitingly chased Ruth's record. But Mantle, somehow, seemed different from earlier pretenders to Ruth's crown and different, too, from slugging contemporaries like Yogi Berra, whose great skill seems almost methodical, and Dale Long, who is still, despite all, an unknown quantity.

The excitement surrounding Mantle goes beyond numbers, beyond homers hit and homers and games to go. Like Ruth, his violent strength is held in a sheath of powerful, controlled grace. Like Ruth, he makes home run hitting simple and exciting at the same time. The distance he hits his home runs (the approved cliché is "Ruthian blast") takes away the onus of cheapness, a word often applied to the common variety of home run hit today, and leaves the spectator aghast, whether he roots for Mantle or against him.

All this holds true despite the hard fact that heretofore in his five years in the major leagues the most home runs Mantle has hit in one season is 37, whereas Ruth hit 40 or more 11 different times, and two dozen others have hit 40 or more at least once.

Yet where others impress, Mantle awes, and even the knowing professional speaks reverently of him. Harvey Kuenn, the shortstop of the Detroit Tigers and a topflight hitter in his own right, listened as Sportscaster Howard Cosell, an eyewitness, described the Memorial Day home run to him.

"Did he really hit it up there?" Kuenn asked, knowing but not believing. "Really?" He shook his head. "His strength isn't human," he said. "How can a man hit a ball that hard?"

Marty Marion, the unexcitable manager of the Chicago White Sox, described a homer Mantle had hit against the Sox with two out in the ninth to tie a game the Yankees eventually won. "It went way up there," Marty said, with a wry little grin, pointing to the far reaches of the upper stands in deep right-center field. "Way up there. He swung just as easy and *whup!* It was gone. Way up there. I never saw anything like it."

As for the nonprofessional, there is no question that Mantle is the new excitement, the new Ruth. Like Ruth, he is known to those who don't know baseball, magically, the way Ruth was. A 7-year-old boy, just on the edge of interest in baseball and in bed getting over the measles, watched part of a Yankee game on television. Later he was not quite sure what teams had been playing and he wasn't positive of the score, but when he was asked if he had seen Mickey Mantle bat, his red-speckled face lit up and he said, excitedly, "He hit a big one!"

Of course, Mantle wasn't the only one to hit "big ones" in this year of the slugger. Some said the 1956 version of the lively ball was responsible for the increasingly bullish market in home runs. Others gave credit (or blame) to the growing popularity of the slender-handled willow-wand bat, which bends like a reed when swung hard and breaks easily but which combines concentrated mass and blinding velocity much the way a golf club does. Mantle uses a 32-ounce bat when he hits left handed, 10 ounces lighter than the bat Ruth used.

Whatever the reason, 19 players had hit 10 or more home runs by June 11, an unprecedented number. But Mantle towered above this forest of hitters both for quality and quantity of his home runs. By June 11 only Ruth had hit more home runs up to that point in a season.

Most of the managers in the American League marveled at Mantle's strength and hoped that the heat of summer and the law of averages would slow him down. Lou Boudreau of the Kansas City Athletics turned to more immediate and dramatic means. Boudreau is an eminently practical man who said sorrowfully of the lively ball that, while other teams must be hitting it, no one ever seemed to throw it to his batters. When the Athletics came into Yankee Stadium a week ago Boudreau carried with him a sheet of paper on which was scribbled a baseball diamond and nine Xs.

When Mantle came to bat in the first inning with two out and the bases empty the Athletics in the field deployed to points approximating the Xs on Boudreau's map. The effect was slightly sensational. It was the Boudreau Shift, with radical variations that included a left fielder playing an extremely deep third base and a third baseman playing a shallow center field. Everyone remembered at once that it was Boudreau, then manager of the Cleveland Indians, who devised the shift in 1946 to stop Ted Williams, and that Manager Eddie Dyer of the St. Louis Cardinals used it in the World Series that year to smother Williams' bat—five singles in 25 at bats in seven games.

But Williams was a slow runner and an unreconstructed right-field pull hitter, whereas Mantle is a switch hitter who knocks the ball well to all fields whether he's batting left handed or right handed. More than that, Mantle is a superb bunter and the fastest man in baseball down to first base.

Everyone waited for Mickey to bunt the Athletics blind, but the pitcher, the erratic Lou Kretlow, had sufficient control of his rising fast ball that night to keep it high and close, with the result that Mantle fouled off all three of the bunts he attempted. He struck out twice (though later in the game, with a man on base and the shift off, he hit a home run) and the next day struck out once more. In the three games against Kansas City he had four base hits in 13 times at bat, which isn't bad: a .308 batting average. But, truth to tell, the shift seemed to affect Mantle's poise at the plate.

The strikeouts were a symptom. Mantle's greatest problem in his first five years in the majors was a tendency to strike out.

This year in spring training he restrained his need to crush the ball with his bat every time he swung, and he struck out only once in the exhibition season. This restraint, applied in the regular season, did not keep his strikeout total quite so dramatically low but it did increase his control of the bat, his ability to meet the ball and, therefore, his domination over the pitcher. Meeting the ball gave him a lot more line-drive base hits and a batting average that has scorched along near or above .400 all season, and his natural strength sent more of those base hits over the outfield barriers than ever before.

Whether or not it was the real or psychological effect of the shift, Mantle's home run pace slowed abruptly in the first week of June. About the shift, Yankee General Manager George Weiss voiced a remark which was something less than a compliment to Mantle's still-maturing self-discipline: "It got him thinking, and that's bad."

Manager Casey Stengel growled around the New York Yankee clubhouse, arguing that the shift made little sense.

"Here's a man can bunt and run down to first base," Stengel said. "If he bunts 10 times he'll get on base five and that's a .500 average. If he hits he'll hit as many home runs as he would anyway because there isn't anyone in the world can catch a ball in the upper stands or the lower stands. Those guys out in left field and right field may catch a couple of long balls, but we have no one on base and we wouldn't score a run anyway and if he bunts who's up next? Berra. Am I right?"

But it seemed to gnaw on Stengel. Here was Mantle, for the first time in his career quietly confident in his own ability, poised and sure of himself, and here was that damned shift and the possibility that Mantle might start to press thinking about it. George Weiss stayed a little worried, too. "I think he ought to just stand up there and hit," George suggested. "Just forget about the shift."

Mantle, while sloughing off from his rapid-fire home run pace, had no cause to worry, not yet, at any rate. All the great home run hitters produced their homers at an uneven tempo. All had one brilliant run (remarkably similar to Mantle's burst of 20 in 41 games), a good secondary cluster (which Mantle, hopefully, will have, too) and a series of dry spells. Jimmy Foxx, who at 24 (Mantle's age) hit 58 home runs in 1932, had one long good surge in May and June (22 in 44 games) and a long lukewarm period in midsummer. But twice he went through 10 straight games without a single homer.

No one was more erratic than Hank Greenberg when he hit 58 in 1938. He went along evenly at first until June 1, when he fell into an abject slump and hit only one home run in the next 16 games. Once that was over he started up like an outboard motor: a sputter of home runs, a brief hesitation, another sputter, another, and then *b-r-r-r-r-r!* through the end of July. He hit 23 home runs in only 38 games, the greatest sustained streak of home run hitting of any of the great sluggers. It ended in a wild crescendo: a home run on July 24, two on July 26, two more on July 27, two more on July 29 and two more on July 30. Then the motor stalled and in the following 17 games Greenberg added just one. In mid-August he came alive again and hit a blistering 20 in the next 40 games. Five days before the end of the season Hank had his 58 home runs. He needed but two more to tie Ruth, three to beat him. What happened? Well, you remember those outboard motors of the '30s. Didn't some of them pick the most frustrating times to konk out?

Ruth himself was erratic. In 1927 he raced through May and into the middle of June, the pace that Mantle has been surpassing. From mid-June until mid-August he slowed down to a comparative crawl. By August 16 the Babe was *29 games behind* his pace when he had hit 59 in 1921. But from then to the end of the season Ruth hit homers at an ever-increasing rate. With nine games to play he was still seven shy of 60. Ruth, ever dramatic, hit the seven, four of them in the last four games.

Some time, maybe, Mantle will have the curiosity to go back some 29 years, to a day of grandeur such as he may live to enjoy himself. If so, this is what he will read in the *New York Times* of October 1, 1927:

"Babe Ruth scaled the hitherto unattained heights yesterday. Home Run 60, a terrific smash off the southpaw pitching of Zachary, nestled in the Babe's favorite spot in the right field bleachers....

"When the Babe stepped to the plate in that momentous eighth inning the score was deadlocked. Koenig was on third base, the result of a triple, one man was out and all was tense. It was the

Babe's fourth trip to the plate during the afternoon, a base on balls and two singles resulting on his other visits plateward.

"The first Zachary offering was a fast one, which sailed over for a called strike. The next was high. The Babe took a vicious swing at the third pitched ball and the bat connected with a crash that was audible in all parts of the stand....The boys in the bleachers indicated the route of the record homer. It dropped about half way to the top. Boys, No. 60 was some homer, a fitting wallop to top the Babe's record of 59 in 1921.

"While the crowd cheered and the Yankee players roared their greetings the Babe made his triumphant, almost regal tour of the paths. He jogged around slowly, touched each bag firmly and carefully, and when he imbedded his spikes in the rubber disk to record officially Homer 60, hats were tossed in the air, papers were torn up and tossed liberally and the spirit of celebration permeated the place.

"The Babe's stroll out to his position was the signal for a handkerchief salute in which all the bleacherites, to the last man, participated. Jovial Babe entered into the spirit and punctuated his kingly strides with a succession of snappy military salutes....

"The ball ... was fast, low and inside. The Babe pulled away from the plate, then stepped into the ball and wham! ... it was about 10 feet fair and curving rapidly to the right.

"The ball which became Homer 60 was caught by Joe Forner, of 1937 First Avenue, Manhattan."

Through the jargon of that anonymous writer seeps the unmistakable hallmark of high sporting drama. Whether Mickey himself will ever know a similar moment depends as much on his ability to emulate Ruth's poise and presence and competitive spark as it does on his bat, but his broad, broad back seems ready to receive the mantle of the Babe.

Aches and Pains and Three Batting Titles

♦

BY MYRON COPE

IN 1966 MYRON COPE SPENT SOME TIME WITH ROBERTO CLEMENTE, THE TALENTED BUT LARGELY UNAPPRECIATED OUT-FIELDER FOR THE PITTSBURGH PIRATES. CLEMENTE WOULD WIN THE MVP AWARD THAT YEAR AND CONTINUE TO PLAY WITH CHARACTERISTIC EXCELLENCE FOR ANOTHER SIX SEASONS BEFORE HIS TRAGIC DEATH IN 1972 ABOARD AN AIRPLANE BRINGING AID TO EARTHQUAKE VICTIMS IN NICARAGUA.

The batting champion of the major leagues lowered himself to the pea-green carpet of his 48-foot living room and sprawled on his right side, flinging his left leg over his right leg. He wore gold Oriental pajama tops, tan slacks, battered bedroom slippers and—for purposes of the demonstration he was conducting—a tortured grimace. "Like dis!" he cried, and then dug his fingers into his flesh, just above his upraised left hip. Roberto Clemente, the Pittsburgh Pirates' marvelous right fielder and their steadiest customer of the medical profession, was showing how he must greet each new day in his life. He has a disk in his back that insists on wandering, so when he awakens he must cross those legs, dig at that flesh and listen for the sound of the disk popping back where it belongs.

Around the room necks were craned and ears alerted for the successful conclusion of the demonstration. Clemente's wife—the tall, beautiful Vera—sat solemnly in a gold wing chair a few feet away. Way out in the right-field seats, ensconced on a $1,000 velvet sofa in what may be called the Italian Provincial division of Clemente's vast living room, were his 18-year-old nephew, Pablo, and Pablo's buddy, Wilson. They sat fascinated, or at least they seemed fascinated, for it may have been that Wilson, who says his hobby is girls, was wishing that minute that Roberto would lend them his Cadillac.

"No, you cannot hear the disk now," shouted Roberto. "It is in place now. But every morning you can hear it from here to there, in the whole room. *Boop!*"

Boop? Certainly, boop. Not only one boop but two, for there is another disk running around up in the vicinity of Roberto's neck. For that one he must have someone manipulate his neck muscles until the sound of the boop is heard.

All this herding of disks, mind you, is but a nub on the staggering list of medical attentions that Clemente has undergone during his 11 years as a Pirate. Relatively small at 5 feet 10 inches and 180 pounds when able to take nourishment, the chronic invalid has smooth skin, glistening muscles and perfect facial contours that suggest the sturdy mahogany sculpture peddled in the souvenir shops of his native Puerto Rico. His countrymen regard him as the most superb all-round big-leaguer to emerge from their island, while many Pittsburghers have concluded that the only thing that can keep Clemente from making them forget Paul Waner is a sudden attack of good health.

Now 31, Clemente over the past five pain-filled years has won three National League batting championships (to say nothing of leading *both* leagues for the past two years) and has averaged .330, a level of consistency that no other big-leaguer has equaled during this half decade. In strength and accuracy his throwing arm has surpassed that of the old Brooklyn cannon, Carl Furillo, and if Roberto's genes are any indication his arm is not about to weaken. "My mother is 75," he says. "Last year she threw out the first pitch of the season. She put something on it, too." Because Roberto smolders with an intense belief in himself, some ballplayers argue that his only real malady is a serious puffing of the head, but the clicking of the X-ray machines, the scraping of scalpels, the trickle of intravenous feeding and the scratching of pens upon prescription pads have mounted to such a fortissimo that Roberto would seem to be a fit subject for graduate research. The moment when Roberto first set eyes on his wife is the story of his life: he spied her in a drug store, where he had gone to buy medication for an ailing leg.

"I played only two innings in the winter league this year," sighed Roberto, having picked himself off the carpet and dumped himself into a chair. "I was having headaches, headaches, headaches, so I had to quit." He had hoped to rest at his split-level Spanish-style house atop a hill in Rio Piedras, a suburb of San Juan. To the left of the living room an open-air tropical garden flourishes in the sun and rain that descend through overhead beams, and along the front of the living room a sunken parlor looks out on a veranda that by night offers a glittering view of all San Juan, clear down to the bay. Roberto had the house built a year ago at a cost of $65,000 and, because of galloping real-estate values, it is worth at least $100,000 today. But now his voice rose and swept out across the veranda and transported down the Puerto Rican hillside all the heartfelt melancholy that has ever been sounded in sad Spanish song and story.

"My head still hurts. The pain splits my head. The doctors say it's tension. They say I worry too much. I've tried tranquilizers, but they don't work. My foot is killing me. I got this tendon in my left heel that rubs against the bone, and I cannot run on it at all. I'm weary, I tell you. All the time it's go here, speak there, do dis, do dat. Always, always, always. When I go to spring training, that's when I take my rest."

On days when Puerto Ricans did not require him to address luncheons and cut ribbons, Roberto lay abed from midnight till noon, then arose for breakfast and returned to bed till 4:30 p.m. He usually got about two hours' sleep in all that time. He is one of the world's great insomniacs because, he explained earnestly, he lies awake worrying that he will not be able to fall asleep.

"When I don't sleep I don't feel like eating and I lose weight," Roberto said.

Has he tried sleeping pills? Yes, he answered, but they kept him awake all night.

Opera companies have performed *Parsifal* in scarcely more time than it takes Roberto to get ready for bed. When the Pirates are on the road he memorizes every aspect of his hotel room. Where is the door? To the right? Is the window to the left? Four paces or five? "Suppose I have a nightmare and jump up. 'Hoo!' I'm screaming, and I rush through the window and my room is on the 13th floor."

Does he have nightmares? "No," said Roberto.

But the point is, he *might* have a nightmare sometime and, besides, when he is memorizing that room he is carefully noting the exact position of the telephone, which is vital. Suppose the phone rings. Roberto is able to pick up the receiver without opening his eyes. When he is forced to open his eyes, he explained, it frequently happens that tears well up in them and then he finds it perfectly impossible to fall asleep. Earlier in his career Roberto roomed with Gene Baker, but Baker snored. Roman Mejias and Alvin McBean, two others with whom he tried rooming, came in too late and awoke him by rattling hangers. So now, management having granted him privacy, he is able at least to hope for a little sleep before it is time to boop his back.

Surely the Lord cannot be punishing Roberto. A generous man and the devoted father of an infant son, he has been the sole support—since age 17—of his parents, a niece and nephew Pablo, to whom he recently gave an 18-foot cruiser. Before that he built a house for his parents. When Pitcher Diomedes Olivo joined the Pirates at age 40, too late to make a pile, Roberto gave him half of all his banquet fees.

"I always try to lead the clean life," says Roberto. He does not smoke and rarely drinks, indulging himself only in his original milkshake recipes. His fruit cocktail milkshake consists of milk, fruit cocktail, the yolks of eggs, banana ice cream, sugar, orange juice and crushed ice. "As much as you want of each," he says. "If I want a peach milkshake, I put a peach in it. If I want a pear milkshake, I put a pear in it."

Sighing and limping through his clean life, Roberto has acquired a reputation as baseball's champion hypochondriac, but his personal physician, Dr. Roberto Busó of San Juan, says, "I wouldn't call him a true hypochondriac, because he doesn't go to the extreme of just sitting down and brooding." Far from it.

Roberto gallops across the outfield making acrobatic catches; with a bat in his hands he is all over the batter's box, spinning like a top when he swings. "I'm convinced of his weakness," says Dodger Vice-President Fresco Thompson. "Throw the best ball you've got right down the middle. If you pitch him high and outside, he'll rap a shot into right field. If you throw one to him on one hop, he'll bounce it back through the mound and it'll probably take your pitcher and second baseman with it." In the past few years, alas, Roberto has become relatively orthodox. "If I have to jump three feet over my head to hit the ball, now I don't do it," he points out, deadly serious.

For all his exertions, Roberto *is* perpetually unfit, because, as Dr. Busó goes on to explain, he has a low threshold of pain, which causes him to take minor ailments for crippling debilitations. "If his back hurts he worries," says Dr. Busó, "and then it becomes a vicious circle, leading to more things. If he has a little diarrhea, he worries that he has a serious stomach difficulty." Roberto is endowed with an exceptionally supple musculature that enables him to race full speed into a base and then stop cold on it—which he likes to do instead of rounding it. But even he pulls muscles, twists ligaments and generally raises hell with his supple musculature that way. "It's his natural style," sighs Dr. Busó.

Still, ballplayers wink and giggle whenever Roberto announces that something or other is killing him; his problem is that he is seldom able to come up with a good, visible injury—say, a nice compound fracture with the bone sticking through the flesh. He spent four of his first five big-league years complaining of an agonizing back ailment that a battery of Pirate specialists could not track down. When a chiropractor, whom Roberto consulted in defiance of front-office warnings, told him he had a curved spine, a pair of legs that did not weigh the same and a couple of wayward disks, Roberto immediately saw why the physicians had overlooked such a mess. "They always X-rayed me lying down," he says. "They never X-rayed me standing up."

Then, a little later, there were chips floating in his elbow. Nobody doubted they were there, because Dr. George Bennett of Johns Hopkins said so, and promised he'd remove them at the end of the season. But when the time came—great

Scott!—the chips had floated off somewhere. Dr. Bennett could not find them.

By all odds, Roberto's most exotic infirmity struck him after the 1964 season, when he fell desperately ill in Puerto Rico. Dr. Busó is not certain to this day whether Roberto had contracted autumnal malaria barnstorming in Santo Domingo or had picked up a systemic paratyphoid infection from the hogs on a small farm he owns, but Roberto himself knows what he had. "Both," he says.

His condition alternated daily between delirium and stupor, says Dr. Busó, and he lost 23 pounds. Alas, none of the Pirates had been in Puerto Rico and been an eyewitness. When Roberto reported to spring camp and began cracking line drives, all hands agreed that if he had had malaria they wanted some.

Clemente bridles at the suggestion that perhaps he only thought he had malaria. "If a Latin player or even an American Negro is sick," Roberto protests, "they say it is all in the head. Felipe Alou once went to his team doctor and the doctor said, 'You don't have anything.' So he went to a private doctor and the doctor said, 'You have a broken foot.'"

For Roberto, life in the big leagues has been a series of outrages. He is by no means anti-gringo—in fact, his relationship with Pittsburgh fans is one of the unwavering love stories of the national pastime—but, as a Latin, he feels persecuted. He is vociferously resentful of the fact that he is the least known, least sung superstar in baseball. "With my eyes blind I can throw to the base," he snaps. "I *know* that. If Mantle have the arm I have you will put it in headlines 'cause he is an American. You never give me credit. How many players in history win three batting titles?" Not including Roberto, only 11 since 1876. "The sportswriters don't mention that. They ask me, 'What you think about dis, what you think about dat?'"

Refusing to underestimate himself, Roberto repeatedly has declared, "For me, I am the best ballplayer in the world." His words provoke indignation on all sides, and his efforts to explain them merely stiffen the indignation. "I say, 'For *me*, for *myself!*'" he shouts. The Stateside listener, taking him literally, can only conclude that in Roberto's own mind he does think he is better than Mays or Aaron or anyone else in the business, and the impression remains fixed until one happens across a man named Libertario Avilés, a worldly San Juan engineer who built Roberto's house and is one of his good friends. Says Avilés: "You have to understand that the Latin is touchy. If you say to me, 'Who is the best engineer in town?' I will say, 'For me, I am the best.' It is a Spanish saying, an expression of self-respect. You are not to underestimate yourself, but that does not mean you are to underestimate anyone else's ability."

Though Roberto's imperfect command of English has prevented him from explaining himself as clearly as Avilés does, he bristles that no amount of fluency would spare him from being portrayed in the American press as a stupid greenhorn. "I'm gonna tell you dis—it's one of the things that kill me most in the States," he says. "I know I don't speak as bad as they say I speak. I know that I don't have the good English pronunciation, because my tongue belong to Spanish, but I know where the verb, the article, the pronoun, whatever it is, go. I never in my life start a sentence with 'me,' but if I start it with 'I' the sportswriters say 'me.' 'Me Tarzan, you Jane.' " For a fact, Roberto is typed, even by ballplayers who dress alongside him daily. Says one Pirate, "Just before he goes out and wears the ball out he'll say, 'Me no feel good today. Maybe me no play.' " During Roberto's one season of minor league ball, at Montreal in 1954, he understood practically no English. A player whom he had robbed of an extra-base hit called him an s.o.b., whereupon Roberto, assuming he was being complimented on the catch, replied, "Sank you." But he worked hard at his English. He still garbles an occasional phrase, says dis and dat somewhat more often than this and that and sometimes is stumped for the word he seeks, yet his conversation is perfectly intelligible. He resents coming off in print like an M–G–M Sioux chief, almost as much as he resented the Pittsburgh woman who once asked him if he wears a loincloth when home in Puerto Rico.

Clemente probably is wrong to think the Stateside press has neglected his talent because he's a Latin, but his batting averages of the past six years—.314, .351, .312, .320, .339 and .329—make it seem incredible that his name has not entered the elite Mays-Mantle-Aaron circle.

In the outfield he has done it all. Although not exceptionally swift, he is the master of the shoestring catch. ("I can run very fast bending down," he explains.) Only last season Roberto fielded a bunt—that's right, a bunt—that had rolled to shortstop. Shortstop Gene Alley had gone to cover third base but, as if from nowhere, Roberto dived headlong at the ball and, with his face in the dirt, threw out Houston base runner Walter Bond at third.

Scarcely credible? Nevertheless, the description suits Clemente's throwing arm, too. From Forbes Field's right-center-field gate, a distance of about 420 feet, he once threw out Harvey Haddix at the plate, on one bounce. "I tear a ligament," he of course recalls.

Roberto's value, so far as Brave Manager Bobby Bragan is concerned, is on a par with that of Hall of Fame players. "The best way to describe Roberto Clemente," says Bragan, "is to say, if he were playing in New York they'd be comparing him to DiMaggio. I would say his greatness is limited only by the fact that he does not hit the long ball consistently and by the fact that he is not playing in New York, or even Chicago or Los Angeles."

In an age of power, the fact that Clemente has never hit more than 23 home runs (and has never driven in more than 94 runs) weighs heavily against his prestige. There is no doubting that his muscular arms and outsize hands are capable of power, for one of his home runs—a shot over Wrigley Field's left-center bleachers—stands as one of the longest smashes ever hit out of the Cub ball park. Yet because he plays half the schedule in spacious Forbes Field, where the man who guns for home runs undergoes traumatic revelations of inadequacy, Roberto wisely has tailored his style to the line drive and the hard ground ball hit through a hole. Thus he hit only 10 home runs last year, but he is certain he can hit 20 any season he pleases, Forbes Field notwithstanding.

"If I made up my mind I'm going to hit 20 homers this year," he bellows with indignation, "I bet you any amount of money I can hit 20." A change of style would do the trick, he claims, but what sort of change? Ah, Roberto becomes tight-lipped. He is one of baseball's most sinister practitioners of intrigue.

"Nothing," he replies. "A little change in the hands, that's all. I don't want to tell you what it is."

In baseball any player who obviously exaggerates simple

moves is labeled a hot dog, and on two counts Clemente seems to fall within this definition. First, he not only favors the basket catch made famous by Mays but lends to it an added element of risk by allowing fly balls to drop below his waist before catching them. Second, when fielding routine singles he often underhands the ball to second base in a great, looping arc instead of pegging it on a line.

Hotly defending himself, Clemente points out that both the low basket catch and the underhand throw are nothing more than natural habits carried over from his youth, for until he was 17 he was a softball player, not a baseball player. Not until a softball coach named Roberto Marin persuaded Clemente that he might earn big money in baseball did he turn to the sport. From the outset he was a natural wonder, and yet a problem.

The Dodgers signed him for a $10,000 bonus but were not quite sure what to do with him. At the time, if a first-year player who received more than $4,000 was sent to the minors, he not only had to stay there for a full season but would be eligible to be drafted by another club in November. The Dodgers could have protected Clemente from the draft by making room for him on their own roster, but they were gunning for a third straight pennant and felt that an untested 19-year-old would be dead weight on their backs. In the end Walter O'Malley's brain trust assigned Roberto to Montreal but told the Montreal manager, Max Macon, to hide him—that is, play him sparingly lest enemy bird dogs take a fancy to him.

Roberto recalls that '54 season with a shudder. "If I struck out I stay in the lineup," he says. "If I played well I'm benched. One day I hit three triples and the next day I was benched. Another time they took me out for a pinch hitter with the bases loaded in the first inning. Much of the time I was used only as a pinch runner or for defense. I didn't know what was going on, and I was confused and almost mad enough to go home. That's what they wanted me to do. That way nobody could draft me."

By religiously discomposing him, Max Macon held Roberto's batting average to .257, but a Pirate scout named Clyde Sukeforth was on to Macon's act. One day in Richmond, Va., before a Montreal-Richmond game, Sukeforth had seen Clemente cut loose with a couple of eye-popping practice throws. He stayed in Richmond four days. Macon countered by keeping Clemente on the bench except for two pinch-hitting appearances, but Sukeforth saw enough of Clemente in batting and fielding practice to be satisfied.

"Take care of our boy," he said to Macon as he prepared to leave town. "You're kidding," Macon said, trying a last-ditch con. "You don't want that kid." Sukeforth smiled and said, "Now, Max, I've known you for a good many years. We're a cinch to finish last and get first draft choice, so don't let our boy get into any trouble." At $4,000, Sukeforth had the steal of the century.

From the Dodger viewpoint, such setbacks are all part of the game, but for reasons the Dodgers had no knowledge of, Roberto has regarded their failure to protect him from the draft as a betrayal of trust. The Dodgers had been his boyhood favorites. Right after he had made a gentleman's agreement to accept their $10,000 bonus the Braves offered him $30,000, he says, but he turned it down. "It was hard," Roberto says, "but I said I gave the Dodgers my word." As he sees it, the Dodgers took a faithful servant and gambled with him in the draft pool as they would with a handful of casino chips. Teaching the Dodger front office the importance of ethics, Roberto in the past five seasons has hit .375 against the pitching staff of Koufax, Drysdale, Osteen, Podres and Company. The only way to pitch him, guesses Koufax hyperbolically, is to roll him the ball.

By now one thing should be clear to Pittsburgh's opponents. For their own good, they ought to warm the cockles of Clemente's heart with praise, commiserate with him when he has a hangnail, elect him to the All-Star team with a landslide vote, punch any sportswriter who does not quote him as if he were Churchill on the floor of Parliament and campaign for him to receive his first Most Valuable Player award. "If I would be happy I would be a very bad player," Roberto himself says. "With me, when I get mad it puts energy in my body."

This business of failing to elect him to the All-Star team (as was the case last year when the malaria and/or paratyphoid caused Roberto to get off to a poor start) only assured that he would win another batting championship. Moreover, he cannot forget that in 1960, when he batted .314 and the Pirates won the pennant, he finished a shabby eighth in the voting for MVP. Dick Groat hit .325 for the Pirates that year, leading the league and winning the MVP trophy, but Clemente drove in 94 runs to Groat's 50, and demands to know why, if he was not Pittsburgh's most valuable player, he was the one the pitchers most often knocked down? When told that Groat sparked the team, Roberto proves that his American idiom is on the upgrade by retorting, "Sparked, my foot!" The point is, however, that he hit .351 the following year. Lest he ever simmer down and acquire a happy disposition, his teammates call him No Votes.

Ignored and rebuffed by baseball's In crowd, Clemente nevertheless leads all popularity polls where it counts—with the paying customers in Pittsburgh. They seem to grasp that, if he is a man who covets recognition, he would rather have it from Joe Doaks than from all the members of the Baseball Writers Association of America. "Winning the World Series in 1960 was not the biggest thrill I ever have in my life," he said not long ago, looking out on the lights of San Juan from his veranda. "The biggest thrill was when I come out of the clubhouse after the last Series game and saw all those thousands of fans in the streets. It was something you cannot describe. I did not feel like a player at the time. I feel like one of those persons, and I walked the streets among them."

Such utterances by Clemente are not a pose for public consumption. Behind closed doors he has urged his teammates to set their sights high, for the novel reason that "we owe these people another pennant." Says Pitcher Bob Friend, a Pirate until traded to the Yankees in December: "He gets pretty windy on the subject, and you wonder how to turn him off. A lot of players leave the game feeling the world owes them a living, but Clemente's an exception to that rule. He knows what baseball's done for him, and he expresses his appreciation."

Puerto Ricans, meanwhile, hold Clemente in an esteem they otherwise tender only to Cellist Pablo Casals and Elder Statesman Luis Muñoz Marín. "He is a glory to the island," says a nightclub guitarist named Frankie Ramirez, whose sentiments are echoed from San Juan to Mayagüez. One recent morning Roberto and his engineer friend, Libertario Avilés, drove into the countryside east of San Juan. Avilés steered his Wildcat convertible past the old sugarcane fields that were now being bulldozed for factory sites. Roberto's father had owned a few acres himself once and at the same time had worked as a foreman of a great plantation and with his wife had run a grocery and meat market for the workers. "My mother and father, they worked like racehorses for me," said Roberto. He has the mid-Victorian morality of the old Spanish families, and his sense of obligation runs strong. "Anybody," he was saying now, "who have the opportunity to serve their country or their island and don't, God should punish them. If you can be good, why you should be bad?"

The Wildcat coursed through the seaside village of Fajardo and, not far beyond, turned up a dirt road where lay a dream that had possessed Roberto's emotions all winter. He was negotiating with the government to lease a lush 20 acres on which he plans to construct a sports camp for boys, plowing the profits into camp scholarships for the underprivileged. He will call the camp Sports City. Tramping through the seaside forest where Sports City will rise, Roberto explained his ambition: "We are known as a good sportsmanship people, and I'm proud to be part of that recognition. But today life is moving too fast for these kids. You see 15-year-old boys and girls holding hands. They hang out on street corners. Maybe if I can keep them interested in sports they will not always be talking about stealing and about gangster movies. I'm proud to do good for my island."

As Roberto spoke of his dream, he seemed no longer the worrier on whose lips are complaints of headaches, backaches, sore feet, sore arms and tired blood. "I like to work with kids," he said. But then he added with a frown, "I'd like to work with kids all the time, if I live long enough."

Citizen Ryan

♦

BY LEIGH MONTVILLE

THE PHENOMENON KNOWN AS NOLAN RYAN CONTINUES TO AMAZE THE WORLD OF BASEBALL. THE FIREBALLING RIGHT-HANDER NOW HAS WON MORE THAN 300 GAMES, STRUCK OUT MORE THAN 5,500 BATTERS, RECORDED MORE THAN 60 SHUTOUTS AND HURLED AN INCREDIBLE SEVEN NO-HITTERS. IN 1991 LEIGH MONTVILLE VISITED THE 44-YEAR-OLD WONDER AT RYAN'S FARM IN ALVIN, TEXAS.

The last 45 minutes of Texas twilight have arrived. The day has been gray anyway, cool, and now the colors begin to fade even further as the unseen sun dips toward the trees at the edge of the pasture. The birds know that night is coming. Hear them squawk? The horses have to be fed. They stand in a group, five of them, behind a brown three-board fence. Waiting. A car passes on the road in the distance. Another. Men coming home from work. Women bringing their children from late practices and meetings at the high school.

"Curveball," Nolan Ryan says.

He stands in the middle of the pasture. This is farmland. The horses have galloped across it and tractors and trucks have been driven across it, and the grass is all knobby and clumpy, certainly

117

unmowed, and yet.... He is at the base of a little grass-covered mound. Mound? His neighbor Harry Spilman, chewing a touch of tobacco, is crouched behind a patch of white that shows through the grass. A patch of white? Nolan tucks his left leg into his chest and accelerates off his right leg and throws the baseball. Harry does not have to move his mitt.

"Good one," Harry says.

There is a rusted chain-link fence, 12 feet high, a few feet behind Harry. Fence? There is the 12-foot-high fence and the patch of white in front of Harry and the mound in back of Nolan and ... yes, sure. The mind and the eye simultaneously bring out the recessed image of a diamond, as if they were solving a puzzle in the Sunday comics. "I built it for my son when he was in Little League," Nolan says. "Little Leaguers never have a place to practice. I built it and they used it for a couple of years. Then I let it all go back. Watch where you walk." He fingers the baseball in his hand.

"Straight," he says.

Nolan's three dogs are fanned out in what could be loosely called an outfield alignment. That is Buster in left and Suzy in center and fat old Bea in right. The fourth dog, tied in the back of the pickup in the driveway, the dog that is barking, is Harry's dog Sarge. Sarge simply can't control himself. Let him loose and he becomes too excited. He chases the ball wherever it goes. He tired to grab it straight out of Nolan's or Harry's hand. Sarge has had a million second chances. Had one just today. Can't control himself. Back in the truck.

"There was something on that pitch," Harry says a second after the ball arrives. "It was traveling."

The first time Nolan was in this field, let's see, he was with the Girl Scouts. Camping with the Girl Scouts. His mother, Martha, was a troop leader, and she wasn't going to let her youngest child, seven years old, stay home while she was taking those girls for a night of outdoor adventure at Mr. Evans's ranch. This was back in 1954, when the bayou over there wasn't straight, before the widening was done and the lake was formed at the other end and the tract development came. Let's see. There were more trees then. The road out there wasn't even a road. There was another road. Yes. Another road.

Smaller. A back road. A further-back road.

"Changeup," Nolan says.

He still is here. How many years later? The land now is his, acquired 13 years ago in a straight trade, a new house that Nolan owned for Mr. Evans's old house and the land. This is a Tuesday, late in February. The game of pitch and catch has been taking place almost every night for a month. Same time. Same place. Training camp is eight days away, and the fastballs are becoming faster and the curveballs are becoming curvier. A stranger, out on the road, might look and squint and see only a couple of middle-aged guys in the middle of nowhere trying to find a few Absorbine, Jr. memories, but there really aren't many strangers out there on the road. These are familiar people. A horn honks. Another. There's old Nolan, tossing with Harry. Getting ready.

"Looked good," Harry says.

"I don't know," Nolan says. "That one might have got hit."

The shades of gray darken, and Nolan is working just a little harder tonight. He has to miss the workout tomorrow. Has to go to the White House. To see the President. Up there in Washington. He will be back in Alvin, Texas, back here, Thursday.

"I don't know how he does it," says Kim Spilman, Nolan's secretary and Harry's wife. "The letters, the invitations, the demands. The businesses. There always is someone who wants him to be a grand marshal in a parade, to talk at Career Day. Something. The White House. How do you stay normal with all of these people pulling at you all of the time? And yet he does it. God, he does. He's everything a person would want to be. He talks with my kids and he's just so nice. They'll ask me, 'Is he supposed to be famous or something?' That's just how he is."

The White House is the latest thing. The White House. The war in the Persian Gulf is at its hottest stretch. The coalition airplanes are pounding Baghdad with their bombs. The ground war will start in four more days. The White House is on television 17 times every day. The President is seen going from meeting to press conference to late-night strategy session. In the midst of all this, the Queen and Prince Consort of Denmark are invited for dinner. Nolan and his wife, Ruth, also are invited for dinner. They are also invited to stay overnight. At the White House.

When will it all stop?

The drumbeat of celebrity always has been in the back-ground—good pitcher, fastest fastball going, All-Star—but in the past two years, since Nolan went to the Texas Rangers, it has become louder and louder. The 5,000th strikeout was a jump in 1989. A record. The sixth no-hitter, spun in Oakland in June of last year against the then-world-champion Athletics, was another jump. Another record. The 300th win, in July, was a capper. How noisy can noisy be for an essentially quiet person practicing a physical craft? The line has shot off the graph paper. The White House.

"Nolan was here when the call came," Kim says in the office Nolan has rented in the Merchants Bank in Alvin to handle the increased demands on his life. "It's funny how that works. As soon as he gets here, the phone starts ringing off the hook. It's like people have antennae or something to tell them he's here. I took the call, and the message was something like, 'Please stay on the line for the President of the United States.' I was so excited I ran into the bank to tell everyone that Nolan was being invited to the White House."

There is the crazy thought that maybe George Bush is going to call this 44-year-old man into the Oval Office and ask him to take a quick trip to the Middle East. Let Saddam Hussein find an emissary to send from Iraq, a solid citizen, someone who represents all the best qualities of Iraqi culture. Let him talk to Nolan, the American representative, to straighten out all of this feuding and fighting. There is the crazy thought that this would not be so crazy.

Who would be better?

"I don't know how it is in the rest of the country," Jim Stinson, Nolan's longtime friend and business partner, says, "but in Texas he is bigger than John Wayne right now. And you will wear out a truck finding someone who's nicer than Nolan Ryan."

John Wayne?

"I talk with ad agencies about him," Matt Merola, Nolan's longtime agent from New York, says. "They will say, 'Well, can he talk?' I will tell them if they're looking for Sir Laurence Olivi-er, they'd better go to Central Casting. But if they're looking for

someone who is honest, who is sincere, who can talk about
things in his way—Jimmy Stewart. If they are looking for Jimmy
Stewart, they want Nolan. He is someone who is really real."
Jimmy Stewart?

In the tie-a-yellow-ribbon Americanism of the '90s, Nolan
somehow has become the perfect oak tree. The fact that he still
can compete with the young and wild-eyed millionaires of his
game and still can make them look silly is only the beginning.
He is Citizen Ryan, a total package. Tired of the fatheads who
spend their first paychecks on sports cars that run on airplane
fuel? Seen too much of the substance abusers and the late-night
carousers and the uncoachable prima donnas? Here is a family
man. Here is a businessman. Here is a cowboy. Here is Nolan
Ryan, cut from a good bolt of denim cloth and served with a
glass of milk and no apologies.

"Do you know what he has?" says Terry Koch-Bostic of the
Slater-Hanft-Martin advertising agency in New York, which
signed Ryan as the spokesman for Bic razors in 1990. "He has
the real stuff of real heroes, the kind of heroes that maybe
we've been missing for the last three decades. That's the kind
of guy he is. When we were making our deal, his first consideration was his family. He said that money was not important,
that he couldn't be traveling around in the off-season. He wanted to be home. I told that to Mr. [Bruno] Bich and he said,
"Well, yes, that's exactly the kind of guy we want. A person
whose family comes first. Absolutely."

After 23 years, the man still is married to his high school
sweetheart, and Ruth remembers when a big date simply was
watching him take target practice with his .22 pistol. They
still live in the same town and their kids attend the same
schools they attended. A big night is still a trip to Baskin-Rob-
bins for ice cream. A big Saturday night still is dancing the
two-step with friends at Eddie's Country Ballroom. Pretty
good two-step, too.

A workday is a workday. Vacations still are mostly for other
people, although there were three days at the end of last year in
Las Vegas for the National Finals Rodeo. There is no real "off"
in the off-season. Nolan is a rancher. Nolan owns three ranch-
es. The biggest, China Grove, in Rosharon, near Alvin, has 550
mama cows and 33 bulls and as many as 1,100 head, total, at

the end of calving season, which is just about now. Relaxation is riding a horse and penning the calves and doing a cattle-rancher's hard work.

"He's a hands-on owner, for sure," Larry McKim, the ranch manager, says. "When he comes here, he gets right into it. He helps us castrate the steers, dehorn 'em, everything. Nothing fazes him. I'll see him reach into the chute with that million-dollar right arm and I'll say to myself, 'Are you sure you want to do that?' But he'll never buckle. He'll go right in there."

"Nolan is as good a cattleman as there is in the state of Texas," Stinson, a partner in China Grove, says. "He's stride for stride with all of 'em. If he'd never picked up a baseball, he'd still be a great success as a cattleman. He's been doing it all his life. I remember his mother telling me once how he saved up enough money when he was a kid to buy four calves. He lived in town, so he had to raise 'em in the garage. Fed 'em all from a baby bottle."

The banking business is another long-term affair. Nolan made news last year when he purchased the Danbury State Bank, about 10 miles from Alvin, but he had been on the board of directors of an Alvin bank for 10 years. Again, he was not just a name on the letterhead. He worked. He sat in on loan meetings. He formulated bank policy. He preached moderation. He still is one of those guys who travel the extra mile for gas at $1.06 per gallon if the local station is charging $1.10. The word is frugal. He did not rush into a deal that translated into "dumb baseball player buys failing bank." He waited and learned, and moved at the proper time.

"I'd use another word for him, 'tight,' " Sonny Corley, president of the Danbury bank, says. "But that's all right, because I'm tight, too. I think he got a great deal here, because under the bank's charter he can expand anywhere in the state of Texas. Nolan knows what he's doing. He's been in the banking business for a while, and he has a great ability to look at a situation and analyze it. He has what I'd call country smarts. Nolan has great country smarts."

His final off-season occupation is being Nolan Ryan. This has become the most demanding job of them all. Until the past two years, his endorsements mostly were local and regional—

Whataburger and Bizmart office supplies—but now he shaves for Bic and takes Advil for headaches and wears Wrangler jeans over his Justin boots when he goes out for a western-wear night. He could sign baseballs forever for charity, especially across the "sweet spot" in the front of the ball, which immediately increases its value. He does not do the autograph shows, signing for money. He does not do speeches for money, but he does talk for certain charities he considers important. The requests are so numerous now that mail arrives at his office in tubs from the Alvin post office. He and Ruth used to handle the mail at home. The tubs began to take control. He has added the office and secretary in the past two years.

"Can you imagine that they did all this at home?" Kim says as Ruth arrives at the office with another tub. "The letters he gets. The requests—he could speak every night of the year if he wanted. Somewhere."

His strength is that he does not go somewhere every night. He usually goes home. The increase in Nolan's celebrity has come at a good time, because his oldest son, Reid, 19, is a freshman at the University of Texas in Austin, and his other children, Reese, 15, and Wendy, 14, are in high school, and his days are free. But he wants to be home for dinner. That is his base. He creates his own orbit around the base, and the orbit rarely leaves Texas in the off-season. He will travel to Arlington Stadium for a day, knock off a series of commitments there and come home. He will go to Abilene or Austin and come home. He works and then he comes home.

"He's just an unassuming, fine guy," Stinson says. "I called him the day after he pitched the no-hitter last year. We talked for half an hour. He never mentioned the no-hitter. Finally, I had to mention it. He said, 'Yeah, I had it going pretty good.' That's it."

"We had to follow him around a bit during the season to complete the [Bic] commercial," Koch-Bostic at the ad agency says. "We finally did it in Los Angeles. He was coming off the disabled list with a bad back. I was thinking about his bad back. The next game, his second start, he's in Oakland, throwing the no-hitter. Reese is rubbing his back in the Ranger dugout between innings."

"The thing I like about him is not so much what he does but the way he does it," McKim says at the ranch. "The only thing fast about him is his fastball. He's so calm, so good-natured, so easy. He's the best rancher I've ever worked for. The other ones were pretty hyper, pretty nervous, always concerned with money. Nolan, he's a people person, not a money person."

The money matters, but it doesn't matter that much. Merola, the agent, tells clients they can have "the sizzle or the steak." Nolan is the steak, and steak is popular. He was asked to run for Texas Agriculture Commissioner last year, thought about it because he was opposed to what he considered the incumbent's anticattleman policies, but finally decided he didn't have the time. The candidate he endorsed, Rick Perry, beat the incumbent, Jim Hightower, in a surprise. The Texas Senate just passed a bill to have a stretch of Highway 288 near Alvin renamed the Nolan Ryan Expressway. There are plans in Alvin to build a Nolan Ryan Museum. Every day there seem to be offers from somewhere to do something involving Nolan. Every day Nolan gives them a look.

He takes his time. Always.

"The big thing with Nolan is that he's hard to pin down," Kim says. "He doesn't like to schedule things in advance because he never knows what's going to come up. Especially with the kids. If Reese or Wendy has a game or something, he'd like to go. If you do pin him down, though, he'll be where he's supposed to be. You can count on it."

The invitation to the White House was typical. Kim came back into the office, still excited at the news. Nolan said he couldn't go. He had looked at his schedule and found he had promised to speak to a cattlemen's civic group in Cotulla to raise scholarships. That was that. Kim told him he was crazy. He said he had turned down trips to the White House in the past. There always seemed to be something.

"Look," Kim said, "if you called the people in Cotulla and said you were invited to the White House, I'm sure they'd understand. They could just schedule you for another night."

"You do it," Nolan said.

The people in Cotulla understood. Duty called for Citizen Ryan. John Wayne, maybe Jimmy Stewart, had to be at the

White House. He would appear in Cotulla the next week if he wasn't in the Middle East.

Nolan and Harry talk while they throw the ball back and forth in the pasture. Harry is not exactly the average next-door recruit, some accountant who bought himself a baseball glove just to help the famous pitcher get ready. Not at all. Harry played, too, 12 years of scuffling on the fringes of four different teams in the major leagues and six in the minors. He is 37 years old now, and he retired with bad knees at the end of last season, which he spent with the Houston Astros' Triple A team in Tucson. He will be working this year as a roving hitting coach in the Cleveland Indians' minor league system.

"So Roger Clemens is getting five million dollars," Nolan says, shaking his head. "If Roger's worth five million, what's Wade Boggs going to be worth?"

Straight fastball.

Splat!

"What about Jim Deshaies?" Harry says. "He's making two million-something. He won seven games last year. Seven games and he's making two million. Isn't that something?"

Curveball.

Splat!

"I know one thing," Nolan says. "I'd like to be about 25 years old now and have about 5,000 innings ahead of me."

Changeup.

Perfect.

Harry remembers the first time he saw Nolan pitch, in 1980. Harry was playing with the Cincinnati Reds, and Nolan, after eight years with the California Angels, had just arrived back in the National League with the Astros. It was an occasion, seeing the great fireballer for the first time. Harry had a great seat on the bench. He really wanted to see the first confrontation between Nolan and Johnny Bench. Everyone did. Bench dug in at the plate. Nolan stared from the mound. All the players moved to the far edges of their seats. Nolan threw a slow, lazy curveball that bounced about a foot and a half in front of the plate. Bench swung so hard that the temperature must have dropped 5° in the ballpark. A curveball! Beautiful.

Harry soon moved along to the Astros himself, and that was where he became friends with Nolan. Harry is from Dawson, Ga., so he is another small-town Southern guy who talks with the accent. He has the same likes and values as Nolan. He likes to hunt. He likes to fish. He likes horses and riding and, of course, talking baseball. When it came time to decide where he would live in the off-season and the rest of his life, Harry picked Alvin, even though he had moved to the San Francisco Giants. Nolan worked out a deal for the land and house next door. What could be better? In the other years, when they were both playing, Nolan would throw batting practice to Harry down at the high school. Batting practice from Nolan Ryan. What could be better? Kim works for Nolan. Harry works with Nolan. Harry is one of 10 current or former teammates who have named a son after Nolan. Everybody is friends.

In the big leagues, Harry faced Nolan twice. The first time, Harry hit a homer, a grand feat considering Harry had only 18 homers lifetime. The second time, Nolan struck out Harry on a high, 3–2 fastball. Then, again, there is an argument about this.

"When Nolan got his 5,000th strikeout, *USA Today* ran a list of all the guys he'd struck out in his career," Harry says. "I looked for my name. It wasn't there. I remembered the strikeout and Nolan remembered it, but since my name wasn't there, I say it never happened. Nolan even checked with the Rangers public relations department. They said there must have been a mistake, because I pinch-hit. I say it never happened."

"It happened," Nolan says.

"Not if my name isn't on the list," Harry says. (It is now. The '91 Rangers media guide lists Harry as one of Nolan's victims.)

Curveball.

Splat!

The workout began in the driveway. Nolan stretched and then started throwing a football with Harry, long and straight spirals. This is part of the conditioning process encouraged by Rangers pitching coach Tom House. Nolan had told House two years ago, his first day as a Ranger, that he hoped House wouldn't be upset if he didn't throw the football with everyone else. House said a sure-bet Hall of Famer could do what he wanted. One week passed and then two weeks and then Nolan suddenly was throwing the football. He did what he does with everything. He studied the concept. He decided for himself. He threw the football. No big deal. He liked the mechanics. He liked the way the motion loosened his arm and shoulder. Logic. He threw the football.

"We're finding it's harder than it looks," Nolan says.

"Maybe we remember ourselves being better than we were," Harry says. "I thought I could throw that thing in high school."

Nolan played two years of football in junior high and one year in high school. He was an end. His biggest memory is of an eighth-grade scrimmage down at Danbury, where he now owns the bank. The farm boys at Danbury were so poor they didn't even have shoes. Didn't have shoes! The Danbury coach said it wouldn't be fair if his team didn't have shoes and the other team did, so the Alvin coach had his players take off their shoes. No matter. Who couldn't beat a team that was so poor the players didn't have shoes? Danbury killed Alvin, 42–0. Nolan quit football after the next year. Stinson begged Nolan to stay because he thought Nolan would help the team. Help the team? Stinson says now that "Jim Thorpe couldn't have helped that team." Stinson and Nolan laugh about that.

"I liked basketball," Nolan says. "I could play a little. I could dunk."

After throwing the football, Nolan and Harry threw a baseball in the driveway for a while. Easy tosses. After that, Nolan put on his blue Rangers cleats to throw out in the pasture. Hard tosses. The workout began a little before five o'clock, and now the time is a little after six. The light is almost gone. The dogs have lost interest, running into the woods in what would be dead centerfield. Nolan says, "They're probably looking for yesterday's game ball." A pitcher's grim joke. Think about it. Nolan says this is the kind of light he wouldn't mind having for all baseball games all of the time. Think about it. He asks Harry if there is enough light for one more pitch. Harry says that there is.

"Straight," Nolan says.

Splat!

"The funniest thing, to me, is when we drive by the Bizmart billboards," Ruth Ryan says. "There's one on the Gulf Freeway

127

and there's one on the freeway in Austin and one in Arlington. They're huge. You look up and there's Nolan. Thirty feet high. I look up, every time, and I say, 'This isn't real.' The kids always start to make fun of him."

There wasn't any grand plan for him to play this long. There wasn't any grand plan for him to become this famous. There wasn't even any grand plan for him to lead a life that would be held up as a model for family men everywhere. Everything sort of evolved. Happened. Nolan figured he would pitch for four years or five and then his arm would go dead and he would come home and maybe begin school and become a veterinarian. Or maybe not. Ruth remembers wondering 15 years ago, when he was with the Angels and was having arm surgery, if he ever would throw a baseball again.

One pitch somehow was followed by another pitch and then another. One family crisis led to the next crisis. There was a balancing act that somehow led across a high wire to here. Twenty-six years of professional baseball. Twenty-six years of living. Twenty-six years?

"I was watching a television show the other night," Nolan says. "Carol Burnett was hosting a special about The Ed Sullivan Show. I remembered I was on The Ed Sullivan Show. With the Mets, when we won it in 1969. We all came on together and sang some song."

He has survived, he figures, on a combination of luck and work and those country smarts. He studied what he did, studied from the beginning. He remembers the first time he ever sat in a big league clubhouse, just a kid, up for a moment in 1966. The Mets were still an expansion team, filled with older rejects from established teams. He remembers the old-timers just coasting, taking the paychecks, gliding out the door as effortlessly as possible. He remembers thinking to himself that he would never do that. He never has.

"I figured things out for myself," he says. "I always wanted to keep in shape, especially after I turned 30. I always had my workouts. I started lifting weights in 1972. Nobody was doing that back then. They told you not to lift weights. I thought it would help me. The older I got, the more I worked out ... to the point now that I work out more than anyone on our team.

I have to do it. To compete with kids who are half your age, you have to do a whole lot more than they do."

He stuck with three pitches. Fastball. Curve. Change. The fastball began to slow about 10 years ago, but not enough to make hitters comfortable. The curve improved. The changeup improved a lot. He stayed away from the slider, a pitch he always has thought is a killer of arms. In California, Angel coach Marv Grissom tried to get him to throw the slider. Nolan nodded, said he would try it out. He never really tried. Never wanted to take that chance.

The Rangers pitching coach, House, is sort of a New Age baseball experimentalist. He uses computers, tests pitching theories. He finds again and again that Nolan figured out this business in his head before the computers did. Nolan, for instance, will mention that he thinks if his back is loose and his left leg is extended just a little higher, his fastball will be better. House will test the proposition on the computer. Whir and hum. Nolan is right again.

"I sometimes think he's the only one who understands me," House says. "He's my translator. He takes what I'm saying in scientific language and puts it into English for the rest of the guys. He'll say, 'This is what he's saying....' Everyone else will start nodding his head."

The idea of staying in Alvin never really came to debate. Why not stay? Isn't this where everyone we know always has lived? The idea of staying married never came to debate. Why not? Isn't that what you're supposed to do? The idea of raising a family was ingrained. Wasn't that what our parents did? Raise families? One year has led into another. Last year, Nolan and Ruth went to the 25th reunion of the Alvin High Class of '65. Everyone hung out at Dairyland on Friday night, the way they had in school. There was a dance at the country club on Saturday night, a picnic on Sunday.

"He is the one who has kept everything together," Ruth says. "Him. It would be so easy for him to go off, to just say, 'You take care of the kids while I go do this business.' He never says that. He always tries to make us a part of everything. He is going to Abilene on business this weekend. He could just go. He doesn't want that. He wants us with him."

"I think you learn so much more from your parents than you

ever thought possible," Nolan says. "It just comes through. I find it comes through again and again."

The lessons of long ago do not leave. How can he go to the gym early every morning of the year, to the free weights and torture machines inside a little room he built off his barn? How can he fight through the everyday soreness, refuse to stay in bed just once? How can he be strong when his body wants to turn soft? How can he do all that work in the morning and then be throwing at night? He remembers delivering newspapers with his father as a boy. His father had two jobs. Nolan would have to get up at one o'clock in the morning, roll the papers for an hour, then deliver them around the back roads of Alvin, 55 miles of traveling, until four. Then he would go back to bed for a few more hours of sleep before school. Every day.

"You had the feeling that people were counting on you," he says. "If you didn't get up, they weren't going to get their papers. You just did it. You had a sense of responsibility. I guess I never lost it. There are a lot of mornings where I'd just like to keep my dead butt in bed. I just get up."

He says he is so old that he remembers when baseball wasn't the fast road to wealth that it has become. He says he made $7,000 in his first major league season. When the Mets won the World Series, in '69, his share of the winnings tripled his basic salary. He bought his first house. For 10 years, playing baseball was an economic struggle. He remembers installing air conditioners in the off-season. Pumping gas. There weren't always ranches and banks and endorsements.

"I talk about some of this stuff sometimes and kids in the clubhouse look at me as if I'm sort of a codger," he says. "And I guess I am. I look at these kids on our team—we have a young team—and I'm the same age as most of their fathers. I'm like one of the coaches. That's how old I am. The one thing, I think, that age has given me is a sense of history. I see a lot of the young guys and the money they make, and they don't know what went into getting that money. That sort of bothers me. It makes you think about a lot of things we just take for granted."

He remembers a time when there was no television in his house, when he would stand in the dark of Dezo Drive and look through neighbors' windows at this miraculous invention. He remembers his grandmother had outdoor plumbing. Man walking on the moon? He remembers long before that. A bus was taking him to play some game in eighth grade in Houston. The coach pointed out the window and said that a thing called NASA was going to be built in a vacant field they were passing. Cows were in the middle of the field. NASA.

"You think sometimes about all the stuff that has happened," he says. "I was reading somewhere the other day that the Rural Electrification Act is 50 years old. Fifty years ago, people were just getting electricity. Thirty years after that, man was walking on the moon."

He says he has no goals for how long he will pitch. The last few years have been a wonderful bonus. He will pitch this year and see what happens. His wife has a hunch that this will be his last year, but it is only a hunch. His friends think he will pitch as long as he is healthy and successful. House thinks, crazy as it sounds, that Nolan is pitching as well now as he ever did. House thinks Nolan will pitch as long as Nolan wants to pitch, as long as he wants to make the physical sacrifices to fight the aging process.

After that, politics is always a possibility, but Nolan says he will not go looking in that direction. He simply will listen if someone talks. The ranching business always has been interesting. The banking business is turning out to be very interesting. He has plans for expansion. The Danbury bank has grown in less than a year from a $9 million bank to a $13 million bank. Maybe he'll do something in baseball. The baseball business certainly has been interesting.

"I remember going to Houston to watch the old .45s play at Colt Stadium," Nolan says. "I went with my dad, I guess. I remember saying, 'How about this? These guys get paid to play baseball.' I said, 'Look at this guy over here, he doesn't even get to play in the game and he still gets paid.' Then, that's what I did. Played baseball for money. It's funny. I go to the career days at high schools and I tell kids that playing baseball isn't a career. It really isn't. How many players ever make the major leagues, and how long do they stay if they make it? I think the average is something like five years. I tell kids they should plan to do something else, really, with their lives ... and yet, here I am. I've been in it this long, and the last two years, I have to say, have been the highlight."

"His age has brought him all this attention," Ruth says, "and I really think he has earned it. I think people looked past him for a long time. I remember being really aggravated back in '73 when he didn't win the Cy Young award and I really thought he deserved it. I remember hearing some mean things that people would say. About him being just a .500 pitcher. He would always say that everyone is entitled to an opinion. I would get mad. So now I get a lot of satisfaction from the accolades he's getting. He deserves them all."

Harry and Nolan walk out of the pasture carrying their gloves. Harry unties Sarge at last from the back of the pickup, and Sarge barks and runs around like the strange dog he is. Reese, who is in the ninth grade, is home from a baseball scrimmage. He drove the old farm-only truck to the lake and back to check his six trout lines. They were empty. Crabs had eaten the bait. He is talking, talking, a teenager in a rush. That is Reese. He picks up the football and starts throwing it with Harry.

"I'd be a great quarterback," Reese says. "I was the quarterback in seventh grade. You should have seen me. I was awesome. Just awesome. You should have seen me last year, eighth grade, when I was a Tower of Power free safety. Awesome."

"How'd practice go today?" Nolan asks.

"I got hit in the shin."

"You got hit in the chin?"

"The shin. It hurt."

"Did you pitch any?"

"Yes, sir. I pitched to five batters. One kid ... I threw the ball behind him."

"Uh-huh," Harry says. "Like father, like son."

In the house, Ruth can be seen through the lighted kitchen window, moving around the cabinets. She went through the day in a buzz, picking up the tickets to Washington, packing the bags for the White House. She bought a new pleated shirt for Nolan to wear with his tuxedo, because the old one looked a little too shabby for dinner with the Queen and Prince of Denmark, not to mention President Bush. She picked up her new dress, a long gown bought in Houston, from her mother's house. Her mother had sewn the hem.

Nolan still has to feed the horses and Harry will help him, but there is a moment here, a pause. It is the pause at the end of the normal working day. It is the pause at the end of a workout, the job done, the sweat still fresh. It is the reward. Night is here, and there is a fine sense of fulfillment. This is life. This is breathing. This is it. Friends and family and dogs and home and land. Dinner soon to arrive.

Nolan leans on the fender of his wife's car, resting. He is wearing a cap from a feed company, a dark-blue windbreaker and a pair of blue gym-instructor sweatpants. He could be anybody. Just a middle-aged, middle-of-the-road anybody. He looks across his pasture with its subliminal baseball field, and someone points out the similarity of the scene to ones in the baseball movie *Field of Dreams*. See the woods? Isn't that where Shoeless Joe Jackson should emerge, ready to play baseball with the other immortals? What was the line? If you build it, he will come.

"I built it," Nolan says. "He never came. Maybe I should have put in lights."

Tomorrow, the White House.

The Razor's Edge

♦

BY   W I L L I A M   N A C K

THE STORY OF CINCINNATI CATCHER WILLARD HERSHBERGER
WAS UNFAMILIAR TO MOST BASEBALL FANS WHEN BILL NACK
WROTE THIS POIGNANT PIECE IN 1991.

*...and though it said on his chest he was one of the team, he sat
among them alone; at the train window, gazing at the moving
trees, in front of his locker, absorbed in an untied shoelace, in the
dugout, squinting at the great glare of the game.*

Bernard Malamud
The Natural

Alone at last in his room at the Copley Plaza Hotel in Boston,
far from his worried manager and teammates on the Cincinnati
Reds, Willard Hershberger locked the door and turned on his
black portable radio to listen to the game. It was nearly time to
go; he had made his irreducible choice. For Hershberger, 29,
the years of anger and torment were almost over.

It was 1:10 p.m. on Saturday, Aug. 3, 1940, a wilting afternoon on which the Reds, leading the second-place Brooklyn
Dodgers by six games in the race for the National League pennant, were about to begin a doubleheader at National League

Field against the last-place Boston Bees. Hershberger was the Reds' second-string catcher, behind future Hall of Famer Ernie Lombardi, but he was far more than a backup player. In pursuit of their second straight pennant, and their first World Series championship since their tainted victory over the Chicago Black Sox in 1919, the Reds were counting on Hershberger not only to spell Lom in the second game of doubleheaders—Hershberger was mongoose-quick behind the plate and a far rangier fielder than the ponderous Lombardi—but also to hit, particularly in the pinch with men on base.

"As good a hitter as I ever saw at getting a man in from third with less than two outs," says Gabe Paul, then the Reds' publicist and traveling secretary and later the general manager of various teams. "[Hershberger] would find a way to get a man home. A hell of a ballplayer."

In 1939, in 174 at bats over 63 games, Hershberger had hit .345. It was only his second year in the majors. He struck out only four times, for a remarkable ratio of once every 43.5 times at bat. "A real good contact hitter," recalls Gene Thompson, a pitcher for the '40 Reds and now a San Francisco Giants scout. "In my business, that's the kindest thing we can say about a hitter: He gets the bat on the ball."

At 5' 10½" and only 167 pounds, Hershberger was, next to Lombardi, a runt who never hit for power. But before the Reds-Bees series started in Boston that August, Casey Stengel, the manager of the Bees, had wailed to reporters about the damage that Hershberger had done to the Boston team in its last set-to at Cincinnati's Crosley Field. "It might seem good to play the Reds in the second game of a doubleheader knowing that Lombardi wouldn't be trudging up to the dish with that big bat of his, but that's an illusion," said Stengel. "Actually, that Hershberger is about as hard to get out as Big Lom."

At the beginning of the Reds' East Coast road trip late in July, Hershberger had been hitting .353. But heading into the Aug. 3 doubleheader with the Bees, he was haunted by old demons and was slipping gradually into a deep, unmanageable melancholy. His average had melted to .309. He was supposed to catch one of Saturday's games, but on Friday he had played as if in a trance—expressionless except for his excited, bulging eyes—and that night he had broken down and wept uncontrollably in the suite of the Reds' manager, Bill (Deacon) McKechnie. The next morning, as Hershberger sat in a chair in the hotel lobby and stared ahead, his teammates called his name as they passed by, heading out the door to pile into cabs for the ballpark.

"Come on, Hersh, let's go," said second baseman Lonnie Frey.

"Yeah, yeah," Hershberger said. "I'll be along."

Pitcher Paul Derringer was the last player to see him. It was 11:55 a.m. when Derringer swept past Hershberger toward the door. "Aren't you coming, Hershie?" Derringer asked.

"Not yet," Hershberger said. "I'm waiting for a friend."

The day before, he bought a bottle of iodine in the drugstore of the Copley Plaza, but he changed his mind about drinking it, even if he could not shake the impulse that had led him to buy it. After the players had left, Hershberger drifted back to his room. At 1:10 p.m., as he sat there thinking, the phone rang. At McKechnie's urgent request, Paul was trying to reach Hershberger from a public phone booth at the ballpark. "The phone rang a long, long time," recalls Paul.

When Hershberger finally answered it and Paul identified himself, the usually gentle, soft-spoken catcher snapped: "What do *you* want?"

"Bill asked me to call you," Paul said. "He's worried about you, and he wants you to come to the ballpark."

"I'm sick," said Hershberger.

"You don't have to put on your uniform," said Paul. "Bill says you can come out and sit in the stands. He's concerned, and he just wants you out here."

Hershberger hesitated. "All right," he said. "I'll be right out...."

Paul was the last person known to have spoken to him. Hershberger never made it to the ballpark. Around 2 p.m., he stripped off his shirt and undershirt and shaved with his brand-new electric razor, which he had bought just before this road trip. In the bathroom, Hershberger then gathered up all the towels from the racks, got down on his hands and knees and, as meticulously as a mason laying tiles, unfolded and spread out the towels, wall to wall, on the bathroom floor. He was too polite and thoughtful a man to make a terrible mess for the maid to clean up. No, he would leave nothing like that. Nothing like the mess his father, Claude, had left 12 years before, when Willard was a high school boy of 17 living at home in Fullerton, Calif., and one dark November morning was jolted awake by the thunderous roar of the shotgun exploding in the bathroom at the bottom of the stairs.

Hershberger finished laying out the towels. The game at the park was in the seventh inning, with the Reds winning 2–1, when he picked up the used single-edge blade that he had taken from his roommate's safety razor. He turned his back to the tub.

Peering above the basin into the reflecting glass, Willard McKee Hershberger looked into the face of the only man who ever really wished him ill.

He was born on May 28, 1911, in Lemoncove, Calif., but Willard and his younger sister, Lois, started school and grew up in Fullerton, 40 miles southeast of Los Angeles, where their father had gotten a job in the drilling fields of Shell Oil. From the time he was a boy, Willard's world was immutably fixed: sports, guns, hunting and tinkering with shortwave radios. Girls only loitered on the edges of this world. "I always had plenty of older girls coming over to the house asking for me, but it was Willard they really wanted to see," Lois recalled in September 1989, eight months before she died. "He never seemed interested in any one girl, particularly. Maybe because the girls were more interested in him than he was in them."

Instead, Hershberger developed into a playground rat who worked endlessly at sports and games, everything from baseball and basketball by day to kick-the-can at night. Baseball was his abiding love. "Willard always had a baseball in his hand and a mitt tied to his belt," said Lois. "He wanted to be a ballplayer all his life."

"A catcher," recalls his cousin, Blanche McKee Maloy, whose father was the brother of Hershberger's mother, Maude. "Cousin Lois was a strong, athletic gal, too. After school, she would throw to him in their backyard. When she got to high school, none of the girls wanted to catch her because she threw too hard."

By the time Willard reached his senior year at Fullerton Union High School, an athletic mecca in Southern California, he had become not only the school's surpassing athlete but a model student and leader as well. The year before, he had been elected president of his junior class and president of the Varsity Club, a group for athletes who had earned six letters. He was the only junior among them. He was a dominant figure in three sports: a runner and kicker in football ("The boy with the magic toe," according to the school's yearbook), a basketball letterman and a baseball player ("The best little catcher ever to wear a Fullerton High School suit").

To be sure, Hershberger was not the only kid at Fullerton in 1928 who was looking to the future and sharpening his spikes. In the tradition of old grad Walter (Big Train) Johnson, who won 416 major league games in 21 years of pitching (1907–27), Fullerton shortstop Arky Vaughan, just a year behind Hershberger and one of his closest friends, was but four years away from launching a major league career in Pittsburgh in which he would hit between .300 and .385 for 10 straight seasons on his way to Cooperstown. And then there was that young Fullerton underclassman, the boy with the full crop of brown hair and the print tie, as he was pictured in the '28 yearbook with this note: "Special mention should be made of the excellent work of Richard Nixon, the high school representative in the National Oratorical Contest on the Constitution."

Coming to his last year—in which he served as the senior class vice-president and as captain of the basketball and baseball teams—Hershberger was a popular, pleasant, affable young man with exceptional athletic ability. He had a quick white-piano-key smile and a cackly, catching laugh that he passed around among the knots of students he met in the halls of Fullerton. At 17, he had everything before him.

"A very lovable human being," recalls Florence Dysinger, 90, a phys-ed teacher at Fullerton then. "Very happy and well-adjusted until ... that terrible thing happened with his father."

Blanche Maloy always saw Willard in contrast to his father, whom she remembers as a figure hovering in the background, looking grainier and more remote than anyone else. "Two of Claude's cousins had killed themselves," recalls Blanche. "One of them hung himself. Willard's father was a strange, moody man. Withdrawn. A little odd. He had these home remedies that he used on Willard and Lois. Willard always had real bad earaches. His father would light up his pipe and draw hot smoke and blow it in Willard's ear. That was supposed to cure the earache. If the kids had a bad cold, he'd kill a skunk and render out the oil and rub them with skunk oil. I don't know where the man came from."

But she remembers how he left. At 2:30 a.m. on Nov. 21, 1928, about two months after Willard had begun his senior year in high school, his father picked up a shotgun that Willard had inadvertently left leaning against a downstairs wall. What he did next was reported the same day by the Fullerton *Daily News*:

Claude E. Hershberger, 54, 222 N. Yale Ave., father of Willard Hershberger, prominent high school athlete, committed suicide in his home ... today by shooting himself with a shotgun.

The decedent had been despondent for several weeks it was believed, brooding over financial worries brought on by changes in personnel of the oil company for which he was employed and which were said to have left him in an inferior position to that which he formerly held.

Retiring to the bathroom of his home, Hershberger is said by police to have pointed at his breast while seated on the edge of the bath tub. The trigger was pushed by means of a cane. Death was believed instantaneous.

"Willard's bedroom was directly above the bathroom, and he was the first one to reach his father," says Maloy. "He ran down the stairs and there [Claude] was. It had blown him into the tub."

Lois, then 15, followed Willard in to see if her father was breathing. She remembered standing there with her brother's arms around her. "I was the strong one," Lois said. "Willard blamed himself for not putting the gun upstairs where it belonged. He hugged me for strength. I guess we were both so upset that we never mentioned it again. We absolutely never spoke a word of it to each other for the rest of our lives."

Of course, the unending horror of the experience—the crashing of the gunshot and the sight of the blood, the void it created and the feelings of anger and betrayal it aroused in the boy—more than altered the course of Hershberger's life. It left him with a widowed mother for whom he would become chief provider and protector, a woman who worshiped him and all he did, in return for which, Lois said, he vowed never to marry while his mother was alive. It also left him with the memory of a father who had shown him not how to be a man but how to be a victim—an unspeakable legacy that ineluctably led him, 12 years later, to that bathroom in the Copley Plaza Hotel. "You can imagine how it affected Willard," says Maloy. "You know, to my knowledge, he never took a bath in a tub again. Only showers."

"Lois adjusted very well," recalls Dysinger. "She came in and talked to me the day after her father killed himself. She said that Willard had found him and he was terribly shocked. Something snapped. It didn't go away. It ate into him. It changed his life."

Indeed, throughout his entire professional baseball career—eight years on seven teams in the minors and 2½ years with the Reds in The Show—Hershberger would never be known as the lighthearted lad he had been in Fullerton. Not that his playing suffered. He hit better than .300 in six of the seven minor league years for which there are records, and in 1937, his final year with the legendary Newark Bears, he hit .325 in 314 at bats, striking out only six times, and had 62 RBIs. At season's end, he was voted the International League's Catcher of the Year. The Bears, owned by the New York Yankees, won the '37 Junior World Series and were regarded by some as the greatest minor league club ever assembled.

Pitcher Jack Fallon was the only '37 Bear not to make it to the bigs. Newark was the third minor league team on which he had played with Hershberger, and he had come to know the catcher as an uncompromising perfectionist. "Everything he did he wanted to do right," Fallon says.

Failure, or even mediocrity, was like poison to Hershberger. "If he went oh-for-four, or was in a slump, it worried the hell out of him," says Atley Donald, another '37 Bears pitcher. Hershberger became a hypochondriac, hoarding pills and predicting his illnesses two weeks in advance. "Hershie was popular when he got to the ballpark, but a lonesome man away from the game," says fellow Newark catcher Buddy Rosar. "And lots of bottles of pills. He had a nervous condition."

Despite the manner of his father's death, for which he continued to blame himself, Hershberger built a vast collection of guns—"He carried one in his suitcase on road trips and usually bought a new one in each city," says Fallon—and he took target practice regularly at the Cincinnati police shooting range. He was a crack shot in rifle, pistol and skeet. Some days he even took target practice in his hotel. In Binghamton, N.Y., he and Fallon had adjoining rooms. "The hotel room was papered in a daisy pattern," Fallon recalls. "Hershie had this pump gun, an air rifle that shot .22-caliber pellets. He shot the center out of every daisy on that wall. He set bottle caps on the edge of the bathtub, and from his bed across the room he shot the caps off the tub. All you heard in the next room was *Peeez! Peeez!* Hershie was an odd person in many ways."

Hershberger's mother could see the changes in him in the off-season when he came home to Three Rivers, Calif., 10 miles west of Lemoncove, to ride the ranges and hunt for quail and deer. Earl McKee, Blanche's brother, recalls Maude Hershberger telling him of how her son began brooding silently. "I'd find him up late at night, sitting in the dark by the window, smoking cigarettes," Maude said.

The reason he rattled around for so long in the minors, from El Paso to Erie to Oakland, was one of those odd turns of fate that seemed to plague Hershberger. Back in 1930, having heard sensational reports about Hershberger, Pirate scout Art Griggs set out from Los Angeles to Fullerton to see him play. At the same time Yankee scout Bill Essick took off in the same direction to look at Vaughan, the shortstop phenom. Instead of going straight to Fullerton, though, Essick detoured through Long Beach to have a look at another player. That left Griggs grazing alone in Fullerton. When he saw Vaughan, Griggs signed him immediately, becoming so distracted by his find that he forgot about Hershberger. When Essick arrived a few days later, he saw that Vaughan was gone and, in his place, signed Hershberger. If Essick hadn't chosen to swing through Long Beach, chances are the two scouts would have gotten what they originally had come for; Vaughan would have joined Lou Gehrig and Joe DiMaggio on the Yankees, and Hershberger would have been a Buc, teaming with future Hall of Famers Pie Traynor and the Waner brothers, Paul and Lloyd. In the 1930s, the Pirates changed catchers regularly, and Hershberger would have made the majors long before 1938, his first year up.

As things turned out, Hershberger played all his minor league years for the Yankees, a dead-end career path for any catcher while the great Bill Dickey was performing in the Bronx. With all the teams that could have used Hershberger as a starter, the Yankees sent him in the winter of '37 to Cincinnati, where he would be a sub, in exchange for $25,000, shortstop Eddie Miller and an option on another player.

They loved Hershie in River City. He and Lombardi were a pair—the wiry Hershberger and the 6' 3", 230-pound Schnozz, who had hands like picnic roasts and an ornament of a nose that raised snoring to a performing art. Everywhere Lombardi went, the lovable oaf fell asleep, and everywhere he fell asleep, he snored—at parties, in darkened movie theaters, on trains. Players would gather around him just to watch him snore. To watch the first flutters coming from his lips, like a light breeze that foretold the storm. "Here it comes!" someone would say. And then the gathering of vibrations, the deeply inhaled breath and, finally, the climactic explosion, an eruption from an abyss that left the audience slapping knees in laughter and Lombardi waking with a start to thunder: "What's so funny?"

"He was the loudest snorer I ever heard," recalls utility infielder Eddie Joost. "Terrible. But a great guy. As kind a person as you'd ever want to meet in your life. And could he hit! One year he hit .342 to lead the league, and he couldn't run to first base in 10 minutes. If he could have run, he'd have hit .400." Indeed, shortstops played him so deep that Lombardi once said to Pee Wee Reese, the Brooklyn shortstop, "You'd been in the league for five years before I learned you weren't an outfielder."

While Hershberger had a quick, accurate arm, Lombardi had a cannon. Nevertheless, "Lom threw the lightest ball I ever caught," says Frey. "You hardly knew you had it in your hand. Just put your glove down, and it was there."

Which is the reason why, as long as Lombardi was around, Hershberger would never start in Cincinnati. Though he and Lombardi could not have been more dissimilar, they were two of the team's best-loved players. In one poll conducted in late July 1940, women fans voted Lombardi the most popular Reds player, with Hershberger second.

While Lombardi moved like a dirigible behind the plate, slow in fielding pop-ups or bunts, Hershberger dashed to back up the first baseman on ground balls to short. He was so active behind the plate that fans began to call him "Herky Jerky." Whenever he came in for Lombardi in the late innings of a game, they applauded him warmly. As much as they admired Lombardi, Crosley fans put the needle to him whenever he failed to get back for a dugout pop-up. "Hershie woulda got it!" they screamed.

Cincinnati was a meat-and-potatoes town, and players recall how the crowd would stir whenever Hershberger came to the on-deck circle with men on base. "Boy, he was tough in the clutch," Frey recalls. "And he had a peculiar habit out there. Every time we had men on base and Hershie came up to hit, before he went to the plate he bent down and untied and then retied his shoestrings. But only when it meant something. I remember the guys would see him doing that and someone would say, 'Hershie's bearin' down.... He's tying' his shoes!' "

Good as Hershberger was, it struck Thompson as curious that the catcher seemed content to back up Lombardi. "No doubt in my mind he could have been a starting catcher for most anybody," Thompson says. "I don't think Hershie realized he was near as good as he was. We pitchers just thought he was outstanding. If you find someone with the ability that Hershie had, and he's aggressive at all, he's not gonna be satisfied to catch behind *anyone*. Most guys with Hershie's ability would say, 'Trade me. I want to go to a place where I can catch every day.' He had no confidence. *He was satisfied.*"

The Yankees swept the Reds in the 1939 World Series. Hershberger got into three games and went 1 for 2, with an RBI single in Game 4, and he used his share of the Series money, $4,000, to build his mother a house in Three Rivers. "He dug a well for her," says Maloy. "He built a little bridge over a little creek that crosses the driveway up to the house. He built a fence around the yard to keep the cows out. She was so happy, and so proud of Willard."

In October 1939, some 300 Orange County residents attended a banquet honoring Hershberger in the cafeteria of Fullerton Union High School. The Junior Chamber of Commerce was welcoming home, as one newspaper put it, "the local boy who made good as catcher for the National League champion Cincinnati Reds." It was a highlight of the Fullerton social season. "Everybody loved him," Maloy says. "Just a hero to the kids."

There was no reason to believe, as the 1940 season began, that Hershberger had anything more menacing on his mind than the tying and untying of his laces. But he did. He had never shared his family secret, so far as anyone could recall. In the majors, as in the minors, he sat apart from his teammates off the field—a nervous, distant, often brooding man. "On the train, you'd be talking to people, and he'd be over there looking out the window, never getting involved in what was going on around him," Joost says. "The impression he gave was of sadness, as if he was saying, 'What am I doin'? Where am I goin'?' I can see his face today. Vividly. A somber face. I am walking by him in a railroad car. He is staring out the window."

The late Lew Riggs, the Reds' backup third baseman and Hershberger's roommate at the Kemper Lane Hotel in Cincinnati, saw him as Maude Hershberger had seen him at home. "Whenever I woke up at any hour of the night, I would find him seated in a chair by the window staring out into the darkness and smoking cigarette after cigarette," Riggs once recalled. "I joked with him about his ability to go into a game the following day and hit a few right on the nose ... and he would say, 'It's a gift.' He practically would not get any sleep at all."

Hershberger's insomnia gave him more time to nurse his hypochondria. "He had a big briefcase filled with all kinds of pills," recalls centerfielder Harry Craft. In his locker, there were bottles in boxes, and nose drops and unguents and sprays. Hershberger spent hours with Doc Rohde, the team trainer, in Rohde's hotel room. He would pull down the skin under his eyes, check the whites of them in the mirror, then ask Rohde: "Doc, aren't these eyes yellow-lookin' to you?"

"No, they look fine to me," Rohde would say.

"I never heard of anybody in my life who could predict down the road that he would be sick," says Thompson. "But [Hershberger] could. He'd say, 'By the way I feel now, I'll be down with a cold by next Wednesday.' The oddity of it was, he would get sick on Wednesday."

His hypochondria became the butt of clubhouse jokes. Players filled his locker with bottles of pills. As Hershberger left

Rohde's room, someone would say, "You look a little peaked, Hershie, are you all right?" Hershberger was not laughing with the boys. "He would get upset about it," says Thompson. "Of course, we were gettin' a big kick out of it, laughing."

By July 1940, something far more ominous than insomnia or hypochondria had Hershberger in its grip. Earlier in the season, he had told Riggs and another teammate, Bill Baker, that he planned to kill himself, but they had not taken him seriously. His brooding and sleeplessness became worse. He started dropping into McKechnie's office and threatening to quit. "Bill, I can't go on," he said one day. "I'm a jinx. I'm getting out of baseball." He bought a savings bond, put it in the Kemper Hotel safe and told Riggs, 'If anything happens to me, Lew, I want you to know where it is. See that my mother gets it.' " He purchased a new car, but he also took out a $5,000 life insurance policy.

It was as if Hershberger had seen an omen. Once again, fate played cruelly with him. The eastern road trip began in Brooklyn with a doubleheader against the Dodgers, who were five games behind the Reds. Lombardi started the first game, which the Reds won 4–3, and Hershberger was behind the plate as the Reds took the second 9–2. Noted *The New York Times* the following day: "Bill Hershberger led the attack on the Brooklyn pitchers in this game, getting four hits in five times up." He also had two RBIs. The next day, with Lombardi sidelined by a sore ankle, Cincinnati won 6–3 to sweep the series, but Hershberger went 0 for 4.

All at once he found himself the first-string catcher of the pennant-chasing Reds in the middle of the season. A heat wave, with temperatures hovering in the high 90s, made the East Coast a bubbling caldron. Wearing wool uniforms, ballplayers suffered damnably. In Philadelphia on July 26, the Reds won their seventh straight, 9–5, and Hershberger drove in two runs with a single in the first, his only hit in five at bats. He began to melt away. On July 27, in 100° heat, the Phillies whipped the Reds 5–3 and held Hershberger hitless. The next day the Reds won the first game of a doubleheader against the Phillies 7–2, but lost the second 4–1, with Hershberger going 0 for 4. The grandstands were beginning to close in on him.

In the furnace of New York's Polo Grounds on July 30,

Hershberger went 3 for 4 in the Reds' 6–3 victory over the Giants, but by then he had lost 15 pounds and was beginning to suffer from dehydration and exhaustion. Whatever it was that had been gnawing at him in the night, he finally surrendered to it on July 31. Reds pitcher Bucky Walters had a 4–1 lead over the Giants in the ninth inning, with two out. He was tiring, but McKechnie left him in. Walters walked Bob Seeds, and Burgess Whitehead homered to make the score 4–3. Walters then walked Mel Ott, and up came Harry (the Horse) Danning, who drove an 0–2 pitch into the balcony in left to win the game 5–4.

Hershberger was inconsolable. For the next two days he insisted on taking the blame for the loss, claiming that he had called for the wrong pitch to Danning. Craft says that Walters blamed himself. After the game the Reds climbed into a Pullman car and headed for Boston. Hershberger was sitting in his berth across from Bill Werber, the Reds' third baseman, and shaking his head. "If Ernie had been catching, we wouldn't have lost those ball games," Hershberger told him. "We'd have *never* lost that game tonight with Ernie behind the plate."

Werber waved that away. "You got nine guys out there, Hershie," Werber told him. "Everybody's responsible."

Hershberger would not hear it. "It's just terrible," he said. "Losing those ball games that you've got in your pocket. It's all my fault. All my fault." He had begun to feel, too, that members of the team were lining up against him. While sitting on the bench one day with Morrie Arnovich, a Reds outfielder, Hershberger confided: "There's a lot of fellows on this club who are down on me." Arnovich told him this was not so. Hershberger grew silent. He was drifting out of touch.

McKechnie began to sense how far the catcher had gone only on Friday, Aug. 2, when Hershberger went 0 for 5 in the second game of a doubleheader against the Bees. At one point in the game, he simply failed to field a swinging bunt in front of the plate, forcing pitcher Whitey Moore to come scrambling for it. After the inning ended, McKechnie put his hands on Hershberger's shoulders. "What's the matter, son?" he asked. "Are you sick? Is there anything the matter with you?"

"You bet there's something the matter with me," said Hershberger, his eyes wide. "I'll tell you about it after the game."

Riggs, who may have known Hershberger best, could see

how far he had gone over the edge. "He caught that game through instinct alone," Riggs said. "When he would come back to the bench, he would not say a word to anybody. I don't believe he really knew what plays had been made."

Later that day, McKechnie took Hershberger to the ballpark's deserted grandstand, but Hershberger balked at sitting there. "I can't talk to you here," he said. "I'll break down."

It didn't really matter. Back at the Copley, on McKechnie's couch, Hershberger unburdened himself. "The kid just sat there and cried for a full hour, and I let him, because I wanted him to get it off his chest," McKechnie said. "Then he started to talk."

At one point, Hershberger said: "My father killed himself, and I'm gonna do it too. I was gonna kill myself this morning when we got off the train. I went to the drugstore and bought a big bottle of iodine. I was gonna drink that, but then I thought there were better ways to do it." He told McKechnie that he alone was responsible for the recent losses. McKechnie tried to console and reassure him. Hershberger said that he bore no animosity toward any of the players and that none of this was their fault. The conversation ranged far afield. The Luftwaffe had begun the air war over Britain, and several times Hershberger referred to "that son of a bitch Hitler." At 9 p.m., the two men went to dinner. At around midnight, thinking he had talked Hershberger out of any notions of suicide, McKechnie left him at his room.

"I'm all right now, Bill," the catcher told his manager. "I'll be in there with my old pep tomorrow."

Later that night, Hershberger's road roommate, Baker, returned to find their hotel room dark. He called Willard's name. No answer. He flicked on the light. Hershberger was sitting in the bathroom. "What are you doing, Hershie?" Baker asked.

"Just smoking a cigarette, Bill."

On the floor lay a coil of wire that Riggs had given Hershberger to use as a radio antenna. It had been on the dresser earlier that night. Later Baker saw that Hershberger, relaxed at last, got his first full night's sleep in many weeks. Hershberger knew what he was going to do.

The following afternoon, after watching his teammates leave the hotel, he went upstairs, shaved, set out the towels and, facing himself in the bathroom mirror, felt for the jugular. He found it only after hacking around clumsily with the blade. Once the vein was open, he turned toward the tub, knelt over its rim and bled to death.

Between games of the doubleheader, McKechnie, realizing that Hershberger had not arrived at the park, asked the catcher's friend Dan Cohen, a visiting Cincinnati shoe-store owner who was to have dinner with Hershberger that night, to check on him at the hotel. The door to Hershberger's room was locked, and no one answered. Cohen finally prevailed on a maid to let him in. The room was empty, neat as a watch, and Cohen was about to leave when he decided to peek into the bathroom. Hershberger was leaning over the tub, half in and half out. Cohen raced back to the ballpark. The second game was in the fourth inning. "When I saw Dan Cohen running down to the bench during the second game," said Riggs, "I knew that something terrible had happened to Hershberger. Goose pimples broke out all over me, and the fellows told me I turned as white as a sheet."

On his way out of the dugout, McKechnie told coach Hank Gowdy what had happened and, putting Gowdy in charge of the team, asked him not to tell the players until after the game was over. The Reds lost the nightcap, 5–2, and Craft recalls walking into the clubhouse and hearing Gowdy call the team together.

"All right, now be quiet," the coach said. "I want to tell you something. Willard Hershberger has just destroyed himself."

Craft dropped his head, too stunned to speak. "What?" he thought. "Hershie what?"

Joost was struck dumb. "Why?" he asked himself. "Why would he do a thing like that?"

Thompson was not in the clubhouse, but when he heard what had happened, he wondered if he and the other pranksters had helped drive Hershberger to suicide by making fun of his hypochondria. Says Thompson, "My first thought was, 'Did we have something to do with it?' I've thought about it so many times. I don't think we had any idea how this was hurtin' that young guy. Since then, I've never made fun of anybody. That will stay with me the rest of my life. Perhaps it would have happened anyway, but I don't think we helped it."

In his suite that night, McKechnie gathered his players together.

He told them what Hershberger had said to him the night before—how his father had killed himself, how Hershberger had wanted to kill himself, too, and how he felt he had let down the team. McKechnie also said Hershberger had talked about other personal problems that the manager felt honor-bound not to reveal. McKechnie mentioned that Hershberger had several uncashed paychecks in his pocket. Lombardi, Riggs and a few others were weeping. "I thought I had talked him completely out of it," McKechnie said. "I thought everything was put back together again. I couldn't keep a bodyguard on him."

The meeting lasted about half an hour. McKechnie made one plea. "The thing for us to do now is win the pennant and vote Hershie's mother a full share of the World Series money," he said. "And I know we'll win it." They did indeed win the Series, beating Detroit four games to three, and Maude Hershberger got a full share, $5,803.62

Ironically, Hershberger's death led to the best of all 1940 World Series stories. In mid-September, Lombardi sprained his ankle, and without Hershberger, McKechnie turned to the only man in the organization he thought could handle the job—coach Jimmy Wilson, 40, a former catcher who had caught but two games in nearly three seasons. Wilson caught in six of the seven Series games, and Thompson can still see him hobbling in pain, his thigh muscles knotted up from so much squatting. Between innings, Wilson would teeter to the runway behind the dugout, drop his pants and sit down so that Rohde could massage a scalding salve into his thighs. "Oh, mercy, it was hot," Thompson says. "And his catching hand was so swollen from catching fastballs that he could barely get it in and out of the glove. He was great."

Wilson also hit .353—six singles in 17 trips. It was a rare farewell, a final performance by an old man who rose one more time to honor himself and the game.

The other legacies of Hershberger's act were not so glorious. Maude Hershberger collapsed in the Three Rivers post office, where she was working, when she learned that her son had followed his father's example. She lived only seven more years.

Hershberger's friend Cohen, who had found him dead, committed suicide in 1961. Even Lombardi nearly emulated Hershberger.

In 1953, out of baseball for four years, the Cyrano of the Iron Mask slipped into a deep depression. On their way to a sanatorium in Livermore, Calif., where he was to receive psychiatric treatment, Lombardi and his wife, Berice, stopped at a relative's house, where Lombardi found a razor and sliced open his throat. He begged Berice to let him die and struggled against the sheriff's deputies who came to take him to the hospital.

Those who knew Lombardi say there is no connection between Hershberger's suicide and Lombardi's attempt, but the nature of their acts suggests otherwise. Thompson believes that Hershberger's act was precipitated by the fear of failing when he was forced to become the regular catcher in Lombardi's absence. "When it all fell on Willard's shoulders," according to Thompson, "he said to himself, 'Hey, I can't handle this.' " And that would mean Lombardi's absence helped cause Hershberger's death. Ultimately, the most popular Cincinnati player of his day became as tragic a figure as the second most popular. Lombardi worked for six years as a press box attendant for the Giants in Candlestick Park, until an insult by a young reporter sent him packing in anger and shame. Lombardi next surfaced years later pumping gas in Oakland and railing against those who had allegedly denied him his rightful place in Cooperstown. He died in 1977; he was elected to the Hall of Fame in 1986.

Trivia question: Who is the only catcher in major league history to win two batting titles? (Lombardi, in 1938 and 1942.)

Trivia question: Who was the only active player in baseball history to commit suicide during the season?

Fifty-one years later, the most intriguing question about Hershberger's death remains unanswered: What were the problems he revealed to McKechnie on Friday night that helped drive him to kill himself on Saturday? "He told me what his problems were," McKechnie said at the time. "It has nothing to do with anybody on the team. It was something personal. He told it to me in confidence, and I will not utter it to anyone. I will take it with me to my grave."

True to his word, on Oct. 29, 1965, in Bradenton, Fla., Bill McKechnie took the secret with him.

MANAGEMENT

◆ ◆ ◆

The Bending Branch

BY   RED   SMITH

AN ERA IN BASEBALL CAME TO AN END IN 1954 WHEN BRANCH
RICKEY RETIRED AFTER A LIFETIME IN THE GAME. MOST REMEM-
BERED FOR HIS YEARS WITH THE DODGERS AND FOR HIS ROLE IN
BRINGING JACKIE ROBINSON TO THE MAJOR LEAGUES, RICKEY
ALSO LABORED LONG AND HARD FOR THE CARDINALS AND THE
PIRATES. RED SMITH WROTE THIS SHORT BUT MEMORABLE PIECE
IN TRIBUTE TO RICKEY'S CONTRIBUTION.

In Brooklyn the Dodgers were at the Giants' throats. In Milwaukee close to 43,000 idolators rent their haberdashery over
the Braves, back home and still winning after sweeping through
the National League like trench mouth. In Chicago Jack Harsh-
man and Al Aber pitched each other numb as the White Sox
whipped the Tigers, 1 to 0 in 16 innings. In Cleveland and
New York the Indians and Yankees won and won.

In Pittsburgh, where ball clubs finish last on merit, the week's
most significant news caused no more commotion than the
Pirates themselves. Branch Rickey announced he would retire
"from active duty" in November of 1955 on completion of his
contract as the Pirates' general manager.

They don't care much in Pittsburgh. They didn't care much

152

in Brooklyn when he left the Dodgers, or in St. Louis when he parted from the Cardinals. Baseball fans don't warm to Rickey, though with the probable exception of Babe Ruth and the possible exception of Judge Kenesaw Mountain Landis he has been the game's dominant figure in his lifetime.

He is a curious man, contradictory.

"A man of many faucets," they said in Brooklyn, "all turned on."

Branch Rickey is a God-fearing, checker-playing, horse-trading, cigar-smoking, double-talking, nonalcoholic, sharp-shooting blend of eloquence and unction and sincerity and enterprise and imagination and energy and independence and profundity and guile. His agile mind races ahead and his facile tongue patters after, and obscurities result. "When," he was saying in a speech, "there comes a stoppage of vertical mobility among the society strata..." "Gawd," said a man in the audience, "guys get drunk and don't say things like that."

In a press conference John Drebinger of *The New York Times* asked a question. Rickey responded at length, say like 20 minutes. "Does that answer your question, John?" he inquired. "I," Mr. Drebinger confessed, "have forgotten the question."

Rickey's speech can be as circuitous as a hoopsnake, but get him talking on a subject that commands his interest (such as the theory that against certain weak batters it is wise to call in two outfielders and play six men on the infield) and every word he utters goes directly to the point.

When he was manager of the Cardinals in the early 1920s he befuddled his players with chalk-talks in the clubhouse. Rogers Hornsby, succeeding him, threw out the blackboard and horse-whipped the athletes to the world championship.

Perhaps because Rickey was born to be a horse trader or maybe because competition has been the kernel of his life, it is important to him never to be beaten in a business transaction. He has, consequently, won a fearsome reputation for selling gold bricks in player deals.

Garry Schumacher of the Giants once stated the rules for talking business with Rickey: "Don't drink the night before, keep your mouth shut and your hands in your pockets."

A ballplayer fighting for an increase in wages would rather spit in Rocky Marciano's eye than walk into Rickey's office without a bodyguard. Yet the master persuader hasn't always come off first in these encounters.

When Dizzy Dean was the rawest of rookies he was closeted for many hours in Rickey's lair in St. Louis. It was Rickey who tottered out at last, collar unbuttoned, black hair untidy, black eyebrows twitching.

"Do you know what that boy said to me?" he gasped. "He said, 'Mr. Rickey, I will put more people in Sportsmans Park than anybody since Babe Ruth.' If there were one more like him in baseball, I'd get out of the game."

There was, unfortunately or otherwise, only one like Dizzy. Rickey remained in baseball, and Dean put more people in Sportsmans Park than anybody else since Babe Ruth.

Probably the most widespread conception of Rickey pictures him as a psalm-singing evangelist in a circuit-rider's black hat and bow tie, making a living from the sinful occupation of baseball. This stems from the advertised fact that he does not attend games on Sunday, and it is entirely inaccurate.

It is not religious scruple that keeps him away from Sunday games. When he set out as a professional ballplayer 52 years ago, he promised his mother he would not violate the Sabbath by playing ball. He kept the promise and lost some jobs as a result.

The tallest building beyond the center field fence in St. Louis is the north side Y.M.C.A. On a big Sunday there were always kibitzers watching the game from the Y.M.C.A. windows. It was a standing gag that the room commanding the best view was Rickey's. He could have been in the Y.M.C.A., at that; he was somewhere out of the ball park, still keeping his promise.

He is a strange and fascinating man. At 72, his energy is beyond belief. Always on the go, he always has a secretary and as he goes he dictates letters, memoranda, ideas.

Once he wrote to a sportswriter: "I think you understand me—better than most people do, perhaps." The sportswriter was flattered pink.

This Time George Went Overboard

♦

B Y   S T E V E   W U L F

WHEN REGGIE JACKSON RETURNED TO NEW YORK FOR THE FIRST TIME AFTER LEAVING THE YANKEES AND BECOMING A MEMBER OF THE CALIFORNIA ANGELS, IT GAVE STEVE WULF AN OPPORTUNITY TO ASSESS GEORGE STEINBRENNER'S STORMY TENURE AS OWNER OF THE NATION'S MOST ILLUSTRIOUS FRANCHISE.

Early last week, in the seventh inning of a game in Yankee Stadium, Reggie Jackson of the California Angels hit a titanic home run off the facade in right field. As Jackson admired this blast from the recent past, many in the crowd of 35,458 began to repeat the old familiar mantra "Reg-gie, Reg-gie." After Jackson had taken a bow from the dugout, the crowd turned its attention and vocal chords to the man who had effectively eighty-sixed 44.

"Steinbrenner creates a partial vacuum with his mouth! Steinbrenner creates a partial vacuum with his mouth!" approximates the chant that engulfed Yankee Stadium.

How could they say something like that? Hadn't George showered them with free agents and pennants and championships? Hadn't he given them the best years of his, their and

Reggie's lives? Had they forgotten they were nothing before George arrived?

So what if, in the process, he had taken all the fun out of the game, robbed them of their pride in the Yankees and played them for suckers. How could they say something like that?

"I'm sorry, but what did they say?" asked Catcher Rick Cerone after the game. "I couldn't quite hear it."

"It was about the only fun I had all night," said Ron Guidry, who gave up the home run. Though Guidry later downplayed that comment, it upset George, who said, "I didn't expect that from a man I pay $750,000 a year, who gave up a homer to a lefthander who's usually kept out of the lineup against hard-throwing lefthanders."

These are not happy times for George. At week's end the team he rebuilt to win both the Drake Relays and the World Series was 9–11, fourth in the American League East. It was tied for 10th in the league in stolen bases and dead last in home runs. Even worse, the National League team from Queens had outhomered the Bronx Bombers 18–9 while outstealing them 19–10. If George rode the subways, he would see posters that say: NEW YORKERS ARE CONVERTING TO A NEW SOURCE OF POWER, with a picture of the broad backs of Dave Kingman, George Foster and Ellis Valentine.

George made his eighth managerial move in nine years after a win on April 25. He had promised Bob Lemon a whole season, but his promise fell short by at least 148 games. So Lemon, who replaced Gene Michael last September, was replaced by Gene Michael.

When the Yankees lost three of their first four games under Michael, George didn't panic. "You have to give Stick time," he said. Stop that snickering.

Some 200 years ago, George III of England used to fire his entire household staff two or three times a day. He once stopped a carriage to address an oak tree as if it were Frederick the Great. Late at night, George III was given to running through the castle and howling like a dog.

Nobody has seen George M. Steinbrenner III talking to the big bat that towers outside the Stadium, or anything like that, but his baseball sanity has been called into question lately. Not a few people thought George was out of his mind to let Reggie go in the first place. Not only did he lose the power in his lineup, but he also lost the reason many fans ventured to the Bronx. But all 12—count 'em, 12—advisers, whose sole purpose seems to be to suck up to George, told him that Reggie wasn't worth a four-year $3.6 million contract (plus incentives). "He didn't want to pay me a million at age 39," said Reggie, "but he could be paying Dave Winfield $3 million when he's 39."

Jackson's return promised to be at least interesting, especially after he waited until exactly 6:44 to step out onto the field. In batting practice he put six balls in the seats, to the screaming delight of the fans, most of whom didn't care less that he was hitting .173 with no homers.

Jackson popped to second his first time up, but in the fifth he singled up the middle, then scored the Angels' go-ahead run on Bob Boone's suicide squeeze. In the seventh Jackson stepped to the plate, and Cerone told him he looked good in his new uniform. Reggie said thank you. Guidry's first pitch was a thigh-high breaking ball that didn't, and Jackson turned on it. Whap! The clout was as prodigious in distance as it was in timing. "He just winked at me when he crossed the plate," said Cerone.

Roy Smalley, George's newest infielder, said, "That's the kind of moment that makes little kids baseball fans for life. I felt like a little kid myself, standing on third."

And the chants began. George, who had given instructions to say he wasn't in the ball park, was sitting in a private box. According to eyewitnesses, he just stared straight ahead. "To make it in New York, you have to suffer the slings and arrows of outrageous fortune," said George, who's from Cleveland and lives in Tampa. "I preach mental toughness, so I have to practice it. I thought the word they used was uncouth, though."

After the rain-shortened game, which the Angels and Angel Moreno won 3–1, George had another elevator incident. As Jackson tells it, he was standing in the street-level lobby of the Yankee offices when the elevator doors opened. There was George. Their eyes met. George let the doors close without getting out. A few moments passed, and the doors opened once more. Again their eyes met. Just before the doors closed again, Jackson heard George mutter something about the elevator not working. Rather than embarrass him any more, Jackson left. "Why avoid me?" said Reggie. "He could have walked by me and said something like, 'Way to go, you bastard,' or he could have just walked past me."

The next afternoon Jackson went to the Yankee locker room to visit with his old teammates for about an hour. "They told me I was very lucky to be out of there," Jackson said. "George really ought to own up for a change."

That night Michael broke his maiden as Tommy John shut out the Angels 6–0. But the next night the Yankees lost to Geoff Zahn 2–0. Jackson quite literally had a hand in that one: Leading off the ninth inning of a scoreless game, Reggie was hit on the wrist by reliever Shane Rawley, and his pinch runner was the first man to score. "I wonder who George is going to blame tonight," said Winfield.

Another ex-Yankee, 43-year-old Gaylord Perry, used his great expectorations to dampen New York the following night, as the Mariners made a batting-practice pitcher out of Rich Gossage in a 6–3 victory. "We're making everybody else's pitcher look like Cy Young," said Yankee DH Oscar Gamble. Yet another alumnus, Jim Beattie, held the Yankees to four hits and one unearned run in seven innings on Saturday night. But then Seattle's relievers got roughed up and New York won 5–1. Smalley's grand slam home run was about the best thing that happened to George all week. Another thing was Smalley's two-run single on Sunday when the Yankees won 4–2.

While the Yankees were trying to right themselves on the field, George and the players were using the New York newspapers as a battleground. On the day Lemon was fired, Gossage had some very pointed things to say. Among his most cogent remarks were: "It started in the World Series and went through spring training" and "It's going to be a long year" and finally "We're made to feel like we're little children being spanked every time things go wrong." Gossage doesn't usually pop off like that.

George took to the back pages of the *New York Post* to defend himself. In an exclusive interview with Dick Young, George said of his managerial change, "If it doesn't turn out, they'll rip me a new seat, those buddies of yours. But if the team turns around and goes on to win, you won't see one [uncouth] word. I'll bet you on it." Young then promised that all the writers would give him "two pips and a hooray" when the Yankees clinch the division.

George gave another exclusive to Maury Allen of the *Post*. His best lines were "I'm paying those guys [Guidry, Winfield, Ken Griffey and Dave Collins] a lot of money, and they haven't produced" and "I didn't throw those home-run balls to [Bobby] Grich and Jackson; Guidry did." Way to trash one of the best pitchers in baseball, George.

On Saturday, through Young's auspices, Winfield sounded off: "Things get hot and he leaves town.... Maybe when things aren't going well here, I should take a day off to look over my stocks and things." Actually, George was relaxing far from the madding crowd at his horse farm in Ocala, Fla. In an exclusive interview with SPORTS ILLUSTRATED Correspondent Tom McEwen, George said, "The Goose should do more pitching and less quacking." He promised, "I'll make one more change, and we think that will make it right. We're getting there and fast, and when we do, we'll be hell on wheels."

George has certainly been hell on wheels since last fall. There was that maxi-tirade after Milwaukee tied the mini-series 2–2. His browbeating and meddling may well have cost the Yankees the World Series.

Over the winter George reshaped the team, acquiring Griffey and Collins for speed. (At week's end Griffey had no stolen bases and Collins no position.) He rehired Lemon for the 1982 season and announced that Michael would be back in 1983. He ordered the team to report voluntarily to spring training in the middle of February, and the extra preparation helped the Yankees go 9–16. Baltimore Manager Earl Weaver took one look at the Yankees in Florida and growled, "There's a guy named George Herman Ruth, called the Babe, who must be rolling over in his grave right now."

George called it the best team he had ever assembled, and then he went about disassembling it. The Yankees needed starters, so starter Gene Nelson was sent to Seattle for a reliever, Rawley. He was acquired so George could trade Ron Davis (who had the temerity to seek arbitration last winter) to the Twins for Smalley, a shortstop, which was something the Yankees already had. The move upset the incumbent, Bucky Dent, as well as the captain of the team, Graig Nettles, whom Smalley was going to spell at third base. Again, all 12 advisers concurred. "We're a true democracy," says George. "We sit around a table and I ask each one what he thinks. I don't even vote." The problem was solved for a while when Nettles broke his left thumb. Unfortunately, by Sunday Dent's bat was moping around at .150, and now Larry Milbourne is in the picture.

Who's on first? is also a burning question. Bob Watson was traded, leaving the Yankees with Dave Revering, Butch Hobson and Collins. The latter two aren't natural first basemen. The trade winds last week had either Toronto's John Mayberry or Pittsburgh's Jason Thompson coming to the Yankees. "There's too much mass confusion here," says Revering, who looked as if he had the job won after he batted .465 in spring training. "I don't know *if* I am playing tomorrow. I don't know when I'm playing. Come back in a week and you won't see me here." Incredibly, George blamed Gamble for most of the Yankees' troubles. "There's no doubt in my mind that this team would be in first place if Oscar hadn't vetoed a trade to Texas for Al Oliver," he said. "Oscar promised me he'd be the best lefthanded designated hitter in baseball, and he's batting .130."

With the team so discombobulated, Lemon was a genius to have it at 5–7, which is where the Yankees were when George decided that a change was needed. "The team had no life, no fire," says George. "Lem and I talked. He said it was O.K. He said he didn't take it as a promise, anyway."

So Lemon, a good man, was used as "meat"—the name he gives to nearly everybody. "I though I might go nine this time, but I didn't even get out of the first inning," Lemon said. Actually, he may have been lucky even to get the start. Reportedly, he had threatened to quit in spring training after George threatened to fire him.

Michael was something of a hero when he told George off last August, but he's back, tail between his legs. "People ask me why I want to manage for George," says Michael. "Lem said it best. 'Managing is the closest thing there is to still playing.' George and I had a talk, and we agreed to be more understanding of each other."

George's defense of his firing managers is that they are always amply compensated. "George thinks that money makes everything good," says Jackson. "But money is the root of all evil. It's harder to get a rich man into heaven than it is to get a

camel through the eye of a needle, and I didn't make that up."
He did bobble it a little, but the point's the same.

Some clubs win with patience rather than money. Why, if
George had owned the Royals in 1980 he might have benched
George Brett in May, when he was hitting in the .260s. John
was on the '73 Dodgers when they got off to a struggling start.
"We went through a bad month and everybody was worried,"
John says, "but before we knew it, it was June and we were in
first place until September. Winning really is just a matter of
having patience. It's like rearing your children. You go through
some tough spells, but if you show them patience they'll turn
out to be fine young people. The management doesn't have the
patience here, but the players do."

"I'm no more impatient than the people who booed me the
other night," says George. "I want a winner. Look at the
record, five flags in nine years. Who can match that?"

The Dodgers come pretty close, and they actually have a farm
system. The Yankees haven't gotten a regular out of their
minor league organization since George took over in 1973, and
they have used only a handful of their own pitchers. He seems
to suck the young blood of the minors only to donate it to
Seattle and San Diego, and the whole Yankee system is festering. While the Yankees are trying to pry the 32-year-old Mayberry from the Blue Jays, Steve Balboni is knocking down the
fences in the International League. "It can be very discouraging
in the minors, dreaming you'll wear pinstripes and knowing
you never will," says Beattie, whom Steinbrenner once accused
of having no guts.

"He really should stick to his horses," says Jackson. "At least
he can shoot them if they spit the bit."

There is little or no hope that George will ever see the light,
though he has his historic precedents, one of whom, Richard
Nixon, was at Yankee Stadium Thursday night. But perhaps
none suits him better than George III, a man of some success
even though he lost the Revolutionary War. After all, he did
beat Napoleon with some late-inning relief help from the
Prince Regent. On July 9, 1776, the people of New York tore
down the statue of George III in Bowling Green. That was just
their way of saying that George III creates a partial vacuum
with his mouth.

The Big Cheese
of the Cardinals

♦

BY   STEVE   WULF

JUST DAYS AFTER STEVE WULF'S STORY ON LEGENDARY MANAGER
WHITEY HERZOG, HERZOG'S ST. LOUIS CARDINALS SWEPT THE
ATLANTA BRAVES IN THREE GAMES FOR THE NATIONAL LEAGUE
PENNANT, THEN WENT ON TO DEFEAT THE MILWAUKEE BREWERS
IN A DRAMATIC SEVEN-GAME WORLD SERIES.

The Friday Kiwanis Club luncheon at Grant's Cabin on Wat-
son Road in St. Louis began with a spirited singing of *America*.
Then Monsignor Richard J. Gallagher delivered the invocation.
He threw a changeup.

"... we thank You for the Smiths, for the Hernandezes and
for Whitey Herzog, the Harry Truman of baseball...."

Herzog was being honored on this day as the South Side
Kiwanis' 36th Sportsman of the Year, following in the foot-
steps of such Cardinal luminaries as Stan Musial, Red
Schoendienst, Ken Boyer, Lou Brock, Joe Torre and, oh
well, Mike Tyson. Herzog was given a silver tray by chapter
president Hellmuth (Red) Reninga, which seemed only fair
since Herzog was about to serve to St. Louis, on a platter, its
first baseball title of any sort in 14 years. At the end of last
week Herzog's Cardinals—and these are *his* Cardinals—led the

162

National League East by a commanding 5½ games.

Which is why last Friday he was being toasted by a gathering that included the Big Eagle himself, 83-year-old beer baron and team owner Gussie Busch. "He is one great guy, and I call him The Rat," growled Busch. "He knows more about baseball than you or I will ever know. Congratulations again, and the best of everything to you, my good friend."

Dorrel Norman (Whitey, The White Rat, Relly) Herzog, the Harry Truman of baseball, couldn't have been enjoying himself more. Here he was, in front of an adoring crowd of 240 people, one of whom was his club's owner, 30 miles from the town in which he was raised, just a few days short of clinching a division title for the team he loved in his youth.

Just a little more than two years ago, after Kansas City had fired him, Herzog came to Busch's retreat at Grant's Farm in St. Louis to talk about a job. "I knew we were going to get along," Herzog told the Kiwanians. "He thought almost the way I did. Whenever I ask him about something he just says"—and here Herzog changed his voice to a foghorn—"'Do it.'"

Herzog did it, all right. Taking a team that had forgotten how to win, he cleaned house and guided it to the best record in its division last year and to its present eminence this year over better teams, at least on paper. But then, Dewey looked better on paper than Truman.

"The two men [Truman and Herzog] just struck me as being similar," said Monsignor Gallagher, pastor of St. Raphael's in St. Louis. "Perhaps it was because of the way they both assault the language. Maybe it's because with both men, you know who the boss is. You can tell that when Whitey takes the ball from one of his pitchers."

"Nobody ever called me the Harry Truman of baseball before," said Whitey. "They called me a lot of other things, though...."

Growing up in New Athens, Ill., Herzog was called Relly. He lived and died with the Cardinals and copied Stan Musial's batting stance. "I've been in a slump ever since," he says. New Athens was a small town of 1,500. Herzog's father worked on the highway crew and his mother was a housewife. Mary Lou Sinn gave him a valentine when he was in the sixth grade and she was in the fifth, but they didn't start dating until after high school and didn't get married until he was in the service. Obviously, his eye for talent was still developing. In the meantime, he played baseball and worked at a variety of jobs.

Herzog signed with the Yankees right after graduation. His rise through the minors was interrupted when he joined the Army Corps of Engineers and was stationed at Fort Leonard Wood, Mo., where he managed the baseball team and once beat a Fort Carson, Colo. team managed by Billy Martin. "In two years we went 85–6 and 86–5," says Herzog. "Of course, you could become a free agent after only two years." The team's bat boy was Mike McKenzie, whose father was an athletic and recreation officer at the base. "Once Herzog's troops wanted a holiday pass to go to a game in St. Louis but had a doubleheader scheduled," recalls McKenzie, a writer for *The Kansas City Star*. "So Herzog got some soldiers to flood the field with hoses during the night, and the games had to be canceled because of wet grounds on a day the temperature went over a hundred degrees."

After the service, while on the Yankees' Denver farm club Herzog came under the influence of Manager Ralph Houk, of whom Herzog says, "Nobody could handle players better than he could." Herzog also got a nickname that would last a lifetime. "Johnny Pesky, our coach, said I looked like a pitcher named Bob Kuzaba," says Herzog. "And they called him the White Rat."

In Denver, Herzog and Mary Lou had bought a mobile home. In 1956 the Yankees traded him and four other players to the Washington Senators for Mickey McDermott. The Herzogs took the mobile home with them to Washington; the unusual quarters earned Whitey his first national publicity.

Herzog was a useful major league outfielder, playing for the Senators, A's, Orioles and Tigers. While with the A's in Kansas City, he and Mary Lou decided to settle in Independence, Truman's hometown, and they have lived there ever since. One night in 1958 McKenzie and his father went out with Herzog for pizza. Recalls McKenzie, "Whitey told us the A's had obtained a rightfielder with a great arm and bat. 'He's capable of breaking Ruth's record,' Whitey said." Of course, the man Herzog was talking about was Bob Cerv.

164

Just kidding. It was Roger Maris. Herzog's legendary eye for talent did not extend to cars, however. He was driving an Edsel at the time.

Herzog's career was cut short in 1963 when he came down with a virus in spring training with the Tigers. It affected his inner ear, and to this day Herzog can have occasional dizzy spells if he bends down suddenly.

After the ailing Herzog batted .151 for the Tigers in '63, he went back to Independence. He had a lot of work experience to draw from besides baseball, having driven a hearse, dug graves, sold bricks and worked in a brewery and a bakery. By night he studied surveying and by day he supervised a construction crew. "I had 35 guys working for me on this job, and only about 15 of them wanted to work," he says. When the weather got cold, half of the crew had to be laid off, but to make sure they were the right half, Herzog laid them all off and told the ones he really wanted to come back on Monday. This violation of seniority rules didn't sit well with the union. Rather than put up with the rules, Herzog quit. Seventeen years later, though, he would do the same thing with the Cardinals and succeed.

Hank Peters, now general manager of the Orioles and then the farm director of the A's, offered Herzog a scouting job for $7,500 a year. "I signed 12 players for $120,000 and seven of them eventually made the major league roster," Herzog says. "The best was Chuck Dobson, the pitcher. I could have had Don Sutton for $16,000, but Charlie Finley wouldn't give me the money." Herzog later became an A's coach but quit when Finely wouldn't give him more money.

Herzog went to work for the Mets in 1966 and served them for seven years as a coach, a scout and the director of player development. Some of the talent he spotted or taught included Jerry Koosman, Jon Matlack and Amos Otis. He worked with Joe McDonald, the director of minor league operations; last spring Herzog handed McDonald the general manager's hat he wore while restructuring the Cardinals.

After the 1972 season Herzog accepted an offer from Texas General Manager Joe Burke to take over the Rangers. With typical bluntness, Herzog called them "one of the worst major league teams I've ever seen." They justified his appraisal by going 47–91 before owner Bob Short fired him and hired Billy Martin with 23 games to go in the '73 season.

"It really wasn't fair," Mary Lou was saying last Friday evening during the Cardinals' 3–1 victory over the Chicago Cubs. "If he'd known that his job was on the line ... hurry, Tommy [Herr], hurry! ... he'd have managed completely different."

Mary Lou is a splendid woman, as candid and talkative as her husband. They must have some wonderful fights. They fish and ski together, and even talk baseball. She sits right behind the plate and roots, roots, roots for the home team: "He does bring the game home with him, and he'll sit around the table talking things over with me and our sons, David and Jim.... C'mon, John [Stuper], don't lose him!–John's having control problems tonight, probably nervous.... I don't think he takes my suggestions very seriously. I did tell him he should use Mike Ramsey a little more, but that was about the time Ozzie Smith got injured anyway.... Pop him up, John!"

Herzog may take the game home with him, but he once forgot to take his son home. "When Whitey was managing in the Instructional League for the Mets, he once took Jim, who was about nine, to the ball park," says Mary Lou. "At the end of the day Jim told Whitey he had to go to the bathroom.... C'mon, Lonnie! [Smith strikes out]. Oh, baloney! ... and Whitey forgot about it and left him."

Although Whitey doesn't mind being called Rat, Mary Lou is not too crazy about it. "In school they'd call our children the little white mice," she says. "One of our neighbors in Independence used to put a sign on our lawn that said WHITE RAT. Whenever Whitey went away, I'd take it down. People thought we were selling them critters.... I never noticed Darrell [Porter] crouching that low before."

Actually, zoologists tell us that the white rat has some admirable qualities. He is easily handled if not misused, and he will fight to protect his nest.

Herzog is even proud of some of the Rat caricatures drawn of him by 70-year-old cartoonist Amadee Wohlschlaeger of St. Louis. They hang on an office wall with the pictures of Casey Stengel, Stan Musial and current Cardinal players, a gag trophy honoring Herzog as New Athens Man of the Year 1980 and a reminder from a Marine general that says DFIU–Don't

Foul It Up. "I'm going to have a lot of moving to do when I get my butt canned from this job," says Herzog.

Burke knew Herzog had gotten a raw deal in Texas, so after he became general manager of the Royals, he hired Herzog to replace Jack McKeon as manager in the middle of the '75 season. Kansas City finished second that year and then won the next three American League West titles. Herzog installed Frank White at second, made George Brett his No. 3 hitter, put Larry Gura in the rotation, started Willie Wilson, etc. He made a lot of changes, stressing speed and defense, and the Royals still bear his stamp. Indeed, the Cardinals were made in the Royals' image.

After K.C.'s second division title in 1977, Herzog was honored on the courthouse steps of Independence. The only other to have that honor was Truman. Actually, Herzog had met Truman several times when he played for the A's. And he was in the Truman house shortly before the President died in 1972. "It was eight days before Christmas," says Herzog. "I was quail hunting on a friend's farm just north of Independence when an ice storm hit. The friend asked me to do him a favor. He said he sent a turkey to the Trumans every year at Christmas, but that he was afraid he couldn't get through, and he asked me to take it. I said sure, but when I was driving back, I realized I couldn't go to the Truman house dressed in my hunting clothes. So I put the turkey in the freezer, and the next day I put my suit on and took the turkey over there. I just drove around to the back. Bess answered the door; she was on the phone at the time. Harry was upstairs, I guess. When she got off the phone, she thanked me—they were terrific people—and asked me to wish my friend a merry Christmas. Then I left.

"What bothered me was how easy I got into their house. But that spring I was playing golf in a foursome down in Texas. When I introduced myself to this guy, he said, 'Yes, Whitey Herzog. You delivered a turkey to the Trumans on December 17.' Turns out he was a Secret Service man stationed in the house across the street. The Trumans didn't want any more surveillance than that."

On the day Herzog was honored in Independence he was

given a Jeep and an English pointer, and Royals owner Ewing Kauffman said, "He can be my manager forever."

Forever lasted two more years. Burke and Herzog quarreled over some personnel moves in 1979, and Herzog also openly criticized the one-year contracts the Royals always offered him. Kauffman chided Herzog for bunting too much, once in the manager's office, once in the press hospitality room. Herzog had lost the respect of some of his players for his harsh treatment of First Baseman John Mayberry, who was also a Kauffman favorite. Hostilities built and never disappeared, and Herzog got fired. He actually criticized Burke for not firing him earlier, when the Royals could have used the spark a new manager often brings.

Herzog still remains a very popular figure in Kansas City, both in the community and in the clubhouse. "He was a great strategist, even on defense," says White. "All the guys enjoyed playing for him." Brett, a friend of Herzog's, says, "If I ever managed, I'd try to do the things Whitey did. He gave the players confidence, but he wasn't afraid to stand up to them. He'd play hearts with you. I remember once going to his house for a quail dinner. Next game I went four-for-four. Later in the season I was struggling a little and one day Whitey walks into the clubhouse with a couple of quail that Mary Lou had sent me."

That ability to be a player's friend and still be his boss is Herzog's secret. A lot of managers know talent and a lot of them know when to hit and run, but Herzog combines those assets. "He's a great manager," says Reliever Bruce Sutter, who Herzog admits has been the Cardinals' salvation. "He tells everybody straight out what their job is. He doesn't put any pressure on you or second-guess. And he's one of the guys." Leftfielder Lonnie Smith says, "The only thing I don't like is we can't have music in the clubhouse. But at least we can have Walkmans."

One day recently Herzog took Sutter, Porter and utility man Gene Tenace to his favorite fishing spot in Freeburg, Ill., not far from New Athens. The four of them were fishing from a pontoon boat when Tenace, reeling in his line, accidentally snagged Herzog's line. "Whitey's there shouting, 'I got one, got a big one,' " says Tenace. "When he finds out what's really going on, we all start laughing. I wish I had it on film, you know, *This Week in Fishing*."

On some mornings when the Cardinals are at home Herzog will get up at five, drive out to his friend Herb Fox's cabin in Freeburg and fish for large-mouth bass by himself till 9:30. A week ago Wednesday he had a good day, bringing home 14 bass. "First of all, I like to eat them," he says. "Second, it's the most relaxing thing I can think of. No phones, no baseball, just some deep thinking. I also like the challenge of finding out what they're hitting on." Just then Porter stops by to recommend a green jig with a black frog. "They must be down deep," says Herzog.

Herzog's coaches are even more taken by him than his players. "In all the years I've been with him," says Third Base Coach Chuck Hiller, who was on Herzog's staff in Texas and Kansas City, "I've never known him to mistreat a player." Says Red Schoendienst, who was the Cardinal manager for 12 years and is now a coach, "He doesn't criticize players. He talks to them. He knows what he's doing, I'll tell you that. Except when he's fishing. He always yells, 'That's a keeper,' and then pulls up a fish four inches long." Butch Yatkeman, the clubhouse man who's retiring this year after 59 years with the Cardinals, says, "He's the best man I've worked for, and there have been a lot of nice ones. Last year I was supposed to retire. When we were about to resume the second season, Whitey and I were alone in the clubhouse one day, and he said, 'Butch, you don't want to retire after this kind of a season. Why don't you stay on another year?' It wasn't like I was indispensable—he was just thinking of me."

Gussie Busch rarely talks to his manager about baseball. "When he hired me that June," says Herzog, "I was afraid he might bring in a general manager who I couldn't get along with. I think he was thinking along the same lines when he offered to make me general manager." At the winter meetings that December, Herzog set about clearing house, acquiring Sutter and assorted others. During the season he added Joaquin Andujar. Before this season he got Lonnie and Ozzie Smith. Lonnie has a chance to be the first player since Ty Cobb to have 70 RBIs and 70 stolen bases in a season, and Herzog estimates that

Ozzie's spectacular play at shortstop has saved the Cardinals 100 runs. Andujar, who wasn't a regular starter in Houston, was 15–10 through Sunday. Somehow Herzog traded away the 1981 American League Cy Young and MVP winner, Rollie Fingers, and a strong 1982 Cy Young candidate, Pete Vuckovich, and came up smelling like a rose.

On Friday he told the luncheon crowd, "I've got a wife who's been pretty good to me, five of the greatest coaches a manager could have and my players. Good players make a good manager, and you can't be a smart manager without a good bullpen. I am worried about our hitting, though. We haven't done much yet, unless we win the world championship."

Give 'em hell, Whitey.

Yogi

♦

B Y   R O Y   B L O U N T   J R .

IN 1984 GEORGE STEINBRENNER MADE A TRULY POPULAR MOVE
AS OWNER OF THE NEW YORK YANKEES: HE HIRED YOGI BERRA
AS HIS NEW MANAGER. AND WHILE BERRA FAILED TO BRING A
PENNANT TO THE BRONX, HIS HOMECOMING DID PROVOKE THIS
UNFORGETTABLE PORTRAIT OF THE MAN BY ROY BLOUNT JR.

*Yoga consists in the stopping of spontaneous activities of the
mind-stuff.*   —YOGI PANTANJALI

How can you think and hit at the same time?
—YOGI BERRA

Is the new manager of the New York Yankees a true yogi?
That may seem an odd question. Lawrence Peter Berra is the
most widely known Yogi in the world, or at least in those parts
of the world where baseball is played. (When the Yankees
appeared in Tokyo in 1955, "the biggest ovation, including
screams from bobby-soxers, went to Yogi Berra," according to
the Associated Press.) He loves to sit around reflecting in his
undershorts. He almost never loses his cool, except in ritual
observances with umpires, during which he has been seen to

levitate several inches. And he's being counted on to bring peace and unity—*yoga* is Sanskrit for union—to baseball's most rancorous team.

Yet, yogis don't tend to appear in a form that is 5' 7½" tall and weighs 190 pounds. Jimmy Cannon, the late sportswriter, said Berra was built like a bull penguin. When Larry MacPhail, the Yankee president from 1945 to 1947, first saw Berra, he was reminded of "the bottom man on an unemployed acrobatic team."

Whereas yoga springs from Hinduism, Berra is a Roman Catholic who tries to attend Mass every Sunday and who once visited the Pope. Yogi told of his meeting with Pope John XXIII in a now-famous interview:

Reporter: "I understand you had an audience with the Pope."

Yogi: "No, but I saw him."

Reporter: "Did you get to talk to him?"

Yogi: "I sure did. We had a nice little chat."

Reporter: "What did he say?"

Yogi: "You know, he must read the papers a lot, because he said, 'Hello, Yogi.' "

Reporter: "And what did you say?"

Yogi: "I said, 'Hello, Pope.' "

Yoga is an Eastern study, and Berra is Midwestern Italian. Once, at a dinner held so Japanese journalists could get together with American baseball stars, a Tokyo newspaper editor was ceremoniously reeling off a list of Japanese delicacies that he was sure his American guests would enjoy. "Don't you have any bread?" Berra interrupted.

Berra's parents were born in Italy. (On his passport, Yogi is Lorenzo Pietro.) He was born in St. Louis, and his sayings are in the American grain. For instance, after visiting the Louvre and being asked whether he liked the paintings there, Berra said, "Yeah, if you like paintings." Another time, after attending a performance of *Tosca* in Milan, he said, "It was pretty good. Even the music was nice." These remarks are less in the tradition of the *Bhagavad-Gita* than in that of Mark Twain, who observed that the music of Richard Wagner was "better than it sounds." Berra is also supposed to have said, after someone mentioned that a Jewish lord mayor had been elected in Dublin, "Yeah. Only in America can a thing like this happen."

Berra hasn't followed the traditional regimen of a person who gives his life over to yoga. He has never attempted to assume the Lotus, the Plough, the Fish or the touching-the-top-of-your-head-with-the-soles-of-your-feet position. In his playing days, it's true, he so mastered the Bat Swing and the Crouch that he's now in the Baseball Hall of Fame. And this spring, in the Yankees' new flexibility program, he stretched, bent and folded himself pretty well for a man of 58. But when he's asked whether he knows the body toning postures of yoga, he says, "Nahhh. A couple of people wrote me, 'What exercises do you give?' thinking I was a, you know.... Ahhh, I don't do no exercises."

In traditional yoga, the practice of meditation is of central importance. But Berra says, "Guys talk about doing this meditating when they go up to the plate. If I'd done that I'd've been worse. I went up there thinking about something *else*."

And yet there's something inscrutable about a man who said, when he saw the late Steve McQueen in a movie on television, "He must have made that before he died." There's something mystic about a man who said, "You got to be very careful if you don't know where you're going, because you might not get there." And there's something wise about a man who said, "Slump? I ain't in no slump. I just ain't hitting."

Although yoga is "a definite science," the Yogi Paramahansa Yogananda has written, "There are a number of great men, living today in American or European or other non-Hindu bodies, who, though they may never have heard the words *yogi* or *swami,* are yet true exemplars of those terms. Through their disinterested service to mankind, or through their mastery over passions and thoughts ... or through their great powers of concentration, they are, in a sense, yogis; they have set themselves the goal of yoga—self-control."

By dispelling that ignorance of the true self he has realized the Changeless Total Universal Self as his own true form, and through this realization ignorance has been destroyed.

—THE VEDANTASARA
a 15th-century Brahmanical text

I'd be pretty dumb if all of a sudden I started being something I'm not.
—YOGI BERRA

The dynastic Yankees of the 1940s, '50s and '60s knew exactly who they were. They weren't a projection of their owner's
ego. "In those days, to be a Yankee, in New York," says Berra,
who was the Yankees' best or at least, after Mickey Mantle,
next-best immortal of the '50s, "you were treated like a god."
Yankees were united by aplomb and *esprit de corps*. Yoga, wrote
Jung, is a "method of fusing body and mind together so that
they form a unity which is scarcely to be questioned. This unit
creates a psychological disposition which makes possible intu-
itions that transcend consciousness."

Levitate your consciousness to total nothingness.

—YOGI BHAJAN

In baseball, you don't know nothing.

—YOGI BERRA

Anyone who has followed the Yankees over the last 20 years—
since 1964, when Berra was fired as manager although New
York won a pennant in its first season under him—knows that
the franchise has a karma problem: a festering buildup of the
consequences of past actions.

"The Yankees made the biggest mistake in their whole career,
firing Yogi," says Berra's old teammate Whitey Ford. It took
them 12 years to win another pennant, and although they have
won four in the last eight seasons, those years have been an Era
of Ill Feeling.

"I don't want to play for George Steinbrenner," said star
reliever Goose Gossage last December, before he forsook the
Yankees for the Padres. Steinbrenner, New York's principal
owner since 1973, has fired 11 managers and alienated player
after player. It's about as uplifting to go over his wrangles with
Billy Martin, whom he fired for the third time after last season,
as it is to replay the Watergate tapes. Bad karma accrues when
your manager calls your owner a liar or punches out a marsh-
mallow salesman, both of which Martin did. Also when your
owner gets into a fight either in an elevator, as Steinbrenner
claimed, or with an elevator, as skeptics suggested.

Just this spring training the Yankees' captain, Graig Nettles,
decried Steinbrenner's "big mouth" and demanded to be traded.

174

Dave Winfield, New York's best player, who has had various run-ins with Steinbrenner that still rankle on both sides, predicted that 1984 will see more of the same: "Afternoon soaps will have nothing on us. I think people are tired of that. They want to see baseball."

Ah. Yogi is baseball all over. Says his wife, Carmen, "Everything except baseball seems small to him." That "everything" would seem to include himself. There's not much I in Yogi, whom people often call Yog. Perhaps the true meaning of "In baseball, you don't know nothing" is that baseball is a game that humbles those who presume to be authoritative, as Martin and Steinbrenner have done. "Yogi is perfect for this club right now," said pitcher Dave LaRoche in camp this spring. "Billy always wanted to be the center of attention. Yogi is satisfied to be a wallflower type."

The iron filings of karma are attracted only where a magnet of the personal ego still exists.
—Yogi Paramahansa Yogananda

A good ball club.   *—Yogi Berra*
when asked what makes a good manager

Since 1960, the Yankees and their fellow New Yorkers, the Mets, have won 11 pennants. Yogi, who served with the Mets as coach from 1965 through '71 and as manager from '72 through part of '75, is the only person who has been a player or a coach or a manager on every one of those pennant-winning teams. When he was fired by the Yankees after losing to St. Louis in the '64 World Series and also when he was fired by the Mets in '75 although his '73 team had won a pennant, Yogi's critics said he had lost control of his players. But a yogi doesn't try to control others. "Every individual," says the Maharishi Mahesh Yogi, "is responsible for his own development in any field." Were the Maharishi a baseball fan, he would add "and at the plate." A yogi attempts to control himself.

Too nice a guy, Yogi's detractors have said of him. But "gentleness of mind is an attribute of a yogi, whose heart melts at all suffering," said the Yogi B.K.S. Iyengar. Robert Burnes, a St. Louis baseball writer, once went with Berra to a church father-and-son

banquet. Every son received a bat and a ball and came up to
have Yogi autograph them. At a corner table were some kids
from a local orphanage. They sat there with no balls or bats.
"Aren't they getting anything?" Yogi asked. An organizer of the
banquet told him that a couple of balls were being sent to the
home for the orphans' use. "We think it's enough of a thrill for
them just to be here," the man added.

Yogi got up from the head table, went to the orphans' table,
sat down and began autographing whatever the orphans had.
Someone at the head table finally said, "Yogi, we'd like you to
come back up here and say a few words."

"Go on with the program," Yogi snapped. "I'm busy. I'm
talking to some friends." And he stayed with the orphans the
rest of the evening. As he and Burnes left, Yogi said, "I'll never
forget that as long as I live."

When Yogi was promoted to manager this winter—he'd
rejoined the Yankees as a coach in '76—Boston sports talk show
host Eddie Andelman said that what the Yankees were actually
getting was a "designated schmoo." Yogi's shape and good
nature may resemble a schmoo's, but he may be more than
that. He may be the man of the hour.

The time is now and now is the time.

—YOGI BHAJAN

You mean right now? —YOGI BERRA
when someone asked him what time it was

To speak of the history of the Steinbrenner Yankees is difficult, because who wants to wade through all that again? To
speak of Berra's history is difficult because so much of what's
said about him—no one, including Yogi, seems to know how
much—is legend.

Berra has little inclination to dwell upon the past. "I'm sure
glad I don't live in them days," he once said, after watching a
bloody movie called *The Vikings*. Or he may have said that.
He's said to have said it. Trying to establish which of Yogi's
famous sayings he actually said is an interesting, but hopeless,
endeavor.

Sometimes diligent research pays off. For instance, there's the story about what Yogi told a young Met hitter who had adopted Frank Robinson's batting stance but still wasn't hitting. "If you can't imitate him," Yogi is supposed to have advised, "don't copy him."

But on Jan. 11, 1964, right after Berra had been named Yankee manager and a year before he got to the Mets, a long tape-recorded telephone colloquy between Berra, Casey Stengel and reporter Robert Lipsyte appeared, in transcript, in *The New York Times*. In it Stengel says to Yogi, "If you can't imitate anybody, don't copy him. That's the best advice I can give a new manager." Conceivably, Berra later passed that adage on to a Met, but because Berra spent several minutes one morning this spring chuckling over the kind of things Stengel used to say and wishing he could remember even a few of them specifically, that seems unlikely.

Why not just ask Berra himself whether he said various things he's supposed to have said? Well, I did that. It confused matters. For instance, if I hadn't consulted Yogi, I'd be able to report that I had pinned down the origin of "Nobody ever goes there anymore; it's too crowded" once and for all. I'd always been told that Yogi said that about a place called Charlie's in Minneapolis. On the other hand, I read somewhere that back in the late '40s Dorothy Parker had said it about Chasen's in Beverly Hills. Then I read that John McNulty had written it in a short story. And sure enough, in the Feb. 20, 1943 issue of *The New Yorker*, in a McNulty story entitled *Some Nights When Nothing Happens Are the Best Nights in This Place*, there occurs this passage:

"... a speakeasy, you could control who comes in and it was more homelike and more often not crowded the way this saloon is now. Johnny, one of the hackmen outside, put the whole thing in a nutshell one night when they were talking about a certain hangout and Johnny said, 'Nobody goes there any more. It's too crowded.'"

Because in 1943 Yogi was 18 and playing in Norfolk, Va., we can assume that neither McNulty nor some New York cabdriver stole the line from Yogi.

However. Before I tracked that short story down I discussed Berraisms with Yogi and Carmen. We were relaxing over vodka on the rocks in their nicely appointed parlor in Montclair, N.J.

After their three boys grew up, the Berras sold the enormous Tudor house about which Yogi once said proudly, "It's nothing but rooms," and moved into a smaller but still substantial gray-shingled house a few blocks away. It's a home filled with fine antiques, with dropping-by children and grandchildren and with Berraisms which, however, the Berras don't preserve as carefully as they do furniture.

"The kids are always telling me, 'There you go, you said another one,' " Yogi said with a chuckle.

"He said one the other day," said Carmen. "I thought, 'That's a classic. I've got to write that one down.' But I forgot."

"How about the one I said, 'If I didn't wake up, I'd still be sleeping,' " said Yogi. "I was almost late someplace," he explained. "Another one...," he added, and he said something else that I didn't quite catch.

"No, that one wasn't funny," said Carmen.

"Oh," said Yogi affably.

"How about the one about the restaurant being so crowded nobody ever goes there?" I asked. "You didn't really say that, did you?"

Yogi smiled. "Yeah! I said that one," he assured me.

"You did?" I said. "About Charlie's in Minneapolis?"

"Nahhh, it was about Ruggeri's in St. Louis. When I was headwaiter there." That would have been in 1948.

"No," said Carmen, "you said that in New York."

"St. Louis," Yogi said firmly.

So there you are.

"My favorite Yogi story," says Yankee first baseman Roy Smalley, "is about the time he went to a reception at Gracie Mansion [the residence of New York's mayor]. It was a hot day and everybody was sweating, and Yogi strolled in late wearing a lime-green suit. Mayor Lindsay's wife, Mary, saw Yogi and said, 'You certainly look cool,' and he said, 'Thanks. You don't look so hot yourself.' If that isn't true, I don't want to know it isn't."

Nor do I. I feel bound to report, however, that there's at least one other version of the story. Same dialogue, only between Yogi and someone it would be hard for witnesses to confuse with Mary Lindsay: umpire Hank Soar.

Bill Veeck once maintained that "Yogi is a completely manu-factured product. He is a case study of this country's unlimited ability to gull itself and be gulled.... You say 'Yogi' at a banquet, and everybody automatically laughs, something Joe Garagiola discovered to his profit many years ago."

What Berra says about his sayings, in general, is "I always say I said half of them, and Joe said the other half." This is apt but untrue. Certainly Garagiola, who grew up with Berra in St. Louis on what was known then as Dago Hill and who is working on a book about those days, has done as much for Berra's legend as the Beatles did for the Maharishi's. For one thing, as Berra says, "Joe can remember stories better than I can. I can't remember them." It follows that Yogi isn't the best authority for what he actually said. (And nobody else is, either.) Sometimes he will say, "I could've probably said that." Sometimes he will say he never said things that you wish he wouldn't deny saying. For instance, he claims he never said, "How can you think and hit at the same time?" It's a cold-blooded historian indeed who's willing to take Berra's word for that.

It may even be that Berra did think and hit at the same time. "Any hitter as good as Yogi was had to have an idea up there," says Yankee coach Mickey Vernon, who played against him for years. But when you ask Berra if it's true that he always hit high pitches well, he says, "They told me I did. I didn't know. If I could see it good, I'd hit it. Some of them I'd swing at, and some of them I wouldn't because I didn't see them good." Berra's old teammate Phil Rizzuto claims, "I've seen him hit them on the bounce; I've seen him leave his feet to hit them."

There's no doubt that Berra thought about other people's hitting. Ted Williams says Berra would notice subtle shifts of an opposing batter's feet that no other catcher would notice. "Berra knows how to pitch to everybody in the league except himself," said Stengel. But then, nobody knew how to pitch to Berra. "He could pull anything inside," says Vernon. "They'd try to throw him two pitches inside and hope he'd pull them foul, and then they'd go outside on him. And he'd take that to the opposite field."

Yankee player-coach Lou Piniella, who says, "When I'm feeling good I'm a player, when I'm feeling bad I'm a coach," studies hitting mechanics meticulously with the aid of videotape. He insists that thinking and hitting are thoroughly compatible. However, he concedes that "the paramount thing is to see the damn baseball." And New York outfielder Steve Kemp says, "Baseball is a game that if you think too much, it'll eat you up."

Let us remind ourselves that if Berra did say what he says he didn't say about thinking and hitting, he didn't say you can't think and hit at the same time. He just raised the eternal question, "How can you?" And even if he didn't say it, he deserves to be credited with saying it because he's such a great example of the athlete who doesn't distract himself. Berra was so attuned to his Batting Self that he didn't consciously have to focus his mind on hitting. Asked if he ever studied his swing on videotape, he cringes. "I don't like seeing myself on television," he says. "I don't like it."

Concentration is the narrowing of the field of attention, the fixing of the mental eye upon a chosen object.

—ERNEST WOOD
Seven Schools of Yoga

You only got one guy to concentrate on. He throws the ball.

—YOGI BERRA

Many putative Berraisms are clearly bogus. Jim Piersall, a player of Berra's era, tells banquet audiences that someone once asked Berra, "Why don't you get your kids an encyclopedia?" Yogi answered, "Listen here, buddy, when I went to school, I walked. So can they." In the *New York Mirror* in 1959 Dan Parker wrote that someone once said to Yogi, "Why, you're a fatalist," and Yogi answered, "You mean I save postage stamps? Not me."

There were plenty of firsthand witnesses, however, to Berra's famous remark on the occasion of Yogi Berra Night at Sportsman's Park in 1947: "I want to thank all those who made this night necessary." Isn't that a perfect expression of the ambivalence of one who sincerely feels honored but hates playing the role of honoree? A poetic slip.

Some Berraisms transcend logic because they are simpler than logic. "I'm wearing these gloves for my hands," he said one cold spring-training day.

Others express something too subtle for logic. There was the time when some sportswriters urged Berra to go with them to a dirty movie. "Nahhh," he said, "I don't want to see no dirty movie. I'm going to see *Airport*."

"Come on, Yog, come with us. Let's go see the dirty movie."

"Nahhh. I'm not interested."

"Come on. You can see *Airport* anytime. Let's go see this dirty picture."

"Well," said Yogi, "who's in it?"

Isn't that a trenchant comment on pornography? Dirty movies don't have anyone in them.

There are many stories about Yogi on radio shows. He's supposed to have laid down this ground rule once: "If you ask me anything I don't know, I'm not going to answer." Would that everyone on radio followed that policy.

But my radio favorite is the one about the interviewer who told Berra before the broadcast, "We're going to do free association. I'm going to throw out a few names, and you just say the first thing that pops into your mind."

"O.K.," said Berra.

They went on the air. "I'm here tonight with Yogi Berra," said the host, "and we're going to play free association. I'm going to mention a name, and Yogi's just going to say the first thing that comes to mind. O.K., Yogi?"

"O.K."

"All right, here we go then. Mickey Mantle."

"What about him?" said Berra.

Self-control entails avoiding statements that cause unnecessary to-do. Berra is very careful about that. Ask him how he's going to differ from Martin as manager, and he says, "I don't get into that."

But self-control isn't the same as self-editing. Two years ago in Florida, Vernon played with Yogi in a scramble golf tournament (in which all players in a group tee off but thereafter play only the best of the balls). Berra hit a nice drive up the middle. Vernon followed with an almost identical shot. Vernon's drive was a bit better. But Berra lingered next to the ball he'd hit so well. "If I was playing alone," he said wistfully, "I'd play mine."

Most people would have stopped themselves before they said that. They would have had the same feeling, but they would have reflected, "I'm not playing alone, though, so...." Then they would have sorted out all the contradictions in

their feelings and said either nothing or something less memorable than what Berra said. Berra reacts more quickly and on
two planes of possibility at once.

The posture must be steady and pleasant.

—YOGI PATANJALI

Berra thinks home plate is his room.

—CASEY STENGEL

Berra, who was awkward behind the plate at the beginning of
his career, worked hard under the guidance of guru Bill Dickey—"Bill is learning me all his experiences"—and he became an
extraordinarily heads-up catcher. Between pitches he was full of
chatty hospitality, but while he was distracting the hitter, he
wasn't missing a trick himself. Indeed, Berra is computer-fast at
adding up gin scores. "He would be a brilliant nuclear physi-
cist," says Garagiola, "if he enjoyed that kind of thing."

And when Berra saw a bunt or a steal of home coming, he
would spring forward before the pitch had reached the batter.
"If anybody'd swung," he says, "they'd've creamed me." But no
one ever did. Berra was especially effective on squeeze bunts.
Twice in his career he grabbed the bunt, tagged the batter
before he could get away and then dived back to tag the runner
coming in from third. That ties him with several other catchers
for the lifetime record for unassisted double plays. "I just
touched everybody I could," Berra explained after one of them.

On another occasion, Billy Hunter of the Orioles missed a
two-strike squeeze bunt attempt on a pitch that was in the dirt.
Berra trapped the ball, slapped a sweeping tag on Hunter, who
was entitled to run because the third strike had hit the ground,
and wheeled to put the ball on Clint Courtney sliding in. Alas,
the umpire ruled that Berra had missed Hunter. Otherwise,
Berra would hold the catcher's single-handed d.p. record single-
handedly. "Hunter was out, too," says Yogi today. "Out as the
side of a barn."

The preceding Berraism is one that I just made up. I guess it
won't do. It's Berraesque in that it entails a kind of refreshment
of the concept of "out"—a soft-focus version of what E.E. Cummings called "precision which creates movement." (Cummings'

own, not very pleasant, example of such precision came from vaudeville: "Would you hit a woman with a child?" "No, I'd hit her with a brick.")

But "out as the side of a barn" doesn't linger in the mind like Yogi's famous re-examination of two ordinary verbs: "You can observe a lot by watching." He actually did say that, except that it may have been "You observe by watching" in the original.

It's hard to make up a good Berraism.

One thing you cannot copy and that is the soul of another person or the spirit of another person.

—YOGI BHAJAN

If you can't imitate him, don't copy him.

—YOGI BERRA

I was determined to make up a Berraism for this story. One that would pass for real and go down in lore alongside "How long have you known me, Jack? And you still don't know how to spell my name." (Which is what Berra said—really and truly—when announcer Jack Buck compensated him for appearing on a pregame show with a check made out to Bearer.)

Here is an ersatz Berraism that I worked on for weeks: "Probably what a pitcher misses the most when he doesn't get one is a good target. Unless it never gets there." Nope. It's too busy. A real Berraism is more mysterious, yet simpler. Stengel once asked Berra what he would do if he found a million dollars. Yogi said, "If the guy was real poor, I'd give it back to him."

To come up with a Berraism that rings true, you have to start with some real Berraistic raw material, which, in itself, may *not* ring true. Take the famous utterance, "It ain't over 'til it's over," which is so distinctively descriptive of a baseball game—a football or basketball game is often over with five minutes to go—and which we would like to think is even true of life.

Research through old sports-page clippings indicates that what Berra probably said was, in reference to the 1974 pennant race, "We're not out 'til we're out." That quickly became, "You're not out of it 'til you're out of it," which somehow evolved into "The game's never over 'til it's over," which eventually was streamlined into "It ain't over 'til it's over."

But I wouldn't call that a wholly manufactured product. Berra sprouted its seed. And he did so at a time when the expression "The game is never over till the last man is out" had become hackneyed, even if its meaning still held true. One thing Berra doesn't deal in is clichés. He doesn't remember them.

"Yogi gives short answers. And they're all mixed in with grunts," says Rizzuto, who adds, "but that doesn't mean he doesn't know as much as managers who'll talk forever." Usually these short statements aren't eloquent, and often they're more a matter of finger pointing, nudges, scowls, pats, shrugs and ingenuous grins than of words or grunts. And yet every time I talked to Berra this spring, he said something or other that I couldn't get out of my mind. For instance, giving me directions to the racquetball club he co-owns in Fairfield, N.J., he said, regarding how long I should stay on one stretch of road, "It's pretty far, but it doesn't seem like it."

As I drove to the club, I kept thinking that over. How could he know that a given distance wouldn't seem far to me? I thought it over so much that the distance went by even faster than I'd been prepared for, and I missed the turn. I should have remembered what Berra said about taking the subway to Brooklyn for the World Series: "I knew I was going to take the wrong train, so I left early."

There is a vital difference between an idiot or a lunatic on the one hand, and a yogi striving to achieve a state of mindlessness on the other.

—YOGI B.K.S. IYENGAR

People say I'm dumb, but a lot of guys don't make this kind of money talking to cats.

—YOGI BERRA

on receiving a residual check from his Puss 'n Boots cat-food commercial, in which the voice of the puss was played by Whitey Ford

In his boyhood, Berra was called Lawdie—a shortening of Lawrence. Had that name stuck, would there now be a cartoon character named Lawdie Bear? At any rate, there is one named

Yogi Bear, an amiable, rotund figure who assures people he's "smarter than the average bear."

"They came out with that after Yogi won his third Most Valuable Player award," says Carmen. "And yet they claimed it had nothing to do with Yogi."

"Once somebody came up to me and asked, 'Which came first, you or the bear?' " says Yogi.

But how did Lawdie become Yogi? Historians agree it happened in his teens. At least five people, including Garagiola, have been credited for giving Yogi his name. Garagiola has said, "It was because he walked like a yogi." *The New York Times* once said it was because young Lawdie had taken up yoga-like exercises. According to other accounts, it was because nothing ever upset Berra, or because one day he was wrestling and spun out of his opponent's grasp, and someone said, "He spins like a yo-yo." Then someone else said, "You mean he spins like one of them yogis." The most established version is that Berra used to sit around serenely with his arms and legs crossed, and one of his American Legion teammates, having seen some yogis in a travelogue about India, said he sat like a yogi. Berra told me a few weeks ago that this last version was correct, except, "Nahhh. There wasn't any movie."

And yet this spring I also heard him telling reporters that he had no idea why he'd been dubbed Yogi. "I had a brother they called 'Garlic,' " Berra told one reporter who pressed him for possible explanations of his cognomen, "and his name was Mike." Berra did say that the original dubber was his American Legion teammate Bobby Hofman—one of the few people connected with youth baseball in St. Louis in the '40s who, according to my research, had never been credited before.

So there you are. Taped onto the Berras' refrigerator door in Montclair is a letter from a boy in San Francisco, which Yogi hasn't gotten around to answering:

Dear Yogi Berra,

My name is Yogi, and I am 9. I hate my name because kids at school joke about it a lot. All the time. You are the only other Yogi I ever heard of. Where did you get your name from? My teacher told me about you. I hope that is OK. She said you just

about invented baseball. How long did you play? Will you be my
friend? I sure need one.

Your friend
Yogi Lisac

P.S. What do your friends call you?
Did you ever get so mad you wanted to punch somebody?

When Berra came into organized ball, he, too, was the butt
of cruel kidding—people swinging from dugout roofs and calling him Ape was typical of this kind of humor—and he never
fought back. He says it never bothered him, but that's hard
to believe. Even some of the compliments he got would have
upset most people. Cannon wrote that he and Berra were sitting in a restaurant when a woman stopped by the table.

"I don't think you're homely at all," the strange lady said.

"Thank you," replied Berra, sincerely.

In 1949, Cannon reported that some players had theorized
that Berra swung at bad pitches because he was afraid of being
ridiculed for taking a strike. "Notice how Yogi acts when he
misses a ball?" one player was quoted as saying. "He shrinks
and closes up. They kid him so much he's afraid of looking bad
in the spotlight."

But if that was Berra's motivation for attacking every pitch he
could reach, he turned that anxiety into a strength that caused
opponents to consider him the Yankee they would least like to
face in the clutch. He was always at his best in the late innings.
"You give 100 percent in the first half of the game," he's said
to have said, "and if that isn't enough, in the second half you
give what's left." And you don't look back to add things up.

"He doesn't dwell on mistakes," says Carmen. "When something happens, it's done. His wheels are immediately turning
about what to do next. I guess it's a quality that successful
men have. I read that about David Rockefeller when he made
a bad loan."

Male and female make a union and this complete union is the
greatest yoga.

—YOGI BHAJAN

She wasn't the first girl I had ever asked out, she was the third, but I could hardly believe my luck when it turned out that she liked me as much as I liked her.

—YOGI BERRA

It's clear, in her 50th or so year, that Carmen Berra will always be a great-looking woman. She and Yogi met in 1947 when he was a budding Yankee and she was a waitress at Stan and Biggie's in St. Louis. "He was honest. And simple," she says. "Wasn't a show-off. I was dating a lot of college boys at the time and I liked him in contrast."

Her name was Carmen Short. "My family came from England in the 17th century," she says.

"Yeah," says Yogi. "She's got more aunts and uncles!"

At the time, Carmen's family wondered why she wanted to marry a "foreigner" and Yogi's why he wanted to marry an "*Americano.*" But it has been a happy marriage, by all accounts, for 35 years.

When asked whether it's true that wise investments over the years have made him very comfortable financially, a near millionaire in fact, Yogi shrugs. "*I* don't know," he says. "You'll have to ask Carm." But hasn't he been a remarkably successful businessman? "Well," he says, "I guess I've got a smart wife. She's a, whattayacallit, an inquirer. Where I'd say, 'Yeah, go ahead,' she'll say, 'Let's wait and look into it.' It's like with the furniture for the house. She's patient. She'll leave the room *bare* till she gets just the right thing."

Carmen serves on the board of a regional theater group, is on the committee that is working for the restoration of the Statue of Liberty and stays on Yogi's case. "Carmen said if you chew tobacco today, forget it. You don't have anyplace to come home to," says a young blonde employee at Berra's racquetball center. "She knows you chewed this morning, Yogs."

They have raised three solid sons: Larry Jr., 35, who caught in the minor leagues until he hurt his left knee and is now in the flooring business; Tim, 32, who played one season as a wide receiver for the Baltimore Colts in 1974 and now oversees the operation of the racquetball center; and Dale, 27, who makes $600,000 a year playing shortstop for the Pittsburgh Pirates. Dale, who has always lived with his parents in the off-season, is about to follow his older brothers' example by getting married and buying a house not far from the New Jersey homestead. What with grandchildren and in-laws, there are as many as 17 people around the Berra table at Thanksgiving. Yogi carves.

When his boys were kids, Yogi says, "They'd try to get me to play ball with them, and I'd say, 'Go ask your brothers. I *got* to play.' " Otherwise, they say, he was a warm, normal father. And now they regard him with evident affection. Because he was already in Florida for spring training, Yogi couldn't make Dale's engagement party this February, but he telephoned his best wishes. After he hung up, Yogi said, "And Dale, you know, he's good. He's good. He said: 'I miss you.' "

"He's masculine," says Carmen of Yogi. "Very strong. Physically and mentally, or should I say psychologically. I think he's very sexy."

Yogi smiles. He doesn't look surprised.

"But he's stubborn. Very stubborn. About everything. I don't even think he's Italian. I think he's German. He's Milanese, from the north of Italy. They're very clipped. Very strong. They have a lot of German in them."

Feldmarschall Steinbrenner, please note.

Man suffers for one reason: Man loses his innocence. When you lose your innocence, you end up with dispute. To regain innocence so that universal consciousness will serve and maintain you is the idea of this yoga. —YOGI BHAJAN

How can you say this and that when this and that hasn't happened yet? —YOGI BERRA

Berra won't speculate as to how long he'll last as Yankee manager, except jokingly: "You better get this story out pretty soon." It should be remembered that in 1949 when the Yankees hired Stengel, who lasted as manager for 12 years and 10 pennants, some of the same things were said about him as are said about Berra now: that he was good for public relations, a funny guy, but not really a serious field leader. When Stengel was a player, they said the same thing about him that they said about Berra later: that he wasn't built like a ballplayer.

Stengel used to say of Yogi, "This is Mr. Berra, which is my assistant manager." He also said the Yankees would fall apart without Berra behind the plate, and that Berra was the best player he ever had, except for Joe DiMaggio. Such distinctly ungushy baseball men as Ted Williams, Jackie Robinson and Paul Richards all said Berra was an exceptionally smart player. His managing moves have been questioned in the past, but so have those of every other manager. No one accuses him of not knowing the game.

At the very least, Berra is a link with the old, proud Yankee days. The clubhouse today is full of players whom Steinbrenner acquired for big money after they became established and whom fans tend to think of more as former Reds, Padres and Twins than as Yankees. The team used to be a symbol of permanence. Under Steinbrenner, Yankees have come and gone and been shifted from position to position. Now that the pinstripes are doubleknits, the team lacks real fabric.

Will Berra produce cohesion? "He knows players," says Smalley. "He's made it clear to each guy what's expected. A team takes on the personality of its manager. And Yogi is comfortable."

But not wholly laissez-faire. "Before, we had a Broadway clubhouse in here, all kinds of extraneous people," says Smalley. "Yogi says no visitors except family, and them only at certain times. I asked if I could bring in Bob James, the jazz pianist. Yogi said he'd go out and meet him, he'd give him a hat, but not in the clubhouse. I respected that."

"Everybody likes Yogi," said Steinbrenner when he announced Yogi's appointment, "and ... respects him." The pause was just long enough to make the "respects" sound grudging. When I try to imagine how Berra and Steinbrenner will relate to one another, I can't shake the unpleasant image of a TV commercial for a New York radio station that Steinbrenner and several uniformed Yankees appeared in a few years ago. When Yogi, who was then a coach, began to say something in this commercial, Steinbrenner glared and snapped, "Just sing, Yogi." Yogi smiled, sang and gave no indication that heavy condescension bothered him. Self-control.

"To say that I don't have any worries or nerves is the opposite of the truth," Berra said in his 1961 autobiography, *Yogi*, written with the aid of Ed Fitzgerald. "I worry about getting old. I worry about not getting around on the fastball...."

Indeed, when Tony Cloninger struck him out three times on fastballs one May day in 1965, Yogi immediately retired as a player. "I didn't go out there to be embarrassed," he says.

"I worry," he went on in the book, "about keeping Carm happy so she won't be sorry she married me, about the kids growing up good, and about keeping out of trouble with God. I worry a lot."

He has always had trouble sleeping on the road. In his playing days his insomnia exhausted many of his roommates, including Rizzuto, from whom Berra often demanded bedtime stories. "Three Little Pigs, Three Bears, anything like that," Rizzuto says. "He said the sound of my voice put him to sleep. I often thought of that when I started broadcasting."

"Relaxed?" says Carmen. "I don't know why people think he's so relaxed. He's a basket case!"

But it's a well-woven basket. "Some men are kind of hanging in the balance," Carmen says. "It seems like they just might go off the deep end any minute. I don't have to worry that Yogi is going to have a nervous breakdown.

"I look around at our friends. The men are heads of some of the biggest corporations, they're members of the biggest law firms. And Yogi is the envy of all of them. Since Day One, I saw that Yogi was the only man I knew who loved his job."

That in itself, of course, doesn't make him a true yogi. "I am a yogi because it is in your mind," says the Yogi Bhajan. "The problem with man," the Yogi Bhajan also says, "is that he is asked, 'Are you this or are you that?' But you are not this nor that, you are as you are." Yogi Berra has said quite a few things more thought-provoking than that.

MILESTONES

◆ ◆ ◆

Yea,
Mr. Mays

♦

B Y R O Y B L O U N T J R .

IN 1970, IN HIS 20TH SEASON IN THE MAJOR LEAGUES, THE
INCOMPARABLE WILLIE MAYS REACHED THE 3,000-HIT PLATEAU, A
MARK REACHED BY ONLY 16 MEN IN BASEBALL. ROY BLOUNT JR.
WAS ON HAND TO RECORD THE EVENT.

In 1951 Marilyn Monroe was a starlet, Bobby Orr a baby,
Hubert Humphrey a comer—and Willie Mays very nearly the
same phenomenon he was last week. In harsh heat and foggy
chill, and under the intense scrutiny such a situation demanded,
he chased after his 3,000th hit—and seemed to blossom rather
than wilt under the pressure. He reached the milestone Saturday at home in San Francisco in the second inning against
Montreal, when he stroked an 0-and-2 pitch between short and
third. It was hardly an appropriate hit for the occasion, taking
everything about Willie Mays into consideration, being neat
and solid rather than spectacular and dramatic. But it was
No. 3,000—and then he promptly collected No. 3,001, which is
really what Willie Mays is all about.

In the stretch run to his latest achievement, marvelous old
middle-aged Willie was sprinting all the way. On a six-game
tear that carried him to the magic mark, he went 10 for 23 and

showed the whole watching world that he could still do it all. In one of those games, Mays ranged *past* his rightfielder once to make a running catch. He cut off a drive to deep left-center barehanded. He went from first to second on a fly ball in the ninth inning of a game after playing 14 innings (and hitting a ninth-inning homer) the night before. He stole one game with a burst of 11th-inning speed.

Who else is still flashing a verve that dates back to the Korean war? "The only difference between the young Mays and the old Mays," says Montreal Manager Gene Mauch, "is that it's hard for a 39-year-old man to feel up to playing like Willie Mays every day. But when he feels like it—when I see him up at the plate with the lineup card and he has that look, I say, 'oh, bleep.' "

But time, after all, has passed. This year Mays was the oldest man ever elected to a starting All-Star position, and with 20 homers already he stands a good chance of becoming the oldest man ever to hit his age in home runs. (Babe Ruth hit only 22 at the same stage in life.) It has been 15 years, probably, since Mays last actually said, "Say Hey!" and almost two decades since Leo Durocher listed the five things Mays could do better, all of them put together, than anyone else: run, throw, field, hit and hit with power. Since then, Willie's distinctions have grown more complex. So a new scouting report on the Giants' still-volatile elder statesman seems in order.

RUNNING: Mays has stolen only two bases this year, in two attempts. But Giant Outfielder Frank Johnson says, "I've got pretty good speed, but I'm not so sure I could outrun him if he turned it on. The other night he was running on 3 and 2, and it was a wild pitch, and he turned second and I mean he really ran to third. He ran like a sprinter and he slid hard. A lot of guys wouldn't have done that—especially somebody 39. And the way he runs, his feet flying ... we were behind third, he was bearing down on us and we jumped up on the bench and said, 'Did you see that?' He does things that just thrill me to death."

THROWING: Mays has a wide variety of throws to choose from, depending on what direction and what posture he is running in when he releases the ball. He comes underarm, sidearm, three-quarter and then he has a sort of hook shot. Says Rightfielder Bobby Bonds, "I don't think Willie knows how strong his arm still is on the days when it isn't hurting and it's especially loose. The other day he threw a strike to the plate from the wall in Cincinnati."

FIELDING: Both Bonds and Ken Henderson, being 24 and fleet, might be considered more appropriate centerfielders than a man almost old enough to be their father. It might also be suspected that Mays is kept in center lest his pride be hurt. The truth is that he is still master of his position. "He gets to balls that I didn't think anybody could reach—that I don't think *I* could reach," says Bonds. What Mays has lost in speed he makes up for with consummate judgment of trajectories and fences and an encyclopedic knowledge of where to play all of the league's hitters.

HITTING: Mays has always been death on changeups because his reflexes are too good to be fooled. "He looks jerky up there," says Houston ace Larry Dierker. "He bounces around and doesn't look balanced. So you'd think he couldn't hit an off-speed pitch. You throw him one, though, and he jumps forward but his hands stay back—and then boom. He has such reflexes that he can wait until the last moment before he commits his hands." Traditionally Mays has been almost as deadly against curves, sliders and other off-speed pitches. Fastballs have always given him the most trouble.

"Why don't you throw me some breaking stuff?" Mays grumbled to Houston's George Culver the other evening during batting practice. "You throw it to everybody else. Me, just smoke. I thought sure I'd get a slider from you, George, but no. Smoke."

"Hell," replied Culver, "you hit it 390 feet."

"Naw," said Mays. "I cut it."

In a similar vein last year, when asked whether he liked fastball pitchers, Mays put a counter-question: "Who do?" But the matter is more involved than that. Anyone who waits so long to commit himself on breaking pitches has to make some provision, especially as he gets up in years, for getting around on tight fastballs. Mays, never one to stop at unorthodoxy, has managed to get the meat of his bat in front of inside hummers by "bailing out," or pulling his body laterally away from the pitch. In other hitters this is counted a fault. Willie, though, when he is going good, can bail back in if the pitch breaks away from him, and he is strong enough to hit a ball for distance while leaning away from it.

TEAMMATE: Mays, affectionately called Willie Howard by President Horace Stoneham, enjoys a special status. He decides when he will play, and last year when he had a shoving match with Manager Clyde King in full view of the stands, King's demise was predictable. King's replacement, Charlie Fox, has been friendly with Mays ever since Willie joined the Giants organization.

Mays is team captain, and the Giants call him "Will" or "Buck" or "Cap." "He's a beautiful person," says Johnson. "I don't think anybody on the club dislikes him. If they do they're crazy." Bonds adds, "He's the most nonchalant superstar you'll ever see. He acts just like he draws the minimum."

Mays has taught the young outfielders how to play the hitters and to some extent how to play the ball. He also goes over the hitters with the day's starting pitcher, and when utility Infielder Tito Fuentes was asked how he knew when to call time and go talk with a shaky pitcher he said, "I look to Mays. He gives the sign."

Mays' relations with Willie McCovey are very good, but he and Juan Marichal have never been buddies. Last winter Marichal told a Dominican newspaperman that Mays was not what he used to be and ought to consider quitting, and the story got back to this country. Marichal claimed he was misinterpreted and Mays says he has forgotten the whole thing, but students of the Giants keep looking for signs to the contrary. Last month in Cincinnati when Mays suffered an apparently simple lack of concentration and let a long fly off Marichal fall in for a triple, the radio announcers immediately termed the incident "strange" and "weird."

PUBLIC RELATIONS: Mays would rather not have his significance probed and belabored in interviews with the press, with whom he is wary. The San Francisco writers give him his due as "incomparable," but many avoid him personally because "he never says anything." He is defensive toward writers he hasn't known for a long time. He can also be curt, and what American boy—or sportswriter—wants Willie Mays to have been curt with him?

In Houston a long-faced fan kept yelling "Hey, Willie" at

Mays from the stands, following him around, tonelessly demanding an autograph while Mays was conferring with his peers during batting practice. Finally the man threw his program and pen onto the field at Mays' feet, without a word. Mays tossed them back at him without a word.

When Mays got close to his 3,000th hit the Giants announced that everyone attending the game in which he reached the milestone would win a free ticket to a future game. Last Friday night the weather in Candlestick was frigid and the wind was blowing great billows of fog briskly across the field, but Mays played, with a head cold, perhaps because he felt he owed it to the fans who had come out and perhaps because he wanted to get the 3,000th hit, an ordeal which was making him more and more nervous. After he hit a three-run homer in the eighth, his 2,999th, the crowd chanted "We want Willie," but what they wanted, said the press-box consensus, was free tickets.

EMINENCE: Ironically, Henry Aaron, overshadowed by Mays for most of his career, made Mays' 3,000th hit something of an anticlimax early this season by beating him to the mark. The low-keyed Aaron has blossomed in the last two years as a national figure, whereas Mays has had to live up to an image of ebullient heroism incurred when he was 20. By the time both have retired, Aaron will probably have exceeded most of Mays' lifetime batting statistics, but Aaron himself has said that it is much easier to hit in Atlanta Stadium than in Candlestick Park, where the fierce winds blow in against a right-handed hitter, and that Mays could have been well past 3,000 hits by now and possibly threatening Ruth's 714-homer record (Mays has 620) if he had not spent the last 11 years in Candlestick.

FUTURE: "Have you ever seen a 39-year-old with a body like that?" asks Johnson. Mays is even trimmer than he was last year. He has the kind of compact, slim-legged build that supports a long career. After the All-Star Game, three days before Friday's chiller in San Francisco, Mays looked ghastly, but he is healthier this year than he has been for some time, and earlier in the season he said he could go two or three more years. He has said he wants to manage and that he doesn't want to manage.

When Mays is poised in the outfield or at bat he still seems more eager, or anxious, than anybody else. He has the air of that kid in a pickup game who has more ability and fire than the others and wishes intensely that they would come on and play *right* and raise the whole game to a level commensurate with his own gifts and appetites. Mays does not say so, but it is hard not to suspect that he feels that way toward it all—the fans, the park, the press. And these days he must finally be saying "Come on, play right" to himself, too. When he does, and when he responds as he has over the last two weeks, Frank Johnson is not the only one who is thrilled to death.

End of the
Glorious Ordeal

♦

BY   RON   FIMRITE

IN APRIL 1974, HENRY AARON SURPASSED BABE RUTH TO
BECOME BASEBALL'S ALLTIME HOME RUN LEADER. RON FIMRITE
REPORTED ON THE EVENT AND ON THE HOOPLA THAT SUR-
ROUNDED IT.

Henry Aaron's ordeal ended at 9:07 p.m. Monday.

It ended in a carnival atmosphere that would have been more
congenial to the man he surpassed as baseball's alltime home-
run champion. But it ended. And for that, as Aaron advised the
53,775 Atlanta fans who came to enshrine him in the game's
pantheon, "Thank God."

Aaron's 715th home run came in the fourth inning of the
Braves' home opener with Los Angeles, off the Dodgers' Al
Downing, a lefthander who had insisted doggedly before the
game that for him this night would be "no different from any
other." He was wrong, for now he joins a company of victims
that includes Tom Zachary (Babe Ruth's 60th home run in
1927), Tracy Stallard (Roger Maris' 61st in 1961), and Guy
Bush (Ruth's 714th in 1935). They are destined to ride in tan-
dem through history with their assailants.

Downing's momentous mistake was a high fastball into

Aaron's considerable strike zone. Aaron's whip of a bat lashed out at it and snapped it in a high arc toward the 385-foot sign in left center field. Dodger Centerfielder Jimmy Wynn and Leftfielder Bill Buckner gave futile chase, Buckner going all the way to the six-foot fence for it. But the ball dropped over the fence in the midst of a clutch of Braves' relief pitchers who scrambled out of the bullpen in pursuit. Buckner started to go over the fence after the ball himself, but gave up after he realized he was outnumbered. It was finally retrieved by reliever Tom House, who even as Aaron triumphantly rounded the bases ran hysterically toward home plate holding the ball aloft. It was, after all, one more ball than Babe Ruth ever hit over a fence, and House is a man with a sense of history.

House arrived in time to join a riotous spectacle at the plate. Aaron, his normally placid features exploding in a smile, was hoisted by his teammates as Downing and the Dodger infielders moved politely to one side. Aaron shook hands with his father Herbert, and embraced his mother Estella. He graciously accepted encomiums from his boss, Braves Board Chairman Bill Bartholomay, and Monte Irvin, representing Commissioner Bowie Kuhn, who was unaccountably in Cleveland this eventful night. Kuhn is no favorite of Atlanta fans and when his name was mentioned by Irvin, the largest crowd ever to see a baseball game in Atlanta booed lustily.

"I just thank God it's all over," said Aaron, giving credit where it is not entirely due.

No, this was Henry Aaron's evening, and if the Braves' management overdid it a bit with the balloons, the fireworks, the speeches and all-round hoopla, who is to quibble? There have not been many big baseball nights in this football-oriented community and those few have been supplied by Aaron.

Before the game the great man did look a trifle uncomfortable while being escorted through lines of majorettes as balloons rose in the air above him. There were signs everywhere— MOVE OVER BABE—and the electronic scoreboard blinked HANK. Much of center field was occupied by a massive map of the United States painted on the grass as an American flag. This map-flag was the site of a pregame "This Is Your Life" show, featuring Aaron's relatives, friends and employers. Sammy Davis Jr. was there, and Pearl Bailey, singing the national anthem in

Broadway soul, and Atlanta's black mayor, Maynard Jackson, and Governor Jimmy Carter, and the Jonesboro High School band, and the Morris Brown College choir, and Chief Noc-A-Homa, the Braves' mascot, who danced with a fiery hoop.

This is not the sort of party one gives for Henry Aaron, who through the long weeks of on-field pressure and mass media harassment had expressed no more agitation than a man brushing aside a housefly. Aaron had labored for most of his 21-year career in shadows cast by more flamboyant superstars, and if he was enjoying his newfound celebrity, he gave no hint of it. He seemed to be nothing more than a man trying to do his job and live a normal life in the presence of incessant chaos.

Before this most important game of his career he joked at the batting cage with teammate Dusty Baker, a frequent foil, while hordes of newsmen scrambled around him, hanging on every banality. When a young red-haired boy impudently shouted, "Hey, Hank Aaron, come here, I want you to sign this," Aaron looked incredulous, then laughed easily. The poor youngster was very nearly mobbed by sycophants for approaching the dignitary so cavalierly.

Downing, too, seemed unaware that he was soon to be a party to history. "I will pitch to Aaron no differently tonight," said he, as the band massed in right field. "I'll mix my pitches up, move the locations. If I make a mistake, it's no disgrace. I don't think the pitcher should take the glory for No. 715. He won't deserve any accolades. I think people will remember the pitcher who throws the last one he ever hits, not the 715th."

Downing's "mistake" was made with nobody out in the fourth inning and with Darrell Evans, the man preceding Aaron in the Braves' batting order, on first base following an error by Dodger Shortstop Bill Russell. Downing had walked Aaron leading off the second inning to the accompaniment of continuous booing by the multitudes. Aaron then scored on a Dodger error, the run breaking Willie Mays' alltime National League record for runs scored (after the home run, Aaron had 2,064).

This time, with a man on base, Downing elected to confront him *mano-a-mano*. His first pitch, however, hit the dirt in front of the plate. The next hit the turf beyond the fence in left field.

"It was a fastball down the middle of the upper part of the plate," Downing lamented afterward. "I was trying to get it down to him, but I didn't. He's a great hitter. When he picks his pitch, he's pretty certain that's the pitch he's looking for. Chances are he's gonna hit it pretty good. When he did hit it, I didn't think it was going out because I was watching Wynn and Buckner. But the ball just kept carrying and carrying."

It was Aaron's first swing of the game—and perhaps the most significant in the history of baseball. It was also typical of Aaron's sense of economy. On Opening Day in Cincinnati, against the Reds' Jack Billingham, he tied Ruth with his first swing of the new season. But this event, noteworthy though it may have been, was merely a prelude, and Aaron recognized it as such.

"Seven-fourteen only ties the record," he advised well-wishers at the time. And in yet another ceremony at home plate, he reminded everyone, "It's almost over."

Aaron's innate dignity had been jarred in that opening three-game series by the seemingly irresolvable haggling between his employers Bartholomay and Manager Eddie Mathews, and Commissioner Kuhn. Bartholomay and Mathews had hoped to keep Aaron out of the lineup for the entire series so that he might entertain the home fans with his immortal swats. When Kuhn suggested forcefully that it was the obligation of every team to put its best lineup on the field at all times and that any violation of this obligation would be regarded by him as sinful, Mathews and Bartholomay relented—but only partially. After Aaron tied the Babe, Mathews announced that he would bench him for the remaining games of the Reds' series, saving him for the adoring home folks.

This brought an iron rebuke from the commissioner: Aaron would play or Mathews and the Braves must face "serious consequences." This message was delivered after the Saturday game, in which Aaron did not play. Aaron was in the lineup for 6½ innings on Sunday, striking out twice and grounding weakly to third in three at bats. The stage—and a stage it seemed—was set for Monday night.

It rained in Atlanta during the day, violently on occasion, but it was warm and cloudy by game time. It began raining again just before Aaron's first inconsequential time at bat, as if Ruth's phantom were up there puncturing the drifting clouds. Brightly colored umbrellas sprouted throughout the ball park, a brilliant display that seemed to be merely part of the show. The rain had subsided by Aaron's next time up, the air filled now only with tension. Henry wasted little time relieving that tension. It is his way. Throughout his long career Aaron had been faulted for lacking a sense of drama, for failing to rise to critical occasions, as Mays, say, or Ted Williams had. He quietly endured such spurious criticism, then in two memorable games dispelled it for all time. And yet, after it was over, he was Henry Aaron again.

"Right now," he said without a trace of irony, "it feels like just another home run. I felt all along if I got a strike I could hit it out. I just wanted to touch all the bases on this one."

He smiled slightly, conscious perhaps that his words were not sufficient to the occasion. Then he said what he had been wanting to say since it became apparent that he would eventually pass Ruth and achieve immortality.

"I feel I can relax now. I feel my teammates can relax. I feel I can have a great season."

It is not that he had ever behaved like anyone but Henry Aaron. For this generation of baseball fans and now for generations to come, that will be quite enough.

The Record
Almost Broke Him

♦

B Y   R I C K   T E L A N D E R

SIXTEEN YEARS AFTER HE BROKE BABE RUTH'S SINGLE-SEASON
HOME RUN RECORD, ROGER MARIS SAT DOWN WITH RICK
TELANDER TO TALK OF HIS LIFE SINCE BASEBALL AND OF THE
DAYS WHEN AN ENTIRE NATION HUNG ON HIS EVERY SWING.
MARIS DIED OF CANCER IN 1985. HE STILL HAS NOT BEEN ELECT-
ED TO THE BASEBALL HALL OF FAME.

Sunday, Oct. 1, 1961, Yankee Stadium, Bronx, N.Y. Bottom of
the fourth, nobody on, one out, no score. Roger Maris of the
Yankees steps to bat for the second time in the final game of
the season. Tracy Stallard, a 24-year-old righthander for the
Boston Red Sox, delivers a fastball—"a strike, knee-high on the
outside of the plate," he would say later.

Maris swings and everybody knows the ball is gone. In the
melee in the right-field stands, Sal Durante, a teen-ager from
Brooklyn, emerges with the home-run ball and becomes a foot-
note to history. Maris slowly circles the bases to a standing ovation from the crowd. Yogi Berra, the next batter, shakes his
hand, as does the bat boy and an ecstatic fan who has leaped
out of the stands. Maris disappears into the dugout, comes out
again, doffs his cap and smiles. On the last possible day he has

203

broken babe Ruth's "unbreakable" record and hit 61 home runs in a season.

Wednesday, March 23, 1977, Perry Field, Gainesville, Fla. Roger Maris, beer distributor and 42-year-old father of six, stands in the Yankee dugout watching his old teammates prepare to play a spring-training game against the University of Florida. George Steinbrenner, the owner of the Yankees, approaches. "Hey, Rog," he says, "where's the beer?" Maris laughs and shrugs his shoulders. "You should have asked me earlier," he says.

Steinbrenner chuckles, but then his smile fades a bit. "You know, you're a hard guy to get a hold of, Roger," he says. "You're hard to get to New York for just one day."

There is a pause. Maris' smile continues, but it is artificial now, as though propped up with toothpicks. Steinbrenner is referring to the annual Old Timers' Game, an event Maris has never attended since he left the Yankees in 1966. Maris has refused to visit Yankee Stadium for any reason.

"Why don't you come?" Steinbrenner says in a softer voice.

Maris stares out at the field. "They might shoot me," he says.

Steinbrenner's voice becomes solemn. "I'm telling you, Roger, you won't ever hear an ovation like the one you'd get if you'd come back to Yankee Stadium."

Maris looks at the ground. "Maybe," he says without conviction, and the conversation is over.

After all these years, the man who hit more home runs in a season than anyone else still has not recovered from the emotional turbulence of the summer of '61. Hounded ceaselessly by an aggressive sporting press and by fans who lusted for the long ball, Maris proved himself inadequate to the vast demands of public relations. It is uncertain whether anyone could have been adequate.

At times, 50 or more reporters so packed the Yankee clubhouse to interview Maris that some of his teammates could not reach their lockers. Rather than clarifying his image, many of the reporters garbled it, filling their copy with adjectives as diverse as their own natures. At various times in 1961 Maris was described as "shy," "decent," "hot-headed," "low-key," "easily agitated," "devout and home-loving," "surly," "cooperative," "unselfish," "reticent," "talkative," "trite," "choleric," "self-pity-ing," "sincere," "wonderful," "sensible," "petulant," "honest," "literate," "straightforward" and "morose."

When it became apparent that Maris had a real shot at Ruth's record, the barrage of home-run questions intensified. A hundred times a day he was asked if he thought he could break the record, how soon, what had he done to his swing, what did he think of all this. "You can believe me or not—I don't care—but I honestly don't know," he would answer, when thinking became unbearable.

Never a patient man, Maris told reporters that if they thought he was surly, it was just too bad, because that was how he was going to stay. In one away game, angered by catcalls, he made obscene gestures to the crowd. In every road park, and frequently at Yankee Stadium, he was booed. He was, after all, chasing the immortal Babe, who hit his 60 home runs in 1927, before TV coverage and routine mass postgame interviews.

Autograph seekers grew vicious. "People would elbow up to Rog and yell, 'Give me your John Hancock!'" recalls teammate Moose Skowron, "so sometimes Rog would sign 'John Hancock.' Sometimes they'd say, 'Gimme yer X!' So he'd sign X. I mean, how many hours can you put up with that garbage?"

Though he admitted to having a short fuse, Maris resented being labeled a redneck by the press. He stopped smiling. His mouth always seemed set in a tight line. His hair began to fall out. His wife, visiting New York from Kansas City after giving birth to their fourth child, told him he looked like a molting bird. A private person, Maris found he could never be alone, and his statements became less and less printable. The needs of the public were not his needs, and the chasm of misunderstanding widened. In 1963 a reporter wrote that the trouble with Maris was not that he had problems with the press but that "he has proved to be such an unsatisfactory hero."

As a final dig at Maris' authenticity, Baseball Commissioner Ford Frick, an old friend of Babe Ruth's and a former sportswriter who once ghosted articles under Ruth's byline, decreed that Maris' record must go into the books accompanied by an asterisk. This, explained Frick, was because Maris played in a 162-game season, while Ruth played a 154-game schedule; 1961 was the year that baseball expanded its schedule to 162 games, and Maris' feat was the first baseball record thus qualified.

Since finishing his playing days in 1968, Maris has had little to do with baseball. He came to Perry Field this spring only because he has a few friends on the Yankees and because the team was now on his turf. "Baseball is just like a kid with a train," he told a reporter not long ago. "You got to outgrow it sometime." But there have been signs that Maris has not outgrown baseball, that very cautiously he is coming back to the game he never really wanted to leave. This year when he took his sons to a spring training game in Fort Myers, he even stepped into the batting cage to help the Royals' John Mayberry work on his swing.

Nonetheless, long distance, over the phone, he had still been wary about being interviewed. "I don't know," he said. "I don't need publicity anymore."

Would it help if the conversation had nothing to do with baseball, with the 61 homers or old times? "Well, see, that's another thing they've gotten wrong," he said. "I don't mind talking about baseball. It's just that every now and then I give another interview, and when it doesn't turn out right, I back off again."

Now, several days later, having agreed to talk, Maris sits behind his desk at the Maris Distributing Company near the Gainesville airport, taking business calls and feeling chipper. Judging from the furnishings, it is apparent that discussing baseball does not disturb him. In the foyer, a glass case holds several large trophies, including a metal crown presented to Maris by the Maryland Professional Baseball Players' Association for the most outstanding batting achievement of 1961. Across the front are engraved the words, "Sultan of Swat."

Numerous photographs, plaques and game mementos are on the walls of his office. One photograph shows Maris with President Kennedy. Another shows him and Mickey Mantle with President Truman. A framed blowup of a cartoon depicting Maris in quest of his 61 homers includes an inset of Ruth, looking heroic and somewhat sad. The caption at the bottom makes reference to the 154-game, 162-game controversy and ends with Ford Frick's quote in defense of the asterisk: "You can't break the 100-meter record in a 100-yard dash."

Next to the cartoon is a color photograph of the 1968 World

Champion St. Louis Cardinals, Maris smiling in the front,
flanked by Tim McCarver, Bob Gibson, Lou Brock and Orlando Cepeda, among others. Maris played two twilight years for
St. Louis—1967 and 1968—and he was much happier there than
in New York. The team did well, the press eased off and the
home fans did not boo. Cardinal President August A. Busch Jr.
approved Maris for ownership of the Anheuser-Busch distributorship in Gainesville at the end of the '67 season. Maris, who
had intended to retire, showed his gratitude by playing one
more season. A valuable property in a thirsty college town, the
distributorship (which handles Busch, Budweiser and Miche-
lob) enables Maris to maintain his independence, to stay away
from anything to do with organized baseball.

Rumors once had it that Cepeda, another Cardinal slugger,
was slated for a Busch outlet when his baseball days were over.
Cepeda never got it, and recently ran afoul of the law. Maris,
seeing Cepeda's picture on the wall, recalls his teammate.

"I heard there were some people in Boston who were supposed to help him, to try and get him off or something," Maris
says. "He was from Puerto Rico, you know. Most of those
guys could speak English, but communication can still be
tough. I still remember this one Latin kid who played with me
in the Three-I League. He couldn't speak a word of English.
When he first came up, everybody ordered hamburger steaks
for a meal. And, you know, that poor kid ate hamburger steak
for I don't know how many months—for breakfast, lunch and
dinner. It was the only word he knew for food. I went over to
the Dominican Republic to play winter ball one year, and I
really got mad when I couldn't get things across. I can imagine
what it must be like for them up here."

Paunchier, fuller-faced and less hawk-eyed than the blond,
crew-cut young athlete who, it was said, could have posed for a
Marine recruiting poster, Maris seems at ease now, but somehow misplaced in his role as small-town businessman. He fid-
gets with his tie, pulls at the tight sleeves of his blue blazer. He
is a man of action at a sit-down job.

His hair is now dark and long. When he leans forward it falls
over his forehead and he pushes it back. "This hair in my eyes,
this long stuff, it bothers me," he says with the irritation of
someone who grew up believing in barber shops. "I'm about

this close to getting a crew cut again. I really am. You know, it's hard these days when athletes and professors and everybody has long hair—it's hard for me to tell my kids to get theirs cut."

Maris looks at the family photos on the back wall of his office, the snapshots of his six blond children, aged 11 to 19, and his infant grandson. Always fiercely protective of his family, Maris never considered moving them to New York during his years with the Yankees. "Never, ever," he says quickly. "I knew it wasn't my permanent home. I don't like big cities. I don't like hustle and bustle." Patricia Maris and the kids lived instead in a suburb of Kansas City where Maris returned as soon as each season ended.

"It can be rough on you having five adolescent kids," Maris adds. "I shudder to think what would happen if they got up in the morning with nothing to do. Fortunately, we belong to a country club, and the boys are pretty interested in golf. Oh, they like baseball, too, but the private school they go to is too small to have a team. The only other thing around here is American Legion ball, and that can be rough when you have all those older boys to compete with.

"I don't push my kids into anything, but I think golf is a good clean sport—no broken bones or anything like that. And if you ever make the pro tour, why, you don't even have to win. You can do fine just finishing near the top.

"Roger Jr., my oldest boy, is going to sign a basketball scholarship next week with a junior college north of here. He's 6' 4" and he loves basketball. Of course, he loves baseball, too, but the thing is...." Maris hesitates, his voice becoming harder, his gray eyes taking on a steely look. "Well, some of those coaches are different, and just because he's Roger Maris Jr., some of them started getting on him. And I think he just got tired of it and said the hell with baseball. I'll tell you, if I had it to do all over again I never would have named him that."

Maris spins the large World Series ring he wears on his right hand, one of three championship rings he got during his 12-year career. "The thing is," he says with a shrug, "how would you know?"

It would have been hard to predict that the name Roger Maris would someday be famous. Raised in Fargo, N. Dak., the son of a railroad man, Maris was a star football and basketball player at a school that did not field a baseball team. "I'd have played college football if I'd been smart enough to get into school," Maris told a reporter in 1960. Trying to make a career of baseball, instead, he was told after a tryout with the Chicago Cubs that he was too small for the game. At the time Maris was 5' 11½" and 190 pounds, and the judgment made no sense. But Maris has always looked smaller than he is. Later, managers would say he "undressed big."

After several years of American Legion ball, Maris was finally signed by Cleveland, and in 1957, his first big league season, he hit 14 home runs and batted .235. In 1958 he was traded to Kansas City and hit 28 home runs while batting .240. In 1959 he raised his average to .273, but he hit only 16 homers.

In 1960 he and two lesser A's were traded to the Yankees for Don Larsen, Marv Throneberry, Hank Bauer and Norm Siebern, and he gave the first real indication that power was his specialty. On Opening Day he hit two home runs, a double and a single and drove in four runs. That year he had 39 homers and 112 RBIs and was voted the American League's Most Valuable Player, even though a sore rib caused him to slump badly in August and September.

At the beginning of 1961 even bigger things were expected of him. Before his rib injury in '60, Maris had been ahead of Ruth's pace, and his compact, lashing swing seemed custom-made for Yankee Stadium's short right-field fence. But in April of '61, Maris hit only one homer; by mid-May he had only three. Then he loosened up with the heat, and his production rose dramatically. He had 20 by June 11, 30 by July 2, 40 by July 25. In August, against Washington and Chicago, Maris all but burst into flames, belting seven home runs in six games.

The last two—Nos. 47 and 48—came off Billy Pierce, the Chicago lefthander. Those were significant blows because Maris supposedly could not hit lefthanders. In 1953, while playing Class C ball, he had been struck in the head by a pitch from a lefty, and for a long time afterward he had a tendency to bail out on the close ones. "Getting hit is scary," he says. "The last thing you remember is collapsing over the plate, and the next thing you remember is riding in the ambulance. I can still feel the imprint of that ball on my temple, it's still tender. In '53 we didn't even wear batting helmets."

Pierce claims Maris' home-run total never entered his mind when he was pitching to him in 1961. "To tell you the truth," he says, "I don't even remember giving up those two homers. I do remember that you usually tried to pitch Roger inside. Or if you went outside, you wanted it way outside. And of course, you didn't walk Roger to get to Mantle."

Mickey Mantle, the affable golden boy contrasting with the brooding Maris, was in the midst of an outstanding year himself in 1961. Together the "M & M Boys" blasted 115 homers—61 for Maris, 54 for Mantle—a major league record for teammates. It soon became part of the skeptics' argument that were it not for Mantle's batting cleanup, Maris never would have seen the pitches he did, never would have approached even 50 home runs. (In fact, all the Yankees aided one another. Six different players hit 20 or more home runs in 1961, and the team total of 240 is by far the most ever hit by one club in a season.)

In the team's 159th game Maris finally hit his 60th homer, tying Ruth's record. Five days later he hit the 61st, and as the dust cleared, he said that he was immensely—exhaustedly—relieved, that he could never go through the same experience again. But instead of the public nightmare dissipating, as Maris hoped, it reappeared in a different form. Now everyone wanted to know if Maris could repeat his feat. There were many—fans, reporters, players—who felt he had to, to prove his legitimacy. But in 1962 Maris hit only 33 home runs, and after that he never hit more than 26 in a season. In his last four years he averaged slightly less than nine.

The notion that Maris was a fluke, that he was not in Ruth's class in anything—skill, endurance, personality, charisma—gained credence. He was, to many, not worthy of being considered Ruth's equal. He would never make the Hall of Fame, they said. (He hasn't.) Forgotten were Maris' outstanding arm, his fielding skills, his baserunning, his three years of 100 or more RBIs, his two MVP trophies—he got his second, of course, in 1961—his many debilitating injuries, the fact that he never claimed to be anything more than a man "just doing my job."

After 1961 fans booed him as routinely as they ordered hot dogs. Some sportswriters gloated over his failings, crediting themselves for much of his fame. "If it weren't for sportswriters," said Tommy Devine of the Miami *News* in 1962, "Roger

Maris would probably be an $18-a-week clerk in the A&P back in Missouri." On a "home-run derby" tour in the South after the '61 season, Maris reached one of the low points of his career. Playing before almost deserted stands, he was jeered by children each time he took a pitch or hit a ball that did not clear the fence.

In New York the press continued to pursue him. Though Maris had informed reporters that he led "the most boring existence you can imagine," that he didn't read, didn't drink, didn't go out, that world events held no interest for him, that he tried to get 10 hours of sleep a night, they would not quit.

"Some of the questions they asked me!" says Maris, his eyes narrowing again. "I remember one writer asked what I did on the road. I said, 'What do you mean?' He said, 'Well, do you go out with girls, fool around, anything like that?' I said, 'I think I'm married, if I remember correctly.' He said, 'Well, so am I, but I still go out and fool around.' I said, 'You do whatever you want. I don't do it.' I mean, that's an intelligent question, isn't it? Especially with about a hundred reporters around me. Then another brilliant guy asks, "What would you rather do, bat .300 or hit 61 home runs?' That's a hell of a question. How many guys hit .300 and how many hit 61 home runs? Doesn't common sense tell you what you answer to something like that?"

Maris shakes his head. "I tried to get along with them, but it just didn't work. I think the problem was that at a certain point the baseball writers got to be gossip columnists. I'm not speaking of some of the old, polished writers—I mean this new breed that came in around 1961. They weren't there to write what happened on the field. And the Yankees, with the experience they'd had, they should have been able to see the whole thing coming. But they did nothing. They just let you stew in your own brew, baby.

"I used to sit at the Stadium for three and four hours after games, until the last reporter was gone. That's wrong. I know there was competition among the writers, and I guess there were times when I got things going, too. Like for years, Willie Mays said that he'd play for nothing. I always maintained I was playing for my family and my bread and butter, and when the bread or butter's not there, I'm not there. So the headlines come out that I'm playing strictly for money, which wasn't true, because I loved the game, too. The press was making me a—what do you call it?—a whipping boy.

"What's funny is that when I first came to the Yankees everybody was giving Mantle a bad time. Why, I don't know. But when I got there, all of that stuff just sort of slid off him and came onto me. I was the one assaulting baseball, apple pie, Chevrolet, the whole works. That's when Mickey got to be the golden boy."

Though the potential for conflict between the two stars was there, it never materialized. Maris and Mantle liked each other, even shared an apartment for a time. When the going got particularly rough for Maris, Mantle would often try to soothe his friend, telling him he would have to get used to the pressure.

"I saw Mickey about two weeks ago," says Maris. "The first time in a while. He was in Florida for a golf tournament. Did the papers get any pictures of us together? No, I don't get along too well with the local press. There's a sports editor here who hammered me in a column a while back, so I told him to do me a favor and just leave me completely out of the paper. Now I even see wire stories in the other papers that the Gainesville paper doesn't run." Maris chuckles with glee over the turnabout.

Leaning back, he furrows his brow and thinks for a moment. "Did you happen to see that book Joe Pepitone wrote?" he asks. He whistles softly, obviously pleased the book isn't his own autobiography. "There's stuff about Joe's wife before their wedding and about Joe and other girls and all that. I mean, his children have to read that someday. Joe just wasn't that bad a guy. He had talent. He could sing on stage—when we were at a bar he'd get up there and sing. I thought he was good. He could dance, too. And he was funny. I don't know, I just think you can go to confession without the whole world knowing it."

The subject turns to another athlete-writer, Jim Bouton, the former Yankee pitcher and author of *Ball Four*. In the book Bouton took several shots at Maris, alluding, among other things, to his alleged shallowness and lack of hustle.

"Jim Bouton," says Maris. "Now there's a guy I never had anything to do with. I didn't like him. He had ability, too, but his head was more his problem. He was the kind of guy who, if somebody made an error behind him, would come up with, 'It's all your fault,' instead of just pitching harder. He couldn't get on me, though, because I didn't want him around. In his book he called me the biggest loafer he'd ever seen, which was a compliment compared to what he wrote about the other guys.

"It's strange, but nobody's interested in anything nowadays unless you're knocking people. Sour grapes. Everytime somebody interviews me, that's all they say—Maris is sour about this, bitter about that. I personally have no interest in ever doing a book. All the things that happened, it's water down the drain, right? I don't think anybody is interested in what I have to say now."

Later in the day Maris drives to the Gainesville Hilton to await the arrival of the Yankees for their night game with the University of Florida. In the hotel restaurant he orders a sandwich and a Budweiser Natural Lite beer. The beer is a new low-calorie brew that Anheuser-Busch is test-marketing in Maris' district, and he is certain it will be a success. "Everybody's on a diet, now," Maris says. "I'm up to 230, though people still guess my weight at around 185 or 190." He pats his ample belly. His hands are large and strong, and his wrists are as thick as a blacksmith's.

"I was always a wrist hitter," he says. "Mickey had a hard and big swing, but mine was short and quick. And I always pulled the ball—I hit only one left-field home run the whole time I played in Yankee Stadium. Most of my home runs were line drives, too, but I did hit some towering ones. My 57th and 58th hit the roof of Tiger Stadium in Detroit, and in Kansas City I hit one out onto the street. I think only seven or eight players had ever done that."

The waitress returns and informs Maris that they are out of Natural Lite beer. He drinks water instead, and mentions that he'll have to get on the manager about this. Then the conversation, perhaps inevitably, drifts back to 1961.

"People say '61 was a fluke," Maris says. "But it wasn't. It was *unusual* in that most of the balls I hit hard went out that year. In '62 I hit the ball even better, but they all seemed to be sinking line drives. I mean 'fluke'—what's a 'fluke'? Babe Ruth only hit 60 home runs once, so was that a fluke? How many times do you have to do something?"

A few minutes later the Yankee bus arrives, and Maris stands just inside the lobby doors, eagerly watching the procession of players entering the hotel. He has visibly perked up, now paces back and forth, looking for faces. Dock Ellis, Roy White and Lou Piniella file through the door, and Maris greets each of them. He says hello to Catfish Hunter and then pumps hands excitedly with Yogi Berra and Manager Billy Martin.

Still watching the doorway, Maris' eyes abruptly light up and a large smile spreads over his face. "Well, look who did make it!" he shouts.

Tanned, with an open-necked shirt, young-man blond bangs and blue eyes set in a craggy, weathered face, Mantle walks into the lobby. The two old teammates greet each other warmly and within minutes are comfortably seated in the hotel bar. Martin joins them, and the stories spill out. Drinking stories, golf stories, women stories—locker-room talk. Mantle is traveling with the Yankees as a special batting coach, and Maris is delighted to learn they will be able to sit together in the Yankee dugout.

In the locker room before the game, Mantle dresses in a Yankee uniform. He is 45 now and, despite his broad shoulders and big biceps, he looks ludicrous in the uniform of a young man. "Look at this, Rog," he says, handing his new glove to Maris. "Ain't that just too big?"

Maris inspects the cavernous mitt and agrees that, yes, it is too large. The conversation turns to the old days.

"When did you quit playing?" Mantle asks.

"I was 34. It was long enough, Mick."

"You could've kept playing."

"Naw. In 1968, when they saw my hand was hurt and I couldn't hit the fastball, I was through." Maris grabs a beer from the cooler and follows Mantle into the restroom, never once stopping the chatter. Later, in the dugout, Maris looks at Mantle, who is leaning back eating peanuts. "Hey, Mick," he says. "After signing all those autographs, you gonna take a shower?" They both burst into laughter. Maris stands against the wall, his arms around his youngest son, Richard, enjoying himself hugely. Earlier he had said that one of his biggest pleasures since moving to Gainesville was being able to remain anonymous. But this is different.

In the fifth inning, Centerfielder Mickey Rivers hits a home run over the right-field fence. Maris turns to Reggie Jackson, who is selecting a bat from the rack. Like Ruth and Maris, Jackson is a left-handed-hitting outfielder whose specialty is home runs. Pressure will seek him out, too. Maris points to the fence. "That's what I want, Reggie," he says.

In the eighth Jackson hits a sizzling 360-foot line-drive double that isn't high enough to clear the fence. Later, when he scores, he trots over to Maris. "Rog, that was for you," he says. "I want you to remember me for something. I want to at least get mentioned in the same paragraph with you some day." Reggie Jackson is smiling, but his voice is filled with deference.

After the game Jackson sits on a stool in the locker room and explains how he feels about Maris. "I have so much admiration for the man," he says solemnly. "For the mental part almost more than the physical. I mean, can you imagine what it's like to hit 61 home runs in a season? In New York? It's like hitting .400. With the way the press is today, it would take a new breed of man to do it again, a deaf and dumb man would have the best chance. People don't know what Roger had to go through—he *had* to act the way he did to maintain his sanity. Believe me, people just don't understand."

Maris stands in the center of the locker room, drinking a beer, swapping jokes, rehashing the ball game, relishing the reunion with his old game. If someone were to ask him if he cared anymore whether people understood or not, he would certainly say no. But that would not be the case. He hasn't forgotten the boos. But after more than a decade, it might be time he went back to Yankee Stadium. He would never forget the sound he would hear there now, either.

Lights
On!

♦

BY   RON   FIMRITE

TO SOME IT WAS ANATHEMA, TO OTHERS SIMPLE PROGRESS, BUT
EVERYONE HAD AN OPINION WHEN THE LIGHTS WENT ON IN
WRIGLEY FOR THE FIRST TIME IN 1988. RON FIMRITE, WHO WAS
THERE, OFFERED HIS OWN OBSERVATIONS.

It remained for Harry Grossman, a 91-year-old retired tire deal-
er, to put the Great Event into perspective. In his lifetime,
Grossman has been witness to, among other marvels, the cre-
ation of the airplane, talking pictures, radio, television, the atom
bomb and the FAX machine, but, he said on Monday, night
baseball at Wrigley Field "tops them all." Grossman may be for-
given some prejudice in this regard, for it was he, a Chicago
Cub fan for 83 years, who symbolically pulled the switch that
illuminated the Friendly Confines for the first time in its 74-year
history. "One, two, three," Grossman bellowed into a field
mike, as the capacity crowd of first-nighters chanted along with
him, "Let there be light!" And, lo and behold, there was.

   This touching little ceremony thus transformed baseball's best-
loved anachronism into just another ballpark. Oh, the vines are
still there, and so are the old hand-operated scoreboard and the
bleacher bums, but what most distinguished Wrigley Field from

more conventional stadiums was that the game was never played there after dark. Now it will be. There will be no more games "called on account of darkness," no more "homers in the gloamin'," such as the one catcher Gabby Hartnett hit as darkness descended on Sept. 28, 1938, to give the Cubs a pennant. Monday's game with the Philadelphia Phillies was the first of seven night games scheduled for this season. There will be 18 next year and for every year after that until the year 2002, according to an agreement the Cubs hammered out with city hall earlier this year. Philip K. Wrigley, the chewing gum magnate who owned the team for 45 years and swore that it would never play home games under the lights, is presumably spinning in his grave. Or maybe it was he who sent a furious little windstorm into the artificially lighted park in the third inning Monday night. An inning later, the wind brought rain, and surely to the gum-chewing shade's delight, the game was delayed for two hours and 10 minutes before it was officially postponed at 10:25 p.m., with the Cubs ahead 3–1. Ironically, the first major league night game ever scheduled—between the Phillies and the Reds in Cincinnati's Crosley Field—was also rained out and had to be played the following day, May 24, 1935.

One thing is certain: Light night did not go unrecognized by the national media. There were, in fact, 522 media representatives on hand for the occasion, probably making this otherwise meaningless contest between a fourth- and fifth-place team the most widely covered regular-season baseball game in history. By comparison, there were only 275 newshounds on duty when Pete Rose broke Ty Cobb's career-hits record in 1985. On Monday, 109 newspapers and magazines were represented, along with 49 television stations, 38 radio stations and such popular programs as *Today, Good Morning America* and *Entertainment Tonight*. This invasion of the media horde left Cub general manager Jim Frey bemused and bewildered. "I think we'll have a lot of fun playing night baseball," he said before Monday's game, "when it ceases to be the Event of the Century." Even the Phillies were impressed by the circus atmosphere. Pitcher Don Carman, for example, darted about during batting practice recording the pregame scene with a video camera. "The important thing, of course, is winning the game. But this is history," he said. "I think you have to be from Chicago and be a Cubs fan to understand this," said Phillie manager Lee Elia, who when he managed the Cubs in 1982 and '83 was not nearly so understanding. It was Elia who, feeling the pressure of fan disapproval, once accused Wrigley's daytime patrons of being layabouts incapable of getting worthwhile jobs.

That the lights were turned on at all represented a final defeat for the citizens of Wrigleyville, the neighborhood surrounding the old park. As long as Philip Wrigley was alive, they felt secure in the undisturbed serenity of their evenings. But the old man died in 1977, and four years later, his family sold the team to the Tribune Company media empire. The new owners were not exactly fans of baseball in the sun. Even though the team drew well at home—more than two million in attendance three of the last four years—the Tribune people contended, and commissioner Peter Ueberroth concurred, that the Cubs could not survive in the modern baseball world without night games. They were opposed by the stadium's suddenly aroused neighbors who, under the banner of CUBS (Citizens United for Baseball in the Sunshine), sought protection in the courts. For the better part of five years, the neighbors won all of the battles in court, including one in which Cook County Circuit Court Judge Richard Curry advised the Cubs' owners that "justice is a southpaw, and the Cubs just don't hit lefties." Eventually, though, the Tribune powerhouse mobilized its lobbying forces, and the opponents of the lights lost the war. With the support of, first, Mayor Harold Washington and then, after Washington's death late last year, his successor, Eugene Sawyer, the compromise ordinance allowing limited night games was passed.

And so, on Monday, Harry Grossman, no traditionalist despite his advanced years, happily led the cheering as the lights came on in Wrigley. Then old Cub heroes Billy Williams and Ernie Banks, who said, "I'd rather have lights than no Wrigley Field," threw out the first two balls. It had been a fearfully hot day, approaching 100°, and it was 91° at the 7:01 p.m. first pitch. And then the wind and the rain came, moving one cynic in the press box to suggest, perhaps facetiously, "The next thing they ought to do with this place is put a dome on it and install air-conditioning." Oh horrors!

THEY ALSO SERVE

❖ ❖ ❖

An Old Hand
with a Prospect

♦

BY PAT JORDAN

IN 1971 PAT JORDAN, A FORMER MINOR LEAGUER HIMSELF,
WROTE THIS INFORMATIVE PIECE ABOUT LIFE IN THE BUSHES.
WHILE ONE OF HIS PRINCIPALS, WOODY HUYKE, CONTINUED
TO LABOR IN THE MINORS, THE OTHER, BRUCE KISON, WAS
CALLED UP LATER THAT SEASON AND WENT ON TO WIN A KEY
GAME FOR THE PITTSBURGH PIRATES IN THE 1971 WORLD
SERIES. KISON REMAINED IN THE MAJORS FOR 15 SEASONS, FIN-
ISHING HIS CAREER WITH A RECORD OF 115–88.

Woody Huyke blows Bazooka bubbles as he takes quick,
pigeon-toed steps away from home plate. His shin guards
click between his legs and his chest protector rises and falls
against his gray-flannel uniform. His cap is still on backward,
and his olive-skinned face is streaked with red dirt and sweat
and the light outlines of his catcher's mask. He shakes the
hand of a tall, impassive Negro who has just walked in from
the pitcher's mound. Huyke says something in Spanish and
Silvano Quezada smiles. The Waterbury (Conn.) Pirates'
team crowds into the dugout, slapping Huyke and Quezada
good-naturedly. A voice calls out, "Nice going, you old
goat." The remark could be meant for either man. Together

they have played 25 years of professional baseball, and their combined age is near 70. "God only knows how old Quezada is," Huyke will say with a raised eyebrow. "He is ageless. Me, I am a mere boy in comparison." Soon Woody Huyke will be 34.

The rest of his teammates disappear, but the catcher remains in the dugout of the Elmira, N.Y. ball park. The outfield, which is nothing more than intermittent clumps of grass, is bordered by a wooden fence painted with advertisements. On this muggy afternoon there are less than a hundred fans on hand. Directly behind the home-plate screen is a cluster of eight women, the wives of the Elmira players. Throughout the game they have chattered amiably, and now that it is over they do not seem to have noticed. Woody Huyke looks at them and at the few old men sleeping high in the shade of the home-plate stands and at the young boys fooling around in the third-base bleachers and he shakes his head. Then he steps onto the field and says with just a trace of a Spanish accent, "Thank you, ladies and gentlemen. Thank you for your applause." He pulls off his cap, sweeps it with a flourish across his chest and bows deeply.

The Waterbury Pirates, a farm team of Pittsburgh, have just won the first game of a twi-night doubleheader from the Elmira Royals behind Quezada's four-hit pitching. The victory, a shutout, moves the Pirates into second place in the AA Eastern League.

The team had arrived in town earlier that afternoon after a six-hour bus ride from Waterbury. The players had only enough time to change into their uniforms at the Mark Twain Hotel and wander conspicuously about the streets of Elmira for a few minutes before reboarding the bus for the drive to the shambling ball park.

During the six-hour ride many of the players tried to sleep. They jacked their knees up into their stomachs, flattened their hands into knuckled pillows and closed their eyes to the pines and lakes of the Hudson Valley flashing by. Between naps players drifted in and out of a pinochle game. Before the ride ended, every man but two would be devoured by the game.

Bruce Kison, a 20-year-old pitcher, had no patience for cards, and he had not traveled on enough charter buses to be able to fold his 6' 4" frame into a cramped seat to sleep. Instead, Kison spent the time reading *The Sporting News*. He bypassed the stories about Tom Seaver and Sam McDowell and turned to the back pages, which told of the accomplishments of minor-leaguers like himself. Kison looked first for news of other Pittsburgh farmhands, specifically pitchers, so that he could see just who stood in his way to Three Rivers Stadium.

Woody Huyke did not sleep or play pinochle either. He had been on too many 28-hour bus rides to be impressed by a mere six-hour jaunt. Nor did he read *The Sporting News*. There was no Pittsburgh farmhand either beneath or above him who could cause him anxiety. Instead, as is his custom, Huyke talked ceaselessly to anyone who would listen and finally, after a few hours, he would talk only to himself. He spoke of his winters in Puerto Rico, where for three months each year he played baseball with some of the most famous major leaguers—Roberto Clemente, Frank Robinson, Orlando Cepeda—men he would never meet during the regular season because he had never played one inning of major league baseball. "I played some beautiful games in Puerto Rico," he said. "The most beautiful was when I hit a single off Juan Pizarro in a championship game.... Ah, I would have paid to be part of it." Huyke turned in his seat and elbowed Ray Cordiero, a balding 32-year-old relief pitcher. "Heh, Rook, you know what it means to play in such a game?" Cordiero grunted and went back to sleep. "Rookie!" said Huyke in disgust.

Halfway to Elmira the bus stopped at a roadside diner and the team got out to eat. When the bus resumed its journey the players were still grumbling about the greasy food. Huyke, who sat up front, began smacking his lips and rubbing his stomach. "Man, that was a great meal, eh, Rook?" Cordiero, an 11-year veteran, said it was the greatest meal he had ever eaten. Huyke nodded emphatically. "I loved it, too," he said. "I love it all." The players began to hoot and swear at Huyke, and someone threw a rolled-up *Sporting News* up front. "Bah!" said Woody. "These kids, what do they know? Always complaining. They don't appreciate the finer things in life, eh, Rook?" He nudged Cordiero again. "What they gonna do when they get our age, huh, curl up and die?"

Cordiero put his hands over his ears and said softly, "Why don't you shut the hell up, you old goat?"

After catching the first game of the doubleheader Huyke sits down, too tired to unbuckle his shin guards. Steam rises from his face. He is just beginning to be stocky, although he claims that his waist is the same size as when he was a 20-year-old rookie. What he does not admit, however, is that his uniform no longer fits him in the same way. The buttons seem about to explode and his pants fit his calves like an added layer of skin. The constant squatting and standing of his profession have made Huyke's legs round and muscular, like gigantic bottles of Coke. Because of his age, Huyke ordinarily would not catch the second game, but today is an exception. The team's backup catcher is on reserve duty and furthermore, Bruce Kison, the Pirates' talented right hander, will be making his first start after sustaining a sore arm.

Huyke walks down to the left-field bullpen where Kison is warming up. Woody stands behind Bruce and watches him throw. Kison has a small pink face covered with peach fuzz, which makes him look about 15. His teammates call him "Sweetie." Whenever they call him that in shrill, affected tones he will smile, although his face grows noticeably pinker. He is also called, on occasion, "The Stick," because he has the long limbs and small chest of a stick figure. His uniform billows at the waist like a sail and his pants billow at the calf like harem pants. At no point does his body impose any definition on the uniform he is wearing.

Now with Woody Huyke watching, Bruce is throwing much too hard and rapidly after his layoff. The ball is dipping into the dirt or flying over the head of his catcher, who must repeatedly run back to the fence to retrieve it. After each wild pitch Kison, expressionless, paws the dirt with his spikes, only to throw even harder and more rapidly. He throws with a loose-limbed, sidearm motion somewhat like those great sidearm pitchers Don Drysdale and Ewell Blackwell. It is a motion conducive to sore arms, especially on curveballs. Kison's meteoric rise through the Pirate system was halted two weeks ago by a strained muscle in his right elbow. It was strained on a curveball. This was the first sore arm of his career, and now in the Elmira bullpen Kison is throwing too hard and too rapidly to prove that his arm is no longer sore—and also to punish the arm for having let him down for the first time in his life.

After Kison's sixth wild pitch Huyke relieves the catcher. Kison throws a low fastball. Huyke scoops it expertly out of the dirt, but before returning the ball he says a few words to the previous catcher. The young pitcher takes a deep breath. Huyke returns the ball, and Kison fires it over the catcher's head. Huyke gets up from his crouch and walks slowly back to the fence. He picks up the ball and walks back to the plate and returns the ball to Kison, who by this time has taken three deep breaths. The next pitch is a strike. Huyke walks a few feet toward Kison and shakes the ball in his face, "Atta boy, Bruce. Use your head." Before long Kison is throwing fastball after fastball into Huyke's glove. Finally the catcher calls for a curveball. Kison spins one up cautiously. Huyke calls for another and studies Bruce's face for a sign. A lob. After a few more soft, halfhearted curves, Huyke shrugs and goes back to calling fastballs.

It is not the seriousness of his sore arm that is worrying Kison and the Pirate front office, but the fact that it could be the beginning of an irreversible pattern. Kison knows that if he is still to be considered a prospect he must prove that he will not be a perpetually sore-armed pitcher. That is why this second game is so important.

The game is also important to Huyke, although not in the same way. He will never play in the major leagues no matter what—he knows that—but if he can contribute to the development of a prospect like Kison, if he can guide the young ballplayer out of this sore arm by making sure he warms up properly, by calling the right pitches, by making Kison twist his elbow a little less strenuously on a curveball, then maybe someday Huyke will have a job in baseball, too.

Elwood Bernard Huyke (pronounced "high key") was born in Santurce, Puerto Rico in 1937. When he turned 18 he wanted to sign a professional contract, but his father convinced him instead to go to college. He enrolled at Inter-American

University at San Germän with the hopes of eventually becoming a doctor. In his junior year Huyke batted .408 in the Central American Games in Venezuela. He was offered a number of
professional contracts, and finally convinced his father to let him
sign with the New York Giants for $225 a month. When he left
for spring training Woody promised his father he would finish
school in the off season and become a doctor.

He worked out one month at Artesia, N. Mex. before
being given his unconditional release. But Huyke pleaded
with the Giant scout every day for a week until the man
finally consented to give him a chance at Hastings, Neb. in
the Rookie League.

There Huyke played third base and lived in a hotel that
charged only a dollar a day and had knotted rope hanging out
the window labeled "Fire Escape." Since the ball park had no
locker rooms Woody had to dress in the hotel and walk
through town in his uniform. When he arrived at Elmira for
the first time and discovered the same conditions he said, "I
thought those days were behind me."

In 1959 Huyke had one of the best hitting years of his
career. He batted .311. "I thought I could hit anyone," he
says. "I don't know what happened along the way, but after
12 years I don't hit so good anymore."

Huyke was assigned to Monterrey in the Mexican League
in 1960. The first road trip consisted of a 28-hour bus ride to
Tulsa in 110° heat. Another time, the team arrived in a town
at 7 a.m. after an overnight trip, and the manager drove
directly to the ball park for a workout. There were cities
where the players stayed at YMCAs, sleeping on mattresses
in the halls to keep cool.

Despite such conditions Woody was batting .296 at Monterrey three days before he was slated to play in the league's
All-Star Game. Then he suffered the first of a series of
injuries—a broken finger—that would hamper his career for
the next 10 years.

The following season Huyke played for the Shreveport, La.
and Portsmouth, Va. clubs. He batted .307 at Portsmouth and
was looking forward to the 1962 season when he was drafted
into the Army. He returned to baseball in the spring of 1963
when the Athletics invited him to their major league camp to

help catch batting practice. In three weeks Woody got into only one game, against the Dodgers. He went 3 for 4 off Don Drysdale, Sandy Koufax and Ron Perranoski.

"When it came to batting, I thought I could hit anyone," he says. "It was the confidence of youth, I guess. I didn't know any better."

On being shipped to the minor league camp, Huyke was immediately converted into a catcher, which he hated. "All day long they fired balls out of a machine at my shins. But I was too afraid to complain. Eventually I realized I would have a better chance making it as a catcher, and then I actually began to enjoy it."

Huyke started that year at Lewiston, Idaho in the Class B Northwest League. He was hitting .317 in midseason when he was handed a plane ticket and told to fly directly to Binghamton, N.Y. "It seems like a little thing, flying," he says, "but by then I had taken so many trains and buses I felt the organization had no interest in me. Now that they wanted me to fly I felt they must consider me a worthy prospect."

Huyke caught his first game with Binghamton and broke a toe on a foul tip. When he returned to the lineup a month later he promptly hit two home runs. The next week, however, he caught a foul tip on his throwing hand and broke a finger. He was through for the season. The farm director convinced him to play in the Winter Instructional League in Florida. "He said that it would be my big chance to make the majors," says Huyke. "It was the turning point of my career, all right. I threw out my arm one day, and I have never been a prospect since. I was so ashamed at having another injury that I didn't tell the manager. But it was so bad I couldn't even reach the pitcher. The fans used to laugh at me. It was a terrible thing for my pride. Finally the club found out and told me to go home."

In 1964 Huyke was sent to Dallas, where his contract called for him to stay for at least 30 days. After a week he was sent to Birmingham. He couldn't understand why until he was told that Birmingham needed someone to help out with the Spanish and black players who were finding life very rough in the South.

"At first it didn't dawn on me that they were using me as

an organization man," says Huyke. "In my own mind I still thought I was a prospect. But it didn't take long. Ever since then I've been too ashamed to ask the front office for a raise no matter what I hit. I have always felt I owed them something for just keeping me each year. After all, I was 27 years old, and they had decided I would never make the majors. Now I realize they were complimenting me by telling me I had other talents besides natural ones. The things I had would never leave me. Lots of guys don't have the temperament or intelligence to be organization men. It makes me feel good to know I can adapt to the facts of life. But at Birmingham in 1964 I thought, like all kids do, that there was no sense playing baseball unless you had a chance to make the bigs. I wonder why I didn't quit. Who knows? Maybe I thought I could prove I was still a prospect. Foolish! But I love baseball too much now ever to quit. I am always grouchy when I don't have a uniform on. I even get imaginary pains. These days just going to any ball park will do. For the home games, I always arrive three hours early and get right into my uniform. It's like a pair of pajamas to me. When I have the uniform on I relax. I guess to be like me you have to be born this way, huh?"

Bruce Kison finishes his pregame warmup and he and Huyke walk back to the dugout as the Elmira Royals take the field. In the dugout Bruce dries his face with a towel and Woody gets a Darvon pill from the Pirate trainer and a fresh supply of Bazooka bubble gum. The gum is to keep his mouth moist and the Darvon is to kill any pain he feels in his chronically sore arm. He has taken a Darvon every playing day since 1964.

It is 8 p.m., twilight and considerably cooler, when Huyke trots out to catch Kison's first warmup pitch in the bottom of the first inning. There is a loud click and the lights go on around the park. A female voice behind the visitors' dugout says, "Look at that pitcher! My oh my, he looks so young."

Bruce Kison was born in 1950 in Pasco, Wash., a rich farming community near the Columbia River. By the time he was 12 he had developed into a fine pitcher, having hurled several

227

no-hitters in Little League "like a million other kids," he says. "In one of those games I struck out 15 batters in five innings, and ever since, the possibility that someday I might pitch a perfect game has always been in my head when I take the mound. I dream of games when I strike out every batter I face on three straight pitches—but I guess that is every pitcher's dream, isn't it?"

After hurling three no-hitters in his senior year of high school Bruce was drafted by the Pirates (not very high) and signed to what he calls "a sizable bonus, although I'd rather not say how much." Before he signed, however, he made the Pirates promise to let him finish his spring semester of college each year before joining a club. "I wanted to make sure I finished college," he says. "So many guys drop out and are left with nothing. I was determined that wouldn't happen to me."

After signing, Bruce enrolled at Columbia Basin Junior College as a history major and then was sent to Bradenton in the Rookie Gulf Coast League. When he arrived he found "a hundred guys running around in Pittsburgh uniforms. We had 30 pitchers, and there were supposed to be just 15 by the end of the season. It was like a pressure cooker, everyone trying to cut each other's throat. You would make friends with a guy, and the next day he would be gone. You wondered when it would be your turn. You learn to evaluate yourself and your talent honestly, and in the process you grow up. I was one of the 15 pitchers left at the end."

Bruce posted a 2–1 record and a 2.25 ERA in 10 games, nine of them as a reliever. "When I got back to Pasco," he says, "I thought I was quite the stud. I told everyone I was going to give baseball three years and then quit if I wasn't at the top. Now I've already been in two years, and if I work myself up into Triple A the next few years, I probably will find it hard to leave. Maybe I'll stick it out five years. But I definitely won't stay in as long as Woody. I'll finish college first. This baseball is a nice game and all, but not in the minor leagues.

Kison moved up from the Pirates' Class A team at Salem, Va. to Waterbury in June. After he had watched a few Eastern

League games Bruce decided that it wasn't a very tough league after all. "Any good high school pitcher can win here," he said. He was as good as his word. He hurled back-to-back two-hitters in his first two starts.

"I no longer worry about being released," he says. "I know I'm established. Now all I worry about is how soon I will get to Pittsburgh. Our farm director, Harding Peterson, said I was one of their top prospects, but you can't rely on that stuff. They are never straight with you."

Harding Peterson arrived in Waterbury shortly before the trip to Elmira. He had sat in the dugout immaculately dressed and motionless, staring through dark glasses at the players performing before his eyes. "We usually let young pitchers build their confidence in the lower leagues," he said, "but Bruce Kison already has his. We would like to hurry him along to Pittsburgh. That's why I am here, to talk him into playing in Florida. But whenever we ask him to do things like that he has a thousand questions. Other guys will stammer and hesitate, but in the end you get them to do what you want. But not Bruce. He plans ahead."

Peterson did not hide the fact that he no longer considered Woody Huyke a prospect. "We drafted Woody from Oakland because he is a fine, intelligent fellow with a reputation for getting along with people," Peterson said. "His job is to work closely with the manager in bringing along kids. He is an excellent liaison man between the front office and the Latins. Huyke has never made any money in this game, so I told him if things work out there might be a job for him one day as a coach. But I have never promised anything. We still have some use for him as a player."

The Waterbury Pirates take the field in the bottom of the first. Huyke tells Kison to let him know if the arm bothers him. Kison nods, though he is thinking he will not say a word unless the pain becomes unbearable. Kison's first pitch is a strike. Huyke returns the ball, and the pitcher looks for the next sign. He fires another fastball past the Elmira batter for a strike. After two wasted fastballs Kison strikes out the batter with a fifth fastball.

On the mound Kison does not look so young or awkward

anymore. His pitching motion is spare and quick. It is distilled of all impurities and his thinking is concentrated like a point of light. He throws each pitch from the same sidearmed angle, with the same speed of delivery and with the same amount of time taken between each pitch. He gets his sign, delivers and waits in his follow-through until the ball is returned. Then he turns, takes two steps back to the rubber, turns again and repeats the process. He never, for effect, rubs up a baseball, wipes sweat from his brow or turns to contemplate the center-field flagpole. His face shows neither self-satisfaction after a good pitch nor anger after a poor one. He seems to have no self-conscious desire to call attention to himself as do most young pitchers.

Many inexperienced pitchers have speedy deliveries such as Kison's. Usually such deliveries mask their fear and ignorance of their craft, as if just by moving quickly through all the motions they define themselves as pitchers without having to impose their will on such motions. Kison's movements, however, are quick and consistent, not because he is defined by them but vice versa. He has neither to slow nor vary them, just as a finely tuned watch has neither to slow nor vary its workings.

The second batter goes to a full count before he lines out to center field. Kison is no longer throwing as hard and recklessly as he was in the bullpen. When Huyke calls for a curveball, Kison shakes him off.

"I've never had a sore arm in my life," Kison had said earlier. "When I hurt it, I was more confused than worried. I did not tell anyone and took my next turn. I walked eight guys in three innings, and when the manager, Red Davis, found out the reason, he was frantic. He yanked me right out. He was afraid if anything happened to me it would affect his career. If I were an older pitcher, like Quezada or Cordiero, say, the manager could take chances and no one would care. If my arm doesn't come around soon, I will quit."

Kison retires his third batter on another well-hit ball and walks off the mound. Red Davis, who was smoking a cigarette on the top step of the dugout, goes quickly over to Huyke, who is waiting for him near home plate. Woody can be heard saying, "I think it's sore." Red Davis' head

230

bobs up and down nervously and then he trots out to his third-base coach's box.

John Humphrey (Red) Davis has the sharp features and slack skin of a man who has lost too much weight too quickly. His fingers are permanently stained with the nicotine of a thousand doubleheaders. After 35 years in minor league baseball (he is 55) Davis has acquired an assortment of twitches and abortive gestures that give him the appearance not of a former athlete but of some aged drummer who has stopped too often at Greenville and Mayfield and Corpus Christi.

He has managed 23 consecutive years in the minor leagues, as low as Class D and as high as AAA. And yet in none of those leagues has his front office ever given him complete authority over certain of his players. For instance, Davis had decided to pitch Kison in Waterbury's last home game, to try his arm then, but after conferring with Harding Peterson, Davis postponed Bruce's start until the Elmira trip.

"Bruce is a fragile piece of property," says Davis. "If he gets hurt it will be my fault. If he were an organization man I could take a chance. Often that is the only reason they have a job in the first place, because we can do things with them that we would never do with a prospect. This makes it easier on them, too, because they know they are not getting paid for batting averages or ERAs. If Huyke is hitting .230 it does not bother him. He knows he helps the team in other ways. If an organization man has any personal success it is reflected in the team's success. That is why I would rather have eight organization men on the field any day. They take the pressure off a manager while prospects definitely put it on. And the older men are usually better all-around ballplayers, which makes you wonder why they never made it. Maybe they never got the breaks. Who is to say."

Davis became a minor league manager in 1949. The year before, he had married Estelle Nicholas of Dallas, a girl he met along the way. Since her marriage, Estelle Nicholas Davis has lived in more than 15 cities from Oregon to Connecticut while waiting for her husband to be offered the major league job that has never come. Like so many baseball wives, Mrs. Davis finds it impossible after so many seasons to

let her conversation stray far from talk of her husband's profession. One night after a home game, she stood in the darkened runway underneath the Waterbury stands, waiting for
her husband to emerge from the locker room. At close to
midnight, only a few scouts and three players' wives
remained. Mrs. Davis smiled at the three wives and continued her conversation with a friend who was keeping her
company, a tall, tweedy man, ex-major-leaguer Buddy Kerr.

"Oh, yes," she was saying in a Blanche DuBois voice, "I
root for all of Red's old boys. I've rooted for McCovey and
little Marichal ever since Red had them." After a while
Mrs. Davis asked, "Did you notice the crowd tonight? Do
you think they'll draw here? I do hope they draw, or else
they'll have to pack up and move elsewhere." When her husband emerged from the locker room Estelle Davis took his
arm, said good night to Buddy Kerr and the three wives and
left the ball park.

Of the players' wives, one was a heavily made-up blonde
clutching a gray toy poodle, another was a well-built brunette
in a lavender pants suit and the third was a slender, athletic-
looking girl in a plain green dress. The blonde and the
brunette were in their early 20s and the athletic-looking girl
close to 30, although she actually appeared younger than the
others because of her short, boyish haircut and because she
wore no cosmetics to mar her fine straight features. The
blonde and the brunette were talking animatedly to each
other about the poodle, whom they referred to as "Baby"
and who seemed quite used to being the topic of conversation. The girl in the green dress said little. She stood slightly
apart from the others and only smiled faintly now and then,
as if she were used to her role—the third person in a two-
party conversation. Not only did it appear not to cause her
any discomfort, it seemed actually much to her preference.
Three years ago the girl in green had become Mrs. Elwood
Bernard Huyke, and in that short span she had adjusted nicely to being the wife of a perennial minor league player.

"A baseball wife is very important to an organization man's
career," Huyke once said. "They can make life miserable if
they are always nagging him to quit. But my wife and I are
very compatible. She encourages me to play. I knew I would

stay in baseball all my life; I explained to her before we were married that baseball was everything to me. She accepted that."

When Ann Marie Huyke was 12 and combining wheat on her father's farm in Gardner, N. Dak. she used to dream of marrying an athlete. She was tall and slim even then, and in a small town she naturally gravitated to sports, and to basketball in particular. Often she competed against the boys on equal terms, and she played on a girls' high school team that won the state championship three years. "All through high school I only dated athletes," she says. "I was sure I would marry someone athletically inclined. After college I worked as a bank teller in Fargo."

One winter Ann Marie took her first real vacation, flying to Puerto Rico. Almost the first thing she did in San Juan was to board a bus for an hour's ride to Arecibo to watch a Winter League game. She met Woody Huyke that day, and they were married two years later.

"I don't mind the traveling much after living in Fargo and Gardner most of my life," she says. "I admit, though, that I still carry a picture of the house I would like to settle down in someday. But I have nothing to be disappointed about. I knew what Woody was when I married him. He made that perfectly clear. But sometimes it's difficult to explain it to others. To the wives of prospects, for instance. They are always making comments about when their husbands get to Pittsburgh. When they talk like that, what am I supposed to say? You hate to have people think you do not have faith in your husband just because you know he will never make the majors. But you have to salt your inner feelings with an honest evaluation of what he is. People are always asking me when he is going back to college. I know what they are hinting at, it's certainly obvious, but I just give them a blank look. I would like to say, 'Look, my husband could have been a doctor but he gave it all up to play baseball. This is what he loves. It's his job, and one day he is going to fade into another position in baseball and that is all there is to it.' But I never do."

In the bottom of the second inning Bruce Kison walks the first batter, retires two and then gives up a single. The single comes off a slow, hanging curveball. After the pitch Huyke walks halfway out to the mound and tells Kison to "put something on the damn ball." Red Davis has again moved to the top step of the dugout. He says something to Huyke as he gets down in his crouch. Woody nods. Davis turns immediately to the bullpen and signals for Cordiero to begin throwing.

Kison throws all fastballs to the next batter and gets him to hit a grounder to second base. As the second baseman fields the ball, it rolls off his glove and back into the dirt. Bases loaded. Kison works the next batter to 2 and 2. A hard, sharp curveball that the batter hits for a soft fly retires the side. As he walks off the mound there is a faint smile on Bruce Kison's lips.

In the third inning he gets two outs on fastballs and one on a hard curve. In the fourth he cuts loose on fastballs and curves and strikes out all three batters. He is throwing considerably harder, mixing almost an equal number of fastballs and curves on each batter. After each strike Huyke bounces out of his crouch, fires the ball back and shouts encouragement. After the third strikeout the catcher remarks out loud, to no one in particular, "That kid is throwing some kind of heat."

Huyke walks over and sits down on a small chair outside the dugout as is his custom. It is even cooler now, and he wraps his hand in a towel. "My fingers get numb," Woody explains, holding up his throwing hand. The fingers are fat and discolored. The blood vessels have been broken so many times and the circulation is poor. Huyke tries to warm the hand. Sitting there, he seems only partially occupied with the scoreless game in progress. He turns often to talk with the fans and seems particularly amused by a very fat woman with whom he has been carrying on a running dialogue each half-inning. The woman has neatly lined up 10 empty beer containers on the dugout roof in front of her.

"Hey, cutie, talk to me some more," the woman says to Huyke. He shakes his head and laughs. "Isn't he a cute one," the woman says.

"You know, you remind me of Buddy Hackett," Huyke says. He turns to the other fans. "Really, doesn't she look like Buddy Hackett?" Everyone, including the woman, laughs.

"It is part of my job to be nice to fans," says Huyke. "If they like you, they come to see you play. When I was young like Bruce I was too embarrassed to talk to them, but as an organization man I had to learn otherwise. I had to learn a lot of new things.

"When I was young I never understood the things that happened to me, but now I know where I am and where I am going and what I have to do to get there. I have no concerns. The only complaint I have in this league is that some of the parks are bad; take Pawtucket, R.I., there they have terrible lights. You can get damaged for life under bad lights. When you are young, who worries about playing conditions? And if you get hurt, the organization takes care of you. If you are older and you get hurt and can't play, maybe you don't have a job anymore."

Kison retires the side in the fifth, but in the sixth he gives up two singles with one out. He gets the fourth batter to pop out to third base and then he fires two quick strikes past the potential third out. Huyke crouches behind the right-handed batter and sticks two fingers beneath his glove. Kison flicks his glove fingers. Huyke responds with one finger and Kison nods slightly. Woody then hunches over the outside corner, but before he can set himself Kison flicks his glove again. Huyke shifts to the inside corner and places his glove at a level with the batter's knees. Again Kison flicks his glove. The catcher raises his target until it rests inches from the batter's chin. Kison goes into his motion and fires a fastball directly at the spot where the batter's head would have been if he had not fallen to the dirt. The count is now 1 and 2.

"Woody does not like to call for knockdowns," says Kison. "He knows a lot of these guys and he is afraid I might hurt someone. That doesn't bother me. I hit seven guys in one game, and we won it. I can't afford to feel like him or I will never get anywhere. I always thought the older guys would be tougher but they are more conscious of injuries than anyone. How can they ever expect to get anywhere unless they take chances? But I guess they have to protect themselves because they don't have anything else. There are three or four directions my life can take outside of baseball. I can play it a little looser as long as I keep those possibilities open."

With the bases loaded and the count 1 and 2 Kison throws, and again the batter, who has hunched slightly forward in expectation of a curveball, hits the dirt. This time he does not get up so quickly. He looks back at Huyke and then out to the mound, as if some rule has just been broken and he had not been informed.

With the count 2 and 2 Kison goes into his motion. The ball is headed for the batter's body, waist high, and he jerks his hips away from the plate just as the ball breaks sharply over the outside corner for a called third strike. The batter stands flat-footed as Huyke rolls the ball out to the mound which has just been vacated by Kison. Huyke shakes his head and says, "Man, that Bruce is too tough for me. But I like him. He battles. He only gets bad when a few guys hit him. I told him he can't pitch a perfect game all the time. He says he knows it, but then, two hits and he wants to throw at everybody. He has never seen a guy's career ruined by a beanball. I have. It is a terrible thing. But he is learning to control himself, and now when he throws at someone it isn't to get even, it is because he has an idea. That's what makes him different from most guys. He is smarter."

"I get along good with all the older players," says Kison, "although I don't let myself get too close because you never know when you will have to push one of them for a job. I respect Woody most of all. He has helped me a lot. But I still cannot understand what he is doing here when he could be a doctor. I don't have much to say to his wife or the others, either. I mean, what am I supposed to say? I can't understand why they are here. And the fans! They are something else, I don't bother with them at all. Guys like Woody are nice because they want some friends if they ever have to come back. I don't plan on ever coming back to Waterbury...."

In the top of the seventh, in a still scoreless game, Huyke steps into the batter's box with the bases loaded. He chokes up on his thick-handled bat and hunches over the plate. His feet are close together and his swing is nothing more than a little push emanating from his chest outward. Twelve years ago at Hastings he stood spread-legged, his heavy bat cocked far back from his right shoulders.

Woody works the pitcher to a 3–2 count and then fouls off

three straight pitches. He is thinking that if only he can foul off enough balls the pitcher will walk him and force in the winning run. But the pitcher throws another strike, and Woody hits a high foul ball to the catcher. Without even waiting to see if it is caught, he walks back to the dugout and begins buckling on his shin guards. The ball is caught and the side is retired.

"Man, one of these days I'm gonna kill a cloud," he says. "I don't understand it. I read some of Ted Williams' book, and he said swing up. I swing up, but nothing." He is smiling as he grabs his mask. "Maybe it is because I am not Ted Williams, eh? You think that could be it?"

With two out in the bottom of the seventh, an Elmira batter lays down a perfect bunt. Huyke pounces on the ball and throws him out. Then he hands the bat to the Elmira bat boy and walks back to his dugout. "Extra innings," he says. "We're gonna get them now. I can feel it. Man, I love this. What else could I do that I love so much? This is a beautiful game."

In the top of the eighth inning of this scheduled seven-inning game, Woody Huyke's prophecy is fulfilled. The Pirates score the first run of the game, and in the Elmira eighth Bruce Kison retires three batters on seven pitches to preserve his fifth victory of the year against four losses. As he walks off the mound he meets Huyke at the dugout and they shake hands. Woody says, "Bruce, I had a dream I would catch two shutouts today. No kidding! I dreamt it last night."

No Place in
the Shade

♦

BY MARK KRAM

MARK KRAM'S PROFILE OF OUTFIELDER JAMES (COOL PAPA) BELL
WAS ONE OF THE FIRST STORIES TO BRING THE RICH HISTORY
OF THE SO-CALLED NEGRO LEAGUES TO A NATIONAL AUDI-
ENCE. A YEAR LATER BELL WAS NAMED TO THE BASEBALL HALL
OF FAME.

In the language of jazz, the word "gig" is an evening of
work; sometimes sweet, sometimes sour, take the gig as it
comes, for who knows when the next will be. It means
bread and butter first, but a whole lot of things have always
seemed to ride with the word: drifting blue light, the bou-
quet from leftover drinks, spells of odd dialogue, and most of
all a sense of pain and limbo. For more than anything the
word means *black*, down-and-out black, leavin'-home black,
what-ya-gonna-do-when-ya-git-there black, tired-of-choppin'-
cotton-gonna-find-me-a-place-in-de-shade black.

Big shade fell coolly only on a few. It never got to James
Thomas Bell, or Cool Papa Bell as he was known in Negro
baseball, that lost caravan that followed the sun. Other
blacks, some of them musicians who worked jazz up from
the South, would feel the touch of fame, or once in a while

have the thought that their names meant something to people outside their own. But if you were black and played baseball, well, look for your name only in the lineup before each game, or else you might not even see it there if you kept on leanin' and dreamin'.

Black baseball was a stone-hard gig. Unlike jazz, it had no white intellectuals to hymn it, no slumming aristocracy to taste it. It was three games a day, sometimes in three different towns miles apart. It was the heat and fumes and bounces from buses that moved your stomach up to your throat and it was greasy meals at fly-papered diners at three a.m. and uniforms that were seldom off your back. "We slept with 'em on sometimes," says Papa, "but there never was 'nough sleep. We got so we could sleep standin' up or catch a nod in the dugout."

Only a half-mad seer—not any of the blacks who worked the open prairies and hidden ball yards in each big city—could have envisioned what would happen one day. The players knew a black man would cross the color line that was first drawn by the sudden hate of Cap Anson back in 1883, yet no one was fool enough to think that some bright, scented day way off among the gods of Cooperstown they would hear their past blared out across the field and would know that who they were and what they did would never be invisible again.

When that time comes for Papa Bell—quite possibly the next Hall of Fame vote—few will comprehend what he did during all those gone summers. The mass audience will not be able to relate to him, to assemble an image of him, to measure him against his peers as they do the white player. The old ones like Papa have no past. They were minstrels, separated from record books, left as the flower in Gray's *Elegy* to "waste its sweetness on the desert air." Comparisons will have to do: Josh Gibson, the Babe Ruth of the blacks; Buck Leonard, the Lou Gehrig of his game; and Cool Papa Bell—who was he?

A comparison will be hard to find for Papa. His friend Tweed, whom Papa calls *the* Black Historian, a title most agreeable to Tweed, says that you have to go all the way back to Willie Keeler for Papa's likeness. Papa's way was

239

cerebral, improvisational; he was a master of the little things, the nuances that are the ambrosia of baseball for those who care to understand the game. Power is stark, power shocks, it is the stuff of immortality, but Papa's jewellike skills were the meat of shoptalk for 28 winters.

Arthritic and weary, Papa quit the circuit 23 years ago at age 47, ending a career that began in 1922. During that time he had been the essence of black baseball, which had a panache all its own. It was an intimate game: the extra base, the drag bunt; a game of daring instinct, rather than one from the hidebound book. Some might say that it lacked discipline, but if so, it can also be said that never has baseball been played more artfully, or more joyously. "Before a game," says Papa, "one of our big old pitchers, he'd say, 'Jist git me a coupla runs, that's all.' You see, we played tricky ball, thinkin' all the time: we git a run they got to git two to beatcha. Right?"

The yellow pages of Tweed's scrapbooks don't tell much about the way it was, and they don't reveal much about Papa, either; box scores never explain. They can't chart the speed of Papa Bell. "Papa Bell," says Satchel Paige, "why he was so fast he could turn out the light and jump in bed before the room got dark!" Others also embellish: he could hit a hard ground ball through the box and get hit with the ball as he slid into second; he was so fast that he once stole two bases on the same pitch. "People kin sure talk it, can't they?" says Papa.

Papa says he did steal two bases on one pitch, which was a pitchout. "The catcher, why he was so surprised the way I was runnin' that he just held the ball," says Papa. "I ask him later what he doin' holdin' that ball, and he say he didn't know 'cept he *never* seen a man run like that before in his life." It is also a reliable fact that once in Chicago, on a mushy field, he circled the bases in 13.1 seconds, two-fifths faster than Evar Swanson's major league record. "On a dry field," he says, "I once done it in 12 flat."

Papa could run all right and he could hit and field as well. He played a shallow center field, even more so than Willie Mays when he broke in. "It doesn't matter where he plays," Pie Traynor once said. "He can go a country mile for a ball."

240

As a hitter Bell had distance, but mainly he strove to hit the ball into holes; he could hit a ball through the hole in a fence, or drag a bunt as if it were on a string in his hand. Bell never hit below .308, and on one occasion when he was hitting .390 on the last day of the season he gave his title up; he was 43 at the time.

"Jackie Robinson had just signed with the Dodgers, and Monte Irvin was our best young player," says Papa. "I gave up my title so Monte would have a better chance at the majors. That was the way we thought then. We'd do anythin' to git a player up there. In the final two games of the season, a doubleheader, I still needed a few times at bat. I was short of times at bat to qualify for the title. I got two hits in the first game and sat out the second game. The fans were mad, but they didn't know what we were trying to do. After the season I was supposed to git the $200 for the title anyway, but my owner, he say, "Well look, Cool, Irvin won it, didn't he?" They wouldn't give me the $200. Baseball was never much for me makin' money."

Papa Bell earned $90 a month his first year back in 1922. He would never make more than $450 a month, although his ability was such that later he would be ranked on Jackie Robinson's alltime team in the same outfield with Henry Aaron and Willie Mays. Bill Veeck, who also saw Bell play, puts him right up there with Tris Speaker, Willie Mays and Joe DiMaggio. "Cool Papa was one of the most magical players I've ever seen," says Veeck.

The money never bothered Papa; it was a game, a summer away from the packinghouse. " 'Cept one time," adds Papa, "when one team told me to pay my expenses from St. Louis to Memphis. They'd give it to me back, they said. I git there, and they say no. Owner of the club was a dentist. I say to 'em I didn't come down here 'cause I got a toothache. So I went back home. Owners are owners, whether they blue or green."

Papa spent the winters in the packinghouse until he learned of places like Havana and Vera Cruz and Cuidad Trujillo, which competitively sought players from the Negro League. He will never forget that winter in Cuidad Trujillo. It was in 1937, he thinks, when Trujillo was in political trouble. He had to distract the people, and there was no better way than to give them a pennant. First, Trujillo had his agents all but kidnap Satchel Paige from a New Orleans hotel. Then he used Paige to recruit the edge in talent from the States: namely, Papa Bell and Josh Gibson who, along with Orlando Cepeda, the storied father of the current Cepeda, gave the dictator a pat hand.

The look of that lineup still did not ease Trujillo's anxiety. "He wanted us to stay in pajamas," says Papa, "and all our meals were served to us in our rooms, and guards circled our living quarters." Thousands would show up at the park just to watch Trujillo's club work out, and with each game tension grew. "We all knew the situation was serious, but it wasn't until later that we heard how bad it was," says Papa. "We found out that as far as Trujillo was concerned we either won or we were gonna lose big. That means he was going to kill us." They never did meet Trujillo. They saw him only in his convertible in the streets, all cold and white in that suit of his that seemed to shimmer in the hot sun. "A very frightenin' man," says Papa.

Trujillo got his pennant and his election. A picture of Papa's, taken near a large stream, shows the team celebrating; the dictator had sent them out of the city—along with their fares home and many cases of beer. It had been a hard buck, but then again it had never been easy, whether it was down in Santo Domingo or back up with the St. Louis Stars or the Pittsburgh Crawfords or the Homestead Grays or the Chicago American Giants. East or West, North or South, it was always the same: no shade anywhere as the bus rattled along, way down in Egypt land.

Papa took the bumps better than most. Some, like Josh Gibson, died too young; some got lost to the nights. *Coolpapa*, as his name is pronounced by those who came from the South as he did, well, Coolpapa, he just "went on movin' on." That was the way his mother taught him back in Starkville, Miss., where he was born in 1903; look, listen and never pounce, those were her words, and all of them spelled survival. Work, too, was another word, and Papa says, "If I didn't know anythin' I knew how to work."

Long days in the sun and well after the night slipped across the cotton fields, all that Papa and his friends could talk about was "going off." Papa says, "One day some boy would be there along with us and then he'd be gone. 'Where'd he go?' I'd ask. 'Why that boy, he done gone off!' someone'd say. Next you'd see that fella, why he'd be back home with a hat on and a big, bright suit and shiny shoes and a jingle in his pocket." They would talk of the great cities and what they would have when they, too, went off and only sometimes would they hear about baseball. An old, well-traveled trainman used to sit under a tree with them on Sundays and tell them of the stars he had seen.

"Why, there's this here Walter Johnson," the trainman would say. "He kin strike out anybody who picks up a bat!"

"Is that right?" Papa would ask.

"Sure enough, boy. You'd think I'd lie? Then there is two old boys named Ty Cobb and Honus Wagner. Well, they don't miss a ball and they never strike out!"

"Never miss a ball?" gasped Papa. "Never strike out? Is that right?"

"I'm tellin' ya, boy. I've been to the cities and I know!"

"Well, mmmm, mmmm," Papa would shake his head. "Only one thing botherin' me. What happen when this here Walter Johnson is pitchin', and these other two boys are battin'?"

"Y'all go on!" the old man would yell, jumping up. "Y'all leave me alone. I'm not talkin' anymore. Don't none of ya believe. I should know. I've been to the cities!"

By 16 Papa was up North in St. Louis with several of his brothers and sisters, who were already in the packinghouse. "Didn't want to know 'bout ball then," says Papa. "Jist wanted to work like a man." His brother suggested that he play ball on Sundays. " 'James,' he said, 'you a natural. You throw that knuckleball, and there ain't nobody going to hit it.' " Soon he was getting $20 to pitch, until finally he was facing the lethal St. Louis Stars of the Negro National League. "They were a tough club," says Papa. "And mean! They had a fella named Steel Arm Dicky. Used to make moonshine as mean as he was on the side. His boss killed him when he began to believe Steel Arm weren't turnin' in all the profits."

Bell impressed the Stars, and they asked him to join them. "All our players were major-leaguers," says Papa. "Didn't have the bench to be as good like them for a whole season. We only carried 14, 15 players. But over a short series we could have taken the big-leaguers. That October, I recall, we played the Detroit Tigers three games and won two of them. But old Cobb wasn't with them, 'cause 12 years before a black team whipped him pretty good, and he wouldn't play against blacks anymore. Baseball was all you thought of then. Always thinkin' how to do things another way. Curve a ball on a 3–2, bunt and run in the first innin'. That's how we beat big-league teams. Not that we had the best men, but we outguessed them in short series. It's a guessing game. There's a lot of unwritten baseball, ya know."

The Stars folded under the Depression. Papa hit the road. An outfielder now, he was even more in demand. He finally began the last phase of his career with the Washington Homestead Grays; with Josh Gibson and Buck Leonard and Bell, it was one of the most powerful clubs in the black league's history, or anybody's history for that matter. "I was 'bout 45 then," says Papa. "Kinda sick. Had arthritis and was so stiff I couldn't run at times. They used to have to put me in a hot tub. I had to git good and warm before I could move." Yet, he had enough left to convince Jackie Robinson that he should never try to make it as a shortstop.

"It was all over the place that Jackie was going to sign with the Dodgers," says Papa. "All us old fellas didn't think he could make it at short. He couldn't go to his right too good. He'd give it a backhand and then plant his right leg and throw. He always had to take two extra steps. We was worried. He miss this chance, and who knows when we'd git another chance? You know they turned him down up in Boston. So I made up my mind to try and show him he should try for another spot in the infield. One night I must've knocked couple hundred ground balls to his right and I beat the throw to first every time. Jackie smiled. He got the message. He played a lot of games in the majors, only one of 'em at short."

Papa was named to manage the Kansas City Monarchs' B team in 1948, the agreement being that he would get one-third of the sale price for any player who was developed by him and sold to the majors. He had two prospects in mind for the Browns. "But the Browns," says Papa, shaking his head, "didn't want them. I then went to the Cardinals, and they say they don't care, either, and I think to myself, 'My, if they don't want these boys, they don't want *nobody.*' " The Monarchs eventually sold the pair: Ernie Banks and Elston Howard. "I didn't get anything," says Papa. "They said I didn't have a contract. They gave me a basket of fruit. A basket of fruit! Baseball was never much for me makin' money."

Life began all over for Papa. He took a job at the city hall in St. Louis as a custodian and then a night watchman. For the next 22 years the routine was the same, and only now and then could he go to a Cardinal game. He would pay his way in and sit there in the sun with his lunch long before the game began; to those around him who wondered about him, he was just a Mr. Bell, a watchman. He'd watch those games intently, looking for tiny flaws like a diamond cutter. He never said much to anyone, but then one day he was asked by some Dodgers to help Maury Wills. "He could run," he says. "I wanted to help." He waited for Wills at the players' gate and introduced himself quietly.

"Maybe you heard of me," Papa said, "maybe not. It don't matter. But I'd like to help you."

Wills just looked at him, as Papa became uneasy.

"When you're on base," said Papa, "get those hitters of yours to stand deep in the box. That way the catcher, he got to back up. That way you goin' to git an extra step all the time."

"I hadn't thought of that," said Wills, who went on to steal 104 bases.

"Well," Papa smiled, "that's the kind of ball we played in our league. Be seein' you, Mr. Wills. Didn't mean to bother you."

After that year Papa seldom went to the ball park anymore. He had become a sick man, and when he walked his arthritic left side seemed to be frozen. It was just his job now. In the afternoons he would walk up to the corner and see what the people were up to, or sit silently in his living room turning the pages of his books of pictures: all the old faces with the blank eyes; all of those many different, baggy uniforms. There is one picture with his wife Clarabelle on a bench in Havana, she with a bright new dress on, he with a white suit

on, and if you look at that picture hard enough it is as if you
can hear some faraway white-suit, bright-dress music.

Nights were spent at city hall, making his rounds, listening
to the sound of radio baseball by the big window, or just the
sound of the hours when winter mornings moved across the
window. When it was icy, he would wait for the old people
to come and he would help them up the steps. Often, say
about three a.m., he would be looking out the window, out
across to the park where the bums would be sleeping, their
wine bottles as sentries, and he'd wait for their march on the
hall. They would come up those steps and place their faces
up against the window next to his face and beg to be let in
where it was warm.

"We're citizens, old Bell, let us in," they would yell.

"I know," Papa would say.

"It's cold out here," they would say.

"I know," he would answer.

"No, you don't, you...." and Papa would just look away,
thinking how cold it was outside, listening to all that racket
going on out there, trying to think of all the things that
would leave him indifferent to those wretched figures. Then
it would be that he sometimes would think of baseball, the
small things he missed about it, things that would pop into
his mind for no reason: a certain glove, the feel of a ball and
bat, a buttoning of a shirt, the sunlight. "You try to git the
game out your mind," he says, "but it never leaves ya. Some-
thin' about it never leaves ya."

Papa Bell is 70 now. He lives on Dickson Street in North
St. Louis, a neighborhood under siege: vacant, crumbling
houses, bars where you could get your throat cut if you even
walked in the wrong way, packs of sky-high dudes looking
for a score. They have picked on Papa's house a couple of
times, so now when he feels something in the air, hears a
rustle outside of his door, he will go to the front window
and sit there for long hours with a shotgun and a pistol in his
lap. "They don't mess with Papa anymore," says his friend
Tweed, looking over at Papa sitting in his city hall retirement
chair. "It's a reclinin' one," says Tweed. "Show 'im how it
reclines, Papa."

Now the two of them, Black Historian Tweed and Papa,

who sits in his chair like a busted old jazz musician, torn around the edges but straight with dignity, spend much time together in Papa's living room. They mull over old box scores, over all the clippings in Tweed's portable archives. They try to bring continuity of performance to a man's record that began when nobody cared. They argue, they fuss over a figure here, they assemble pictures to be signed for people who write and say that they hear he will be going into the Hall of Fame; the days are sweet.

"Can't believe it," says Tweed. "Kin you, Papa? Papa Bell in de Hall of Fame. The fastest man who ever played the game."

"Ain't happened yet," cautions Papa, adjusting his tall and lean figure in his chair.

"Tell me, Papa," says Tweed. "How's it goin' to feel? De Hall of Fame ... mmmm, mmmm."

"Knew a fella blowed the horn once," says Papa. "He told me. He say, 'Ya got to take de gigs as dey come.'"

No Bad Hops
with Wally

♦

BY   FRANZ   LIDZ

IN 1987 SPORTS ILLUSTRATED DEVOTED AN ENTIRE ISSUE TO "A
DAY IN BASEBALL." AMONG A VARIETY OF STORIES EXAMINING
THE OVERLOOKED ELEMENTS OF THE GAME WAS FRANZ LIDZ'S
PIECE ON ONE LONGTIME BEER VENDOR IN MINNEAPOLIS'S
METRODOME.

Wally the Beerman looks with disdain on the crowd filing
into the Hubert H. Humphrey Metrodome. "Kids," Wally
mumbles. The first 10,000 fans under 14 who show up
today to see the Twins play Chicago get a plastic fishing-
tackle box with rubber worms. You can't sell cold, frosty
ones to 10,000 children.

Walter McNeil, 52, is the Dome's top beerman. On average, Wally dispenses 18 trays of 20 beers a game, earning
36 cents on every $2 beer sold. His closest competitor, Jerry
the Beerman, sells around 15 trays. Three summer ago Wally
set the Twins record of 33 trays. That's 660 beers. "The Tigers
were in town," he recalls. "Everything just fell into place."

Wally, whose regular job is operations manager in a phar-
maceutical firm, has worked the Dome since it opened in
1982. He merchandises himself like a multinational corporation,

handing out Wally the Beerman business cards and match-
books. Last season he gave away 5,000 Wally the Beerman
baseball cards.

The Metrodome sits on 22 acres of downtown Minneapolis, its fiberglass roof rising like yeasty bread in an outsized
baker's pan. Inside, it is dim and surprisingly cozy for a joint
that seats 55,000. "There are 36 rows in the lower deck, 32
in the upper," says Wally. "The long aisles of the lower deck
are set on a 37-degree angle, with 76 steps that are 18 inches
deep. The upper-deck aisles are at 45 degrees, and have 68
steps that are only 12 inches deep. When you set your tray
down in the upper deck, you've got to take the beers from
the back. If you don't, the tray may flip up on you."

Today, Wally loads up each 34-pound tray of beer in a
vending room behind home plate, the stadium's choicest
location. The lower-deck area is packed with season-ticket
holders who like to have their beer delivered to their seats.
Wally sticks mainly to the rows behind the plate and the visitors' dugout. "Fans on the first base side drink more than
fans behind third," he says sagely. "Third base fans are more
conservative."

At 12:41, Wally makes his first pitch. "Coldbeerhere! Coldbeerhere!" he shouts in a voice that cuts through the Dome
chatter like a metal shredder. Wally negotiates the steps as
adroitly as a Sherpa scaling Everest.

He makes his first sale at 12:43 to a retired bank president
wearing a WALLY'S MY BEERMAN T-shirt. By 12:51, Wally has
covered six aisles and emptied the tray. His Converse low-
tops seem to be spring-loaded. Soaked in sweat, he sprints
back to the vending room.

By the time the national anthem is sung, at 1:10, he's mid-
way through his third tray. He doffs his yellow visor and
holds it over his heart. That's about the only time the whole
afternoon that Wally stands still.

During the first four innings, he catches about seven seconds of action. The Twins have hit four homers, but Wally
has seen only Tom Brunansky's. He descends Section 126 as
the ball clears the centerfield fence. Wally pauses in momen-
tary tribute, then turns around and bellows, "Real big league
baseball beer here, sanctioned by the commissioner of baseball.

Look for his signature in the bottom of the cup." A broad-backed man wearing a Crabby's Oyster Bar T-shirt buys one.

In the fifth, Wally runs into Igor the Peanut Man, who hawks the "Hall of Fame nuts that Harmon Killebrew eats." You'd think Igor would be a good setup man for a beer seller, but Wally doesn't agree. "My theory," he volunteers, "is if a fan's got peanuts in his hand, he may not have another one free to buy beer."

The guy in the Crabby T-shirt has a complaint. "Hey, Wally," he says. "I didn't get the commissioner's signature."

"You'd better get another beer," Wally says. "This isn't Cracker Jack—I don't guarantee a prize in every cup." Crabby orders two more.

Two innings later a foul ball heads roughly in Wally's direction. "I got it. I got it. I got it," he screams. The ball lands in the upper deck. "I got the cold beer right here."

Crunch time comes in the bottom of the eighth. There is no late-inning cutoff on beer sales at the Dome, but beermen have to decide by the end of the eighth whether to take out more brew. They are stuck with any left in their trays at the end of the game. Wally looks at the scoreboard. The game is tied at five. He splits a tray with Tom the Beerman and heads for Section 119.

Gary Gaetti leads off the Twins' half of the eighth by reaching on an error. The crowd roars. "Hey, rally time," yells Wally. "Get your rally beer here." A lady in a black jumpsuit reaches for a rally beer just as the Wave almost swamps Wally's tray. The Wave is one more occupational hazard for beermen.

Brunansky doubles in Gaetti. Roy Smalley singles in Brunansky. Wally sells his last beer. "I think we're done," he says. The Twins are still batting when Wally gets to the pay window. His score is 17½ trays, 350 beers, 50 more than either Jerry or Tom. His take-home will be $126, plus $21 in tips.

Somebody tells Wally that the Twins win 8–6. "Great!" says Wally. "Wanna go to the bar across the street? I'm about ready for a beer."

An American
Classic

♦

B Y   R I C K   R E I L L Y

WHEN TEXAS HIGH SCHOOL STAR JON PETERS WENT FOR THE
ALLTIME HIGH SCHOOL RECORD FOR CONSECUTIVE WINS, RICK
REILLY WAS ON HAND TO RECORD THE EVENT. SADLY FOR
PETERS, HE WOULD SUFFER AN ARM INJURY AFTER HIGH
SCHOOL THAT WOULD PREVENT HIM FROM COMPETING IN
COLLEGE OR PROFESSIONAL BASEBALL.

There is a real field of dreams in this country and it's not at
your local Odeon Cineplex 8. It's a real ballpark with real
grass and a real motel ad painted on the fence and, right
now, about 250 empty lawn chairs waiting on history.

And there is a real baseball legend in this country and he's
not Robert Redford or Kevin Costner. This legend is 18
years old, shaves twice a week and just had a big fight with
his best girl.

His name is Jon Peters, and he's from Brenham, Texas. And
right now, Friday, April 28, 1989, just a few hours before he
attempts to break the national high school record for consecutive pitching wins, a whole town hangs on his bony shoulders.

Pressure? The *Today* show is setting up at the old Band
Hall, waiting to see if you win. There was a camera crew in

your government class this morning. people have been coming to the ballpark since yesterday and nailing their stadium
seats to the bleachers—sort of the Black and Decker approach
to reserved seating—waiting to see if you'll let them down.

Pressure is hearing that tonight instead of one concession
stand, there will be three, and instead of one cop for security
there will be eight, and instead of one photographer down
the third base line there'll be 20. It's knowing that of the
11,000 folks in your pickup-truck, vanilla-ice-cream town,
almost half of them will be sardine-canned into a ballpark that
seats 1,200. The other half will be hunched over radios listening to one of four live broadcasts, and anybody left can
watch the game later, courtesy of one of the eight TV cam-
eras perched on your dugout roof.

"I swear," said Peters the night before the game, "if I had
an ulcer, it'd be fixin' to bust."

And so it was that the 6' 2", 190-pound Peters, 50–0 as a
righthanded starter for the Brenham High School Cubs, prepared to take the immaculately manicured mound at Fireman's Park in Brenham, 73 miles northwest of Houston, and
try to scratch his initials in the park bench of time, just as
the town desperately hoped he would.

Not that he hadn't already done all this before.

On April 12 last year, Peters went out on this same field to
pitch for his 34th straight win. By all accounts the existing
national high school record was 33. Peters tossed a one-hitter
against Oak Ridge, 5–0; he had faced the record, beaten it
and been relieved of it. But a week later, a reporter from
USA Today was on the phone with some distressing news.
Seems that nine years ago, Timmy Moore of McColl, S.C.,
was stopped 1–0 to end his high school winning streak at 50,
an achievement nobody had bothered to report to the
National Federation of State High School Associations, which
keeps track of such things.

Even Moore was unaware of his own immortality. "I
thought maybe I'd held *some* kind of record," said Moore,
now a management trainee with a freight company in Cher-
ryville, N.C. "But I'd never been told anything about it."

Poor Peters. It is one thing to rewrite the record books. It
is another to have to make a carbon.

Could he win 17 more straight? Peters told a friend, Kevin Picone, he didn't think so. But Peters had underestimated his remarkable unhittability. In the remainder of his junior year, he reeled off eight more en route to Brenham's third straight 4A baseball title. He opened his senior season this year with seven wins, including two no-hitters. On April 21 he won his 50th with a dicey 3–1 win over Taylor High of Katy. Now, just over a year since he broke the unrecord, Peters was back, ready to write his name in the books. This time, in ink.

Already, the sequel was playing even bigger in Brenham than the original. So many wanted to be witnesses to history that the city donated extra bleachers. Folks brought lawn chairs the day before and placed them anywhere the benches weren't. Four Santa Fe Railroad security deputies, armed, were brought in to keep people off the nearby railroad tracks. Six porta-potties were imported and allotted: four for women, two for men. The Girl Scouts cooked up 2,000 hot dogs and 100 apple pies. The Future Homemakers of America served up nachos and Brenham's own Blue Bell ice cream. Businesses closed at four o'clock. As dusk approached, most people in town were fully expecting the moon to come up Cub green.

Stage set, the town ached for a most unlikely looking god. Jon Roland Peters has size XL ears and a country face that has barely grown out of its freckles. His walk is late Walter Brennan. His dress consists mostly of extra-long jeans (the way Opie Taylor used to wear them), gray T-shirts and running shoes. He says "sir" a lot, has a 92 grade average, and can throw a baseball past any high school kid alive.

Never mind what the scouts say, that he doesn't have big league stuff yet—his fastball is timed in the low 80-mph range—he has a big-league head. If you set him 60' 6" from a French door, you could name the windowpane and he would put his fastball through it. He'll throw his changeup or his neck-breaking curve on 3 and anything. He has almost 560 strikeouts in his career and less than 100 walks.

But most of all he has a bull-backed will, like that of his role model and idol, alltime major league strikeout leader Nolan Ryan. Didn't Ryan too come from a small town in Texas (Alvin)? And hadn't Ryan pitched right here in Brenham once (1965)? Like Ryan, Peters is nothing if not stubborn.

In the four-year life of the streak, he has won in the rain, won with the flu, won with his best stuff and won with his worst. Says Brenham assistant coach Harry Francis, "He never learned to lose."

He has been good and he has been good and lucky. Three times in the streak he left a game losing, and three times his teammates scraped up enough runs to get him a no-decision. Brenham's other starter, James Nix, knows something about the luck of the draw. As of last Friday, Nix had his own 25-game winning streak going, including four no-hitters. The last one, a perfect game, was seen by 400 people. Nix's problem is that he decided to cross the Atlantic the day after Lindbergh.

When asked what it takes to put together a great streak, Peters answers, "Great teammates." But as this game drew closer, Peters felt mostly alone. It has been his custom on most pitching days to go to his girlfriend's house to relax. He and Brenham tennis team star Jill Becker had been steadies for two years. But with their recent spat and all, Jon had been going home instead.

Still, the rest of his good-luck machinery was in place—the ritualistic pool game with buddies the night before, the wearing of the lucky gray T-shirt to school, the trip to McDonald's for his lucky Big Mac, the donning of the lucky green jersey, complete with his lucky number, 21.

So pregnant with promise was Fireman's Park that six fans had backed up a forklift behind the wooden rightfield fence, stuck a huge crate on the lift, got inside and elevated it to mezzanine height. Moore, flown in from Kings Mountain, N.C., to throw out the first pitch, was impressed. "This is the first high school game I've ever seen with sky boxes," he said. If Moore was impressed, imagine how the visiting team, A & M Consolidated, must have felt. They had been invited to a luau only to find out they were the pig.

Beneath a charcoal-gray sky, Peters finally begins the biggest game of his life. Seated behind home plate is Red Murph, the very scout who discovered Ryan more than 25 years before. Peters gulps, twists through his quirky windup and throws. Ball, too high. He is nervous and slightly pale. His next pitch is low, but swung on for a strike. Then Peters throws two more strikes for a K. He strikes out the second batter. Then the third. Pressure *that.*

Hastily, as if to spare his teammates as much angst as possible, Cubs rightfielder John Schulte lines the first pitch from Consolidated's Brent Ives for a double. One hitter later, Peters singles to right to knock Schulte in. Peters 1, Consolidated 0. Is Jill watching?

The Cubs come up with another for a 2–0 lead, but when Peters returns to the mound, he begins to falter. He walks the first A & M hitter, then, with two outs, walks another on four straight balls. The unthinkable go-ahead run is at the plate. Another ball, his fifth straight. Had he invited the world to his own funeral?

He takes off his cap to wipe his brow. On the underside of the brim, where no one can see, he has written one word: NOLAN.

Two hellacious fastballs later, he moves the count to 1 and 2, wastes one, then punches the batter out on a curve. It is 3–zip in the third when Peters whiffs the side again. And when Brenham lights up A & M for five more runs and an 8–0 lead in the bottom half of the inning, the question is not will Peters get No. 51, it's will he have the audacity to do it with a no-hitter?

"I was standing in the dugout, he would say later, "and I was thinking, Nolan lost his no-hitter the other night [with one out in the ninth to Toronto]. I'm not gonna lose mine."

That settled, he opens the fifth with two strikeouts—his 11th and 12th in 14 outs—then allows Consolidated its deepest penetration of the night, a pop-up to the shortstop no higher than a Pop Warner punt.

In Texas high school baseball, a team that is ahead by 10 runs in the fifth inning is the winner, and now the question is whether the Cubs can secure Peters' no-hitter without his having to go back to the mound. Two runs will wrap it up. Brenham's Tadd Maass triples to start the inning and is singled home by pinch hitter Joel Wellmann. It's 9–0. Another single and an out later, Nix approaches the plate with the game-ending run at second base. "Go up there and end this thing right now, O.K.?" Peters says in the on-deck circle.

But Nix has a better sense of theater than that. He strikes

out, leaving Peters with a delicious chance to consume the night totally. He can not only write the Great American Novel, he can star in the movie, too.

Two outs. The photographers and the minicams creep closer to the base paths. Four thousand or so edge forward on their benches and lawn chairs and roofs and forklifts. Even the Santa Fe guards turn their backs to the tracks to watch.

A hanging curve. A slashing swing. A line drive between third and short. A pinch runner, Dietrich Burks, churning around third and heading home. A throw to the plate too late and too wide. A euphoric Peters, riding a bed of shoulders. An ending to make Frank Capra blush. Peters has knocked in the game-ending run, he has thrown a no-hitter and he has set a record that may be very hard to erase, ink or otherwise.

"Every night before I go out there," he says in the jubilation afterward, "I think, Is this going to be the one? Is this the night I lose? But, really, never in my wildest dreams did I think I'd make it to this record." Now he has done it not once, but twice. Did they ever ask Leonardo to paint another *Mona Lisa?*

But that is not what makes the moment whole. What makes it whole is Jon standing on the mound, swarmed by autograph-, hug- and quote-seekers—and seeing Jill. She is wearing his necklace, and from it hangs a gold "21." She smiles at him. He smiles back. Jon & Jill, consolidated.

Maybe someday Jon Peters will be a major league superstar or maybe he'll be a management trainee. Maybe this summer he'll accept a pro contract or maybe he'll go ahead with the scholarship offer he has already signed with Texas A & M University.

But for right now, on this night, on this very real field, he is the greatest high school pitcher ever, on his way to kiss the prettiest girl in school.

THE GAME

...

'Perfect Day—A Day of Prowess'

♦

BY   R O B E R T   F R O S T

IN 1956 SPORTS ILLUSTRATED INVITED AMERICA'S GREATEST LIV-
ING POET TO ATTEND THE ALL-STAR GAME AND RECORD HIS
THOUGHTS. THE RESULT WAS THIS WHIMSICAL TRIBUTE TO
BASEBALL.

Americans would rather watch a game than play a game. Statement true or false? Why, as to these thousands here today to
watch the game and not play it, probably not one man-jack
but has himself played the game in his athletic years and got
himself so full of bodily memories of the experience (what we
farmers used to call kinesthetic images) that he can hardly sit
still. We didn't burst into cheers immediately, but an exclama-
tion swept the crowd as if we felt it all over in our muscles
when Boyer at third made the two impossible catches, one a
stab at a grounder and the other a leap at a line drive that may
have saved the day for the National League. We all winced
with fellow feeling when Berra got the foul tip on the
ungloved fingers of his throwing hand.

As for the ladies present, they are here as next friends to the
men, but even they have many of them pitching arms and batting eyes. Many of them would prefer a league ball to a

pumpkin. You wouldn't want to catch them with bare hands. I
mustn't count it against them that I envision one in the outfield at a picnic with her arms spread wide open for a fly ball
as for a descending man-angel. Luckily it didn't hit her in the
mouth which was open too, or it might have hurt her beauty.
It missed her entirely.

How do I know all this and with what authority do I
speak? Have I not been written up as a pitcher in *The New
Yorker* by the poet, Raymond Holden?—though the last full
game I pitched in was on the grounds of Rockingham Park
in Salem, New Hampshire, before it was turned into a race
track. If I have shone at all in the all-star games at Breadloaf
in Vermont it has been as a relief pitcher with a soft ball I
despise like a picture window. Moreover I once took an hon-
orary degree at Williams College along with a very famous
pitcher, Ed Lewis, who will be remembered and found in the
record to have led the National League in pitching quite a
long time ago. His degree was not for pitching. Neither was
mine. His was for presiding with credit over the University
of New Hampshire and the Massachusetts College of Agriculture. He let me into the secret of how he could make a ball
behave when his arm was just right. It may sound supersti-
tious to the uninitiated, but he could push a cushion of air
up ahead of it for it to slide off from any way it pleased. My
great friendship for him probably accounts for my having
made a trivial 10¢ bet on the National League today. He was
a Welshman from Utica who, from having attended
eisteddfods at Utica with his father, a bard, had like another
Welsh friend of mine, Edward Thomas, in England, come to
look on a poem as a performance one had to win. Chicago
was my first favorite team because Chicago seemed the nearest city in the league to my original home town, San Francisco. I have conquered that prejudice. But I mean to see if the
captain of it, Anson my boyhood hero, is in the Hall of Fame
at Cooperstown where he belongs.

May I add to my self-citation that one of my unfulfilled
promises on earth was to my fellow in art, Alfred Kreymborg,
of an epic poem some day about a ball batted so hard by Babe
Ruth that it never came back, but got to going round and
round the world like a satellite. I got up the idea long before

any artificial moon was thought of by the scientists. I meant to
begin something like this:

> It was nothing to nothing at the end of the tenth
> And the prospects good it would last to the nth.

It needs a lot of work on it before it can take rank with
Casey at the Bat.

In other words, some baseball is the fate of us all. For my
part I am never more at home in America than at a baseball
game like this in Clark Griffith's gem of a field, gem small, in
beautiful weather in the capital of the country and my side winning. Here Walter Johnson flourished, who once threw a silver
dollar across the Potomac (where not too wide) in emulation of
George Washington, and here Gabby Street caught the bullet-
like ball dropped from the top of George Washington's monument. It is the time and the place. And I have with me as consultant the well-known symbolist, Howard Schmitt of Buffalo,
to mind my baseball slang and interpret the incidentals. The
first player comes to the bat, Temple of the Redlegs, swinging
two bats as he comes, the meaning of which or moral of
which, I find on application to my consultant, is that we must
always arrange to have just been doing something beforehand a
good deal harder than what we are just going to do.

But when I asked him a moment later what it symbolized
when a ball got batted into the stands and the people instead
of dodging in terror fought each other fiercely to get and keep
it and were allowed to keep it, Howard bade me hold on;
there seemed to be a misunderstanding between us. When he
accepted the job it was orally; he didn't mean to represent
himself as a symbolist in the high-brow or middle-brow sense
of the word, that is as a collegiate expounder of the double
entendre for college classes; he was a common ordinary cym-
balist in a local band somewhere out on the far end of the
Eeryie Canal. We were both honest men. He didn't want to
be taken for a real professor any more than I wanted to be
taken for a real sport. His utmost wish was to contribute to
the general noise when home runs were made. He knew they
would be the most popular hits of the day. And they were—
four of them from exactly the four they were expected from,
Musial, Williams, Mays and Mantle. The crowd went wild
four times. Howard's story would have been more plausible if

he had brought his cymbals with him. I saw I would have to take care of the significances myself. This comes of not having got it in writing. The moral is always get it in writing.

Time was when I saw nobody on the field but the players. If I saw the umpire at all it was as an enemy for not taking my side. I may never have wanted to see bottles thrown at him so that he had to be taken out by the police. Still I often regarded him with the angry disfavor that the Democratic Party showed the Supreme Court in the '30s and other parties have shown it in other crises in our history. But now grown psychological, shading 100, I saw him as a figure of justice, who stood forth alone to be judged as a judge by people and players with whom he wouldn't last a week if suspected of the least lack of fairness or the least lack of faith in the possibility of fairness. I was touched by his loneliness and glad it was relieved a little by his being five in number, five in one so to speak, *e pluribus unum*. I have it from high up in the judiciary that some justices see in him an example to pattern after. Right there in front of me for reassurance is the umpire brought up perhaps in the neighborhood of Boston who can yet be depended upon not to take sides today for or against the American League or the Boston Red Sox. Let me celebrate the umpire for any influence for the better he may have on the Supreme Court. The justices suffer the same predicaments with him. I saw one batter linger perceptibly to say something to the umpire for calling him out on a third strike. I didn't hear what the batter said. One of the hardest things to accept as just is a called third strike.

It has been a day of prowess in spite of its being a little on the picnic side and possibly not as desperately fought as it might be in a World Series. Prowess, prowess, in about equal strength for both sides. Each team made 11 hits, two home runs and not a single error. The day was perfect, the scene perfect, the play perfect. Prowess of course comes first, the ability to perform with success in games, in the arts and, come right down to it, in battle. The nearest of kin to the artists in college where we all become bachelors of arts are their fellow performers in baseball, football and tennis. That's why I am so particular college athletics should be kept from corruption. They are close to the soul of culture. At any rate the Greeks thought so. Justice is a close second to prowess. When displayed toward each other by antagonists in war and peace, it is known as the nobility of noble natures. And I mustn't forget courage, for there is neither prowess nor justice without it. My fourth, if it is important enough in comparison to be worth bringing in, is knowledge, the mere information we can't get too much of and can't ever get enough of, we complain, before going into action.

As I say, I never feel more at home in America than at a ball game be it in park or in sandlot. Beyond this I know not. And dare not.

Tricks of
the Trade

♦

B Y   S T E V E   W U L F

IN 1981 STEVE WULF LIVENED UP SPORTS ILLUSTRATED'S ANNUAL
BASEBALL ISSUE WITH THIS DISCUSSION OF THE MANY NEFARIOUS
METHODS USED BY MAJOR LEAGUERS TO GET AN EDGE ON THEIR
COMPETITION.

Kansas City. Sept. 30, 1980. Bill Kunkel, working the night
watch out of bunco, apprehends Rick Honeycutt (male Cau-
casian, 26, 6' 1", 190 pounds) for battery with intent to doctor a
baseball. The facts: Kunkel, an American League umpire, catches Honeycutt, a Seattle pitcher, using a thumbtack taped with a
Band-Aid to the forefinger of his right (non-throwing) hand to
carve up baseballs he is pitching to the Royals. Let's return to
the scene of the crime.

"It was the third inning," Kunkel recalls. "I wasn't looking
for anything in particular, but Willie Wilson had complained
about some of the pitches. I saw the Band-Aid on his finger
and asked him what happened. When I grabbed his hand I got
stuck. I was shocked."

The pitcher's testimony: "I thought the thumbtack trick up
all by myself. Pretty smart, huh? Look, I was desperate at that
point in the season [he was 6–0 on May 8, 10–17 on Sept. 30].

I figured, 'What did I have to lose?' Well, as soon as I see Kunkel coming out to the mound, I tried to get rid of the tack. But I had done too good a job of taping it on. I felt like I was being pulled over for speeding.

"All I wanted to do after that was plead my case. I wanted to tell everybody that I was really sorry, that what I did was stupid and that I'd never do it again. I never wanted this to happen, and I didn't know the consequences. Besides, I'd only scratched three balls that night, and none of them did anything. But before I could say a word, Kunkel told me, 'You're gone.' "

"I'm glad we caught him," says Kunkel, himself a former American League pitcher. "But I'm sad somebody would do something like that."

The surprise in the Honeycutt case is not that "somebody would do something like that," but rather that somebody would actually get caught doing something like that.

Birds do it. A's do it. Even educated Jays do it. Mets do it. Mess ball in glove.

Baseball players also plug bats with cork, cheat on the double play, con runners, bilk umpires and steal signs. There are a thousand tricks of the trade, and they're all done in the name of gamesmanship. They run from the illegal to the immoral to the unethical to the clever. As long as the other team isn't doing them, they're just part of baseball.

BALLS

The granddaddy of all the tricks is the spitball. It has come a long way from that day in 1902 when, during a pregame warmup, an outfielder in the Eastern League named George Hildebrand tried to make fun of a rookie pitcher who went to his fingertips before he threw the ball. Hildebrand loaded up a ball with a generous helping of saliva and threw it to the catcher. "The ball took such a peculiar shot that the three of us couldn't help but notice," Hildebrand once recalled. Like Newton and Goodyear before him, Hildebrand had made a remarkable discovery quite by accident. Word of it got around, and in 1908 Ed Walsh won 39 games with a spitball. The spitter was outlawed in 1920 for sanitary reasons, and Babe Ruth went from 29 homers to 54. However, pitchers already in the major leagues who registered as spitballers could still throw the pitch, so the last legal spitter was delivered in 1934, by Burleigh Grimes, whose drooler got him into the Hall of Fame.

That wasn't the end of it, however. Thanks to the research of such pioneers as Lew Burdette, Whitey Ford, Don Drysdale and Gaylord Perry, the spitball has given way to the mudball, the shineball, the shampoo ball, the pine tar ball, the sandpaper ball, the petroleum jelly ball, the belt buckle ball and the puffball.

Players are willing to reveal which pitchers throw a less-than-kosher cowhide, although they make it clear that nobody on their team would ever do such a thing. Nearly every sinkerball pitcher gets accused—one of the things that burned Honeycutt was that during his unbeaten string at the start of last season, he was constantly being suspected of loading up the ball, even though he was strictly legit. The names most frequently mentioned are those of Perry, Don Sutton, Tom Burgmeier, Pete Vuckovich, Tommy John, Dave Goltz, Jim Barr, Enrique Romo, Ferguson Jenkins, Bill Lee, Mike Torrez, Stan Bahnsen, Mike Caldwell, Paul Splittorff, Ross Grimsley, Bill Castro, Glenn Abbott, Bob Stanley and Doug Corbett, not to mention 99 and 44/100% of the Oakland staff. The A's, under the tutelage of Pitching Coach Art Fowler, are said to be fond of rubbing Ivory soap on the insides of their pant legs at the spot where their throwing hands touch their thighs. When the pants become wet with sweat, the soap just happens to come through to the other side for easy application. The only pitcher on the A's who wasn't accused last year was Dave Beard, who made all of 13 appearances. Apologies to any pitcher left off the above list.

By scuffing, soaping, greasing, etc., a pitcher is able to grip the ball conventionally and throw it with the force of a fastball but achieve exaggerated movement. None of the pitchers has probably ever heard of Dr. Hermann Schlichting, a former southpaw for the Engineering University of Braunschweig, West Germany, but in his 1951 classic, *Boundary Layer Theory,* Schlichting explained the magic behind the spitball as follows: "Integrating the pressure distribution and the shearing stress over the surface of the sphere, we obtain the total drag

$$D = 6\pi\, \mu\, R\, U_\infty.$$

This is the very well known *Stokes equation* for the drag of a sphere."

Got that? In other words, by messing with the baseball, the pitcher creates a kind of a drag (The Buckinghams, 1966) that changes the flow lines around the ball, making them asymmetric. Even the slightest change will give the ball a more pronounced wiggle, producing a funkier pitch than can be thrown without tampering with the ball. For instance, a sinkerball pitcher will most often throw from the side or three-quarters with topspin on the ball. A normal sinkerball drops three or four inches. By scuffing the ball, usually on the topside just behind the horseshoe of the seam, a pitcher can make it drop by as much as half a foot. A fastball pitcher who comes over the top, putting backspin on the ball, can make his pitch take an extra hop by scuffing the underside.

The spitball is often the last refuge of the marginal pitcher, who is either losing his stuff or didn't have all that much to begin with. When erstwhile Oriole Ross Grimsley, in 1975, got in a jam one day, his pitching coach, George Bamberger, went out to the mound and said, "If you can cheat, I wouldn't wait one pitch longer." This wasn't idle talk, because Bamberger is said to have taught his pitchers in Baltimore and Milwaukee "the Staten Island sinker," which is named after Bambi's home borough.

Of course, the mahatma of the debaseball is Perry. Over the years he has progressed from Slippery Elm (pronounced ELL-um) lozenges, all the better for keeping a ready supply of saliva; to K-Y jelly, ideal for lubing a greaseball; to Pillsbury flour, which he mixes with resin to produce the puffball—a dry rather than wet pitch that the batter has to locate amid a cloud of dust. Billy Martin, then managing the Tigers, once brought a bloodhound to the ball park just to sniff out the Indians' ball bag when Perry was pitching. Ralph Houk suspected Perry of supplanting spit with a fly-line cleaner favored by fishermen because it's clear and dries quickly. Such attention no doubt pleases Perry, who believes that a batter's anxiety over the prospect of being thrown a spitball can serve as useful a purpose as the spitter itself.

Pete Rose says that if he were a pitcher, "I'd try to get every edge I could." But Honeycutt has had second, third and home thoughts about what he did: "I hadn't been in any trouble since the last time I was sent to the principal's office. But there I was, sitting in the tunnel after they threw me out. All the other guys were coming up to me, making jokes—the whole season was a joke. Then it hit me. What are they going to do to me? Is the commissioner going to ban me from baseball forever? What an ordeal.

"Crime never pays."

No, it doesn't. Honeycutt was fined $250 and suspended for 10 days, the last five of the 1980 season and the first five of this season. The last pitcher to be suspended for throwing a doctored baseball was Nels Potter of the St. Louis Browns; he was caught by Umpire Cal Hubbard and told to take a walk for 10 days in 1944, which was, perhaps coincidentally, the year Potter had his best season, with 19 wins.

With all the slicing and dicing going on, it seems strange that it took umpires 36 years to catch another pitcher in the act. Actually, Umpire Doug Harvey nabbed Sutton, then with the Dodgers, in 1978 and threw him out of a game. But Sutton threatened to sue if he was suspended, so it was made clear that he was ejected not for doctoring a baseball, but for throwing a baseball that happened to be doctored. Otherwise, Sutton has always enjoyed his outlaw reputation. Once, an umpire went out to inspect Sutton's glove and found a note inside which read, "You're getting warm, but it is not here."

Dave Duncan, the pitching coach of the Cleveland Indians, estimates that close to 50% of the pitchers in baseball do something to the ball. Former Twins Manager Gene Mauch, now in the Angels' front office, says, "More pitchers are doing it than at any time in the 40 years I've been associated with baseball." Honeycutt says, "Every day I heard a new rumor about another pitcher doing it. I figured it was O.K. for me to try, too."

Dick Butler, the supervisor of umpires for the American League, doesn't see any more slippery dealings than normal among pitchers, even though both leagues sent out bulletins last year warning umpires to be on the alert for spitters and scuffers. "There's just more attention paid to it," he says. "Maybe nobody complained before. The umpires don't want to see the rules broken, but it's a lot easier to sit in the stands and say someone is doctoring the ball than to find evidence of it down on the field. If the balls have marks on them, all in the same spot, beyond the normal wear and tear a baseball gets, then the umpire can do something." That something is this: if an umpire discovers a scuffed ball, he can hold the pitcher responsible—because the pitcher was the person who threw it—and issue a warning. If the umpire detects another similarly scuffed ball, the pitcher can be ejected and suspended for 10 days.

Ray Miller, the Orioles' pitching coach, has a unique collection of abused baseballs, selections from which he occasionally sends to the American League office. His most prized relics are a series of scuffed balls handcrafted by Mike Marshall. Not only was Marshall a doctor of physiological psychology, but a doctor of baseballs as well.

"It's getting ridiculous," says Miller, who maintains that the Orioles only throw them on the sidelines. "I suggested last year that the umpires make it an automatic balk on the pitcher every time they find a scuffed ball. That way, if a relief pitcher comes in with the bases loaded, needing a ground ball, he won't be so quick to scuff the ball."

Tiger Manager Sparky Anderson has a different idea. "Myself, I'd like to see it legalized."

"Great," says Miller. "I can now conceive of the day when a pitcher will come out to the mound wearing a utility belt, complete with files, chisels, hammer, nails and hacksaw."

BATS

"I don't begrudge the pitchers," says Yankee Third Baseman Graig Nettles. "But until the umpires have the guts to stop them from marking the ball, I see nothing wrong with using a corked bat."

Of course, Nettles wouldn't use one. Not since Sept. 7, 1974 he wouldn't. That date will live forever in baseball infamy because in the fifth inning of the second game of a doubleheader in Detroit, Nettles hit a bloop single to left and the end of his bat fell off. His single was disallowed, but not his second-inning home run with the same bat. That homer, by the way, produced the game's only run.

The original accounts said that the bat was filled merely with cork. Well, such a legend has grown up around the incident that members of at least three other teams claim Nettles hit the home run against them, and that it wasn't cork inside the bat, but from four to six Super Balls, incredibly lively little devils.

Who can ever forget the sight of Tiger Catcher Bill Freehan chasing after the bat for evidence? The Tigers certainly knew a corked bat when they saw one, because their first baseman, Norm Cash, was particularly proud of his. Nettles claimed he didn't know where the bat came from—some fan had given it to him in Chicago "for good luck." The bat was stained a dark brown, so how could Nettles tell?

"Why that lying sonofagun," says Cash. "I ought to know. I used a hollow bat my whole career." But, Norm, surely not in 1961, the year you hit .361 with 41 homers and 132 RBIs. "I'm afraid so," Cash says. "In fact, I owe my success to expansion pitching, a short rightfield fence and my hollow bats."

How do you cork a bat? Well, Cash's method was to bore a hole about eight inches deep and half an inch wide into the meat end of the bat. He left most of the hole empty, plugging only the top two inches of it with cork, sawdust and glue. Cash, who now works outside Detroit for NORPADIC, a manufacturer's representative, says it took him about half an hour to doctor a bat.

According to Earl Weaver, the Orioles' manager, the best way to cork a bat is to drill a hole 12 to 14 inches down into the barrel without splitting the wood and then pack the hole tight with ground-up cork, leaving a two-inch void at the top. The hole is then closed with a carefully shaped plug of plastic wood. Finally, sand over the top of the bat. "You can't spot a good job with a magnifying glass," says Weaver.

What does hollowing the wood from a bat do? According to Cash, it makes the bat lighter, so that a batter is getting the mass of a 36-ounce bat with the whip of a 34-ounce bat. And, of course, it stands to reason that a bat with a cork center will be livelier than a bat with a wood center. Players say they can get an extra 20 to 50 feet with corked bats.

There are other things a hitter can do to coddle his bat. Old-timers used to put nails in them. Some even honed one side of the bat to make it flat and thus increase the hitting surface. Other bats are grooved and the grooves filled with wax. Nettles remembers a player in the minors who used to fill his bat with mercury, on the assumption that the force of the mercury traveling to the barrel head increased the power of the bat. Unfortunately, the player couldn't hit, mercury or not.

Weaver says he used a corked bat when he played for New Orleans in 1955 and tied his career-high in homers with six. "I cried when they found us out," he says. But would his Orioles pull something like this? You bet, says Bamberger. In 1979 he publicly accused Ken Singleton and Rick Dempsey of using corked bats against the Brewers. Weaver, on the other hand, thinks that Cecil Cooper of the Brewers wields a doctored bat. Weaver became convinced after Cooper, who stands 6' 2" and weighs 190 pounds, hit a ball out of the park one-handed. "No way a guy his size can do that with a legal bat," said Weaver. "It's a standing joke between us," says Cooper. "Earl always comes over and looks in our bat rack before the game."

The Phillies and Royals are also suspect—perhaps because they were the most successful teams in baseball last year. Then again, maybe they were the most successful teams in baseball because they used corked bats. A couple of years ago one Phillie play-er—an All-Star—was overheard at the batting cage telling a bat company representative, "I'll take one of the super-cork mod-els." He was probably just kidding.

John Mayberry, now with the Blue Jays, recalls that a corked bat was available when he played for Kansas City. Reportedly, an undercover craftsman used to service the bats in the Kansas City clubhouse, charging only $1 apiece to cover the cost of cork. Hal McRae, the Royals' designated hitter, is sometimes accused of using a bat that floats, but the one time he was checked—the bat was cut in six pieces—he was clean. Some of the other names bandied about are Mike Schmidt, Davey Lopes, George Foster, Tony Armas, Bobby Grich, Darrell Porter, Buck Martinez, Jose Cardenal and Vic Correll. "I'm sure it goes on," says Rose, who also says he has used one in practice but never in a game. "I always thought that if I got caught, every one of those damn hits I got, people would think I cheated."

The one current player who has admitted to swinging a bogus bat is Andre Thornton, a first baseman/designated hitter for Cleveland and a very religious man. After the 1978 season, Thornton made his confession: "I was approached to use a corked bat. I used it two weeks. It gave me a tremendous emo-tional problem. I hit one home run with it. But I couldn't find peace with that, even though a lot of players use them. I just couldn't use something illegal and live with myself. It was a dark bat, and no one would ever have known.

"I felt so much joy when I discarded that bat, you can't imagine. My flesh told me to go ahead and use it. All men face such decisions, in any walk of life. Do you cheat? Or do you rise above it?"

So guess what most baseball players would answer.

GLOVES

Thornton is so honest that he's probably the only first baseman not mentioned by players when they discuss who cheats while tagging the bag, *i.e.,* pulls his foot off before the fielder's throw arrives. This is intended to make the umpire believe that the throw got to first before it really did. The list is long, but the best at the cha-cha are Cooper, Jim Spencer, Willie Montanez, Rod Carew, Eddie Murray, Keith Hernandez and the old guard of Rose, Willie Stargell, Tony Perez, Carl Yastrzemski and Lee May. Rose has been playing the position for only two years, but he picked up the knack about two minutes after he became a first baseman. He says Willie McCovey was the best he has ever seen. "He was so good at it," says Rose, "that I was hesitant to try and bunt for base hits on him, because you could be safe by a step and a half and he'd still make you look out." Old-timers say that nobody could compare to Gil Hodges of the Dodgers and Joe Adcock of the Braves for cheating on the bag. Darrell Johnson, the former Seattle and Boston manager and now a coach with the Rangers, says all first basemen do it. "But like Orson Welles says, they only do it when it's time."

"We don't cheat as much as second basemen do on the double play," says former Second Baseman Rose. Bump Wills, Willie Randolph, Jim Morrison, Frank White, Davey Lopes, Mike Tyson, Joe Morgan and Rich Dauer are considered the best—or worst, depending on one's point of view—second basemen at studiously avoiding the bag on the pivot. The phantom double play is sometimes a matter of survival, which is why the umpires rarely acknowledge it, but there are other times when it's just plain cheating. The second baseman hopes to cover up for all manner of faux pas—bad throws from the shortstop, bad timing on his own pivot and the like.

When asked last season what percentage of the time he cheats on the DP, Phillie Infielder Ramon Aviles said, "All the time.

B A S E B A L L
♦ ♦ ♦

Last Sunday I participated in four double plays. I cheated on three of them. What happens is that when I play second base, I'll put my left foot on top of the bag as I'm waiting for the throw. When the ump sees my foot on top of the bag, he figures I'm there the whole time. But by the time I catch the ball, I'm not there."

Bobby Grich, the Angels' second baseman, is sometimes cited for cheating on the double play, but he says it ain't so. "I'm a former football player, so I like contact. Besides, I'm bigger than most second basemen. The guy, though, who gets away with it more than anyone is Randolph. He was even doing it during infield practice at the All-Star Game. He straddles the bag. I don't know why he does it that way, but he does it often."

The shortstops most frequently accused of ignoring the bag are Fred Patek, Tim Foli, Larry Bowa, Dave Concepcion and Rick Burleson. "Guys like Phil Garner say I cheat," says Concepcion. "I no cheat. I'm just quick." Retired Umpire Hank Soar says, "Burleson is a master at cheating on the bag. So you have to call it on him to make him stop. I did one time in something like a 15–2 game, and he told me, 'I'll get your job for this.'"

Grich is a wizard at many infield tricks. Three or four times a year on flyballs he will fake fielding a grounder to the detriment of the runner going from first to second on a steal or hit-and-run. "If the runner's not watching the ball," says Grich, "he'll get confused. I learned that trick when I was a 9-year-old bat boy on my father's softball team. I love stuff like that. It breaks up the monotony of the game and, after 14 years in pro ball, sometimes I need it." Grich is also adept at positioning his feet to block a runner from getting back to the bag. "It's just as much mine as his," he says. Grich is very good at sneaking up behind runners on pickoff plays, and he has faked more than a few runners into sliding into second when they should have been wheeling on to third.

The *pièce de résistance* of all infield tricks is the hidden ball. "I've never pulled it off, although I try a couple of times every year," says Grich. "The third base coach or somebody will usually yell and spoil it. I don't know how Gene Michael did it with the Yankees, but he worked it successfully four or five times a year. He's not about to tell me how, now that he's manager of the team. But that's the one remaining goal of my career—to pull off a hidden-ball trick."

Some first basemen are good at it. Spencer and Mayberry among them. With Ron LeFlore, then of the Tigers, on first, Spencer, a Yankee, once instructed his pitcher to throw over eight times in a row. LeFlore didn't even notice that the eighth time Spencer kept the ball, and when Leflore stepped off, Spencer had him. Mayberry uses a different approach. "Big John is so nice and easygoing," says Grich, "you don't suspect anything when he asks you to take your foot off to kick the dust away—until he tags you."

Grich was exaggerating, but he wasn't far from the truth. Mayberry once nailed a Minnesota rookie by asking him to step off the base for a minute so Mayberry could use the bag as a prop while tying his shoe. Mayberry took his glove off—with the ball in it—hee, hee!—and while lacing up, he tagged the rook.

But you don't have to be an experienced hand to pull it off. Kansas City's young shortstop, Tim Ireland, did it to Cincinnati 10-year veteran Larry Biittner in a spring training game this year, killing a Reds rally in the 11th. After receiving a relay throw from the outfield, Ireland kept the ball in his glove instead of returning it to the pitcher. A few moments later he simply sneaked up behind Biittner, who was leading off second, and tagged him out to end the inning. "It's just a logical thought process," said Ireland. "You play all your life and see guys off base. No big deal."

Then there is the Goodrich Blimp School of Trickery. Last year in a game between the White Sox and the Yankees, Chicago rookie Outfielder Rusty Kuntz was on first when Alan Bannister hit a ground ball just inside the first-base line. Yankee First Baseman Bob Watson scooped up the ball and touched first. In the meantime, Shortstop Fred Stanley signaled to Kuntz, who had left with the pitch, to hold up because the ball was foul. As Kuntz casually walked back to first he was tagged out to complete the double play. "I couldn't even be mad at Stanley," said Kuntz. "It was brilliant." Kuntz was soon sent down to the minors for more seasoning. Chris Speier of the Expos tried the same thing on the Cubs' Mick Kelleher a few years ago, and Kelleher didn't think it was brilliant. "I thought it was bush," he said.

Catchers have their own bag of tricks. They'll try to coax strikes from the umpire by ever-so-smoothly pulling their gloves into the strike zone as they catch a pitch that's a bit off the plate. Gary Carter is highly, or lowly, regarded for his deftness at this, as are Jim Sundberg, John Stearns, Bob Boone, Steve Yeager, Joe Ferguson, Barry Foote, Johnny Bench and Rick Dempsey. Art Kusnyer, a former catcher and the bullpen coach of the White Sox, reveals how it's done. "Jerking the glove sideways or pulling it down won't work. The ump won't fall for it. But if I caught a pitch on the corner with the palm facing out I'd flick my wrist and turn the glove in, so it would be perpendicular to the pitcher. It was just an illusion, but it helped sometimes."

Catchers also have no qualms about doctoring the ball for their pitchers. Birdie Tebbetts used to wear thumbtacks in his shin guards for those very special occasions, and the late Elston Howard would help Ford, when the heat was on, by putting mud in the ball's seams or scratching it on his shin guards. Kusnyer claims that he could scuff a ball simply by scooping up a low pitch and slamming it off the ground quickly so that the umpire wouldn't notice. "I've also loaded up for pitchers," says Kusnyer. "A little K-Y jelly on the forearm just above the wrist."

Catchers also chatter to throw a batter's concentration off. Thurman Munson was very good at this, as was Ray Fosse. "Thurman would talk a little rough at times," says Fosse. "My psych was praise. Brooks Robinson, I remember, came to bat once, and I said, 'Here's my idol, the greatest third baseman in the history of baseball. I love your style. You're poetry in motion.' He turned around and threatened me."

"When you're talking to the catcher or the first baseman, it's hard to concentrate on the third-base coach," says Al Oliver of the Rangers. "But then, you don't want to seem antisocial."

Outfielders don't get as many opportunities for trickery as infielders and catchers do, but they do the best with what comes their way. Sometimes an outfielder will try to freeze a base runner by pretending he's about to catch a fly ball even though he knows he can't reach it. One of the cagiest outfielders is Milwaukee's Gorman Thomas, who says, "I've worked that maybe 10 times. I was taught by the master, Ken Berry.

The reason I learned my lesson so well is that he put a decoy on me when he was with the Angels. I was on first base and a bloop was hit to center. I froze, and he caught me by 85 feet." Berry is also legendary for carrying an extra ball in his back pocket. When Berry was with the White Sox, the story goes, he once leaped for a home run that made it into the first row of outfield seats. Berry didn't catch the ball, but he did pull the second ball out of his pocket and hold it up. The umpire ruled it a catch. Cub outfielders have been instructed to pretend they've lost the ball in the Wrigley Field vines. That way, sure triples become ground-rule doubles.

Most outfielders say that short-hopping a ball so that it looks as if it was caught is more an accident than an art form, but Coach Joe Nossek of the Indians actually tells his charges to hold up the ball after shoestringing it on the off chance that the umpire might be fooled. "Sometimes it's justice," says Nossek. "You get enough of those to make up for the catches that they mistakenly rule as traps."

ET CETERA

Nossek is also the acknowledged master of that most arcane of baseball skills, sign-stealing. "Nossek probably knows our signs better than we do," said Bill Mazeroski, a Mariners coach last summer. "Sign-stealing is really a misnomer," says Nossek. "It's nothing more than educated guessing. You watch the opposing third-base coach, and then check out the manager, and things start falling into place. For instance, if you've been watching a team the first two games of a series and it hasn't tried anything in the way of stealing or the hit-and-run, and then you suddenly pick up a whole new series of signs, well, you just assume the runner's going, and you call a pitchout. If I'm right on 50 percent of my pitchouts, I figure I'm doing pretty good. I'd trade a ball for an out anytime.

"I learned an awful lot from Gene Mauch when I coached under him at Minnesota. Plus, I picked up a lot of tips from other players. I'd trade tidbits of information. In general, a team's signs will follow the same pattern throughout the season. Eventually, you build up a pretty good book." Nossek is also good at anagrams and crossword puzzles.

There are more nefarious ways of stealing signs. When Martin was managing the Rangers, he was suspected of relying on electronics. He's said to have had a closed-circuit camera installed just beyond the centerfield fence in Arlington Stadium. The camera was hooked up to a television set in Martin's office, and a player, usually Jim Fregosi, would decipher the catcher's signs. When Fregosi had the code broken, he'd relay his findings to Martin via walkie-talkie. Martin would then be able to tell the batter what was coming by whistling or yelling a prearranged phrase.

But some batters don't want to know what's coming. Norm Sherry, a coach with the Expos, remembers a game against the Cubs in 1978. "Larry Cox was catching, and he was putting his signs down so low that I could see every one from the third-base box," Sherry says. "I told the guys, 'I've got all his signs.' Nobody wanted them."

Some clubs have trick plays. The White Sox will sometimes switch cutoff men on balls hit to the outfield to confuse base runners. First Baseman Mike Squires will move toward the mound as if he's going to cut off the throw, then circle behind the runner and take the throw at the bag. Sometimes they catch the runner in a rundown between first and second. Conversely, the Expos use a base-running ploy called the Sleeper Rabbit, thought up years ago by George Moriarty, third baseman on the Ty Cobb Tigers. With runners on second and third, the man on second takes his time walking back to second after the first pitch. By doing it a second time, he hopes to induce the catcher to throw to second. But just as the catcher releases the ball, the runners break for home and third. The Orioles have a special base-running ploy of their own known as "the famed play." The purpose is to score a run from third by having a runner at first draw a throw from the pitcher. The play, which is practiced during spring training in secret, has been used successfully in recent years against Cleveland, Chicago and Boston.

For some tricks, there is an equal and opposite re-trick. Carew, among others, doesn't like to be fenced in by the batter's box. He erases the back line of the box, so he can plant his rear foot pretty much wherever he wants. But then, some pitchers don't even bother to touch the rubber. One member of the Cub staff says he digs a deep hole in front of it and pushes off from there while in the stretch. "It gives an extra foot to my fastball," he says.

Occasionally, a pitcher will try to cheat on his pickoff move, but that's one trick umpires are always on the lookout for. "The important thing is to be consistent," says Pitcher Dave Roberts of the New York Mets, "or else the umpire will call you for a balk." Roberts suggests that a pitcher with a particularly good pickoff move confer with the umpires before the game or even in spring training, just to let them know what to expect. Pirate Reliever Enrique Romo has a very good pickoff move to first, but he's always being called for balks because he doesn't communicate with umpires. When called for a balk, he gets angry, and the umpires only get angrier.

Chicanery isn't confined to players, coaches and managers. Sometimes, the home-team groundkeeper gets in on the dirty dealing. In Kansas City, George Toma makes the batter's box extra large because the Royals like to stand well back. In the early '70s, when the Tigers were very slow afoot, the Detroit ground crew would water down the base paths, particularly the takeoff area next to first, to neutralize the speed of opposing teams. By the same token, fast teams keep hard, fast tracks. Clubs that still play on living fields and have a lot of sinkerball pitchers keep the grass high to slow down ground balls. Good bunting teams keep the foul lines tilted inward. Artificial turf has taken much of the fun out of groundkeeping.

Baseball has come some way from the days when the turn-of-the-century Baltimore Orioles would grab hold of runners' belts to delay their departure from a base or take a shortcut between first and third when the umpire—and there was only one on the base paths at that time—had his back turned. But the rule of thumb still is: if you can get away with it, do it. The fiercest competitor of all, Ty Cobb, once coached in a high school all-star game in Chicago opposite Babe Ruth. Cobb, who had the West team, delivered an impassioned speech to his players about fair play and sportsmanship. Then the players took the field for a workout. Cobb stood behind the catcher and watched his throws. "Very good," said Cobb. "But here's a little trick for you. Just before the pitcher throws, grab a handful of dirt, and after he throws, flip the dirt up into the batter's eyes."

The Sky's
the Limit

♦

B Y   S T E V E   R U S H I N

IN 1991 SPORTS ILLUSTRATED SENT STEVE RUSHIN TO INVESTI-
GATE TORONTO'S SKYDOME, THE SITE OF THAT SEASON'S ALL-
STAR GAME AND PERHAPS THE MOST SOPHISTICATED OF TODAY'S
DOMED STADIUMS. HEREWITH HIS REPORT.

The disembodied head of Mookie Wilson grinned at me as I
came to. Thirty-three feet tall and 25 feet wide, the outfielder's
noggin hovered high above the crowd like a helium-filled bust
broken free from Mount Rushmore. I had passed out in a seat
in the sun after 51 hours of voluntary confinement at SkyDome,
the retractable-roofed restaurant, ballpark, bar, hotel, health
club, cinema, self-contained city and sold-out curiosity shop
that Mookie and the rest of the Toronto Blue Jays call home.
Heat stroke, no doubt, was causing me to hallucinate.

   For three days, I called SkyDome home, viewing a weekend
series of baseball from all those venues that have become so
venerated in the somehow venerable two-year history of the
park that will host baseball's All-Star Game on Tuesday. I
watched from the windows of Windows on SkyDome restaurant in centerfield (Oakland's Jose Canseco tattooed it with a
grand slam on May 22, 1990) and from the Hard Rock Cafe

in right (touched by ex–Blue Jay Fred McGriff, April 23, 1990). I watched from section 540 in the fifth deck, just inside the leftfield foul pole (reached by Canseco's near-600-foot homer, Game 4 of the 1989 American League Championship Series), and I watched through windows of a room at SkyDome Hotel (site of an unidentified couple's inside-the-park home run, May 15, 1990).

I was shown "the brains" of this $583 million building (they're located in its bowels), and I stood on a catwalk 20-some stories above the field as the roof literally brushed my hair while retracting. In short, I explored every superlative feature of SkyDome (never, in stadium literature, "*the* SkyDome"), not the least of which is its amazing, overwhelming, inexhaustible Cholest-O-Plex of snack stands, a collection unlike any other in the world. In fact, I took a culinary tour of them just before, sated, I slipped from consciousness in the sunshine.

Now that I mention it, my vision of Mookie in the Sky above the Diamond may have had something to do with the 18 mini-donuts I snarfed on the heels of a McFrankfurter, which was preceded down my gullet by a Labatt's, which had washed away the Nachos Grande I had consumed for starters. The Nachos Grande is a laundry basket full of chips slathered in "cheez"—I would say from a dozen or more "cowz"—an order so formidable that my sombreroed server told me to enjoy my "meal" after he had the thing hand-trucked from behind the counter for my consumption.

This, I know now, is the gigundo scale on which all things SkyDome are done. For instance: Mookie's giant mug, it turns out, was not an indigestion-induced hallucination after all, but the ballplayer's real life bean projected onto the Sony JumboTron in centerfield, a 110-foot-wide scoreboard three times larger than any other in the world. But that is hardly the beginning. The rest of this SkyJoint is equally....

"Magnificent," murmured 49-year-old Jimmy Riggio of Tampa, as he panned the stadium with his camcorder. "I will never see anything else like this in my lifetime. And I've got it all on videotape for my kids."

A good thing, for Riggio probably couldn't have gotten seats for the kids even if they had made the trip to Toronto. More mammoth than the centerfield Sony is the attendance zenith being approached this year by the division-leading Blue Jays, who had sold out 20 consecutive home games as of Sunday, and who, by season's end, may surpass the absurd attendance frontier of 4,000,000 fans. Last season the Blue Jays drew a major league record—smashing 3,885,284 folks to SkyDome.

Or did SkyDome draw them to the Blue Jays? "I think it's a combination of the two," Jays president Paul Beeston was forced to admit following four consecutive SkyDome sellouts (of 50,000-plus) for a four-game set against the Cleveland Indians, baseball's worst team by a Canadian kilometer. "How does SkyDome compare to Cleveland Stadium?" I asked a man in an Indians cap and T-shirt while the Jays were beating the Tribe in the final game of the series to complete the sweep. "In Cleveland," replied Mike Bennett, 33, of Chatham, Ont., "you call and ask what time the game starts, and they ask you, 'What time can you make it?' An old joke, but it's true."

There are no old jokes about SkyDome, but there are stories that already seem old. And they're true. Indeed, that's the beauty of SkyDome: It's all true. Everything alleged to have happened here actually *happened* here. You can't make this stuff up.

Toronto was playing with the top down on June 7, 1989, when a biblical rain began falling on the Blue Jays and the Milwaukee Brewers. The roof was in the process of being closed, but before the last panel slid into place, the sky opened up. A 20-foot gash, running the width of the stadium, left home plate exposed to the elements. Thus, while the rest of the players on the field remained bone dry, sheets of rain drenched and blinded Toronto batter Lloyd Moseby, Milwaukee catcher Charlie O'Brien and home-plate umpire Rich Garcia, who finally called time and took one step backward, where it wasn't raining a drop. Not so O'Brien, who by habit sprinted from his position behind the plate and didn't stop until he was beneath the shelter of the visitors' dugout.

Shake another tree, out falls another memorable SkyDome moment. Todd Anderson, an assistant manager at Windows, prefers the story of Canseco's 500-foot bomb that landed atop the glass that curves high above the white-clothed tables in the elegant 650-seat restaurant in deepest centerfield. "I watched him hit it," Anderson recalls. "The ball kept coming and coming. Then it just went *boink!* off the glass." When

Anderson says "*Boink!*", an entire shift of busboys gets misty-eyed at the memory.

Windows, by the way, is open for every SkyDome event. Which means that when SkyDome recently hosted a Mötley Crüe concert, ticket holders with reservations in the restaurant could select, say, a $95 bottle of Mumm Cordon Rouge Brut from the champagne list to enhance their enjoyment of the world's consummate heavy-metal band. That is, if any leather-headed customers were so inclined. Which raises the question: Were any leather-headed customers so inclined? "You mean, did anyone sit at the window sipping Perrier?" asks Anderson. "No."

In any event, I've digressed—but barely. For Mötley Crüe and the Blue Jays go together as comfortably as the Blue Jays and those other musicians whose memories are enshrined in the Hard Rock Cafe, built into the third deck in rightfield. Just before the Jays' final game against the Tribe, those of us at the bar in the Hard Rock squinted through the glass and down at the field, where a children's choir sang what was presumably a heartrending rendition of *The Star-Spangled Banner,* except that instead something like *Rock and Roll Hootchie Koo* came from the mouths of these cherubs.

The song was actually coming from the Hard Rock's own sound system, which was then turned off in favor of SkyDome's P.A. system as soon as the children swung into *O Canada.* After Toronto starter Jimmy Key struck out Cleveland's Mike Huff to begin and—these being the Indians—to effectively *end* the game, the attention of some fans in the stadium quickly turned to the baseball trivia quizzes posed on the JumboTron. Those of us in the Hard Rock, however, could learn more substantial stuff by examining the very walls we leaned against. Mine purported to display Jimi Hendrix's actual hotel bill for the three days of Woodstock, during which he stayed at the Hotel Elysée in New York City. At a rate of *$28.62* per night. Now: Would you rather know *that,* or that Matt Merullo committed the last error at Exhibition Stadium?

Joe Ofiara, for one, considers the latter more essential knowledge. The 40-year-old Torontonian has owned Blue Jay season tickets since 1979, when the team played at the Ex. "There are some things about that place I do miss," he says. "You got to know your neighbors then. Here, things are subdued. It's like the corporations have taken over. If you stand up to heckle here, people look at you like, 'What's wrong with *this* guy?'"

"These fans aren't that into it," concurs Blue Jay rightfielder Joe Carter, an erstwhile Indian, who is quick to add: "But they show up 50,000 every night. So I got *no* problem with that."

Many in this land of the low key are still uneasy about celebrating the through-the-roof cost of this complex, which is owned by a partnership made up of government and private investors. Beeston says the money will be recovered five times over in the next 10 years, what with the dough being dropped all over downtown Toronto during each home stand.

And anyway, what's a few hundred mil when it's going toward something that has brought so many together? "I'm not just saying this because I work here," says control room operator Steve MacCormack as he turns on the lights in all 88 SkyDome washrooms with the push of four computer keys in this field-level room that he calls "the brains" of the building. "But there is nothing else like this place anywhere."

"There may never be another one built," says Beeston. "Because of the cost. And that's something that's a part of the Canadian psyche. There are cities in the U.S. where despite the cost, people would say, 'We've got something that no one else has.' But here, we worry about the expense."

Not everyone does, mind you. Many fans *are* into it here, Carter's comment notwithstanding. You *can* get to know your neighbors at SkyDome, Ofiara's complaint aside. The place really *has* brought folks together. Want proof? For $7 you can rent a pair of binoculars at souvenir stands in the ballpark. Then simply point them toward the windows of any of the 70 guest rooms at SkyDome Hotel that face the field.

"Once our guests check in, their room becomes their residence for the duration of their stay," says Gerry Brooks, the hotel's director of marketing and sales. "We cannot infringe upon their privacy." Thus, there is nothing to prevent a repeat of the episode during which wandering SkyDome eyes fell upon that now famous pair of corpulent fans—naked as jaybirds—getting busy in the window of a suite. For one night, the Blue Jays were back at Exhibition Stadium.

The most frightening vista *I* encounter at SkyDome is on my walk around the exterior rim of the roof, on my way to the interior rim of the roof. My roof guide is Scot Muncaster, who looks exactly like Don Mattingly but who is recognized in Toronto as the Guy Who Opens the Roof. "It gets to be a bit much," Muncaster says of the burden he must bear at cocktail parties and such. "I never initiate conversations about it." *It,* of course, is the roof. At 10 a.m., we are going to tear the sucker off SkyDome.

It is usually less dramatic than this. Ordinarily, local TV weatherman Harold Hosein faxes in his forecast, Muncaster phones SkyDome director of stadium operations George Holm with the outlook, and Holm decides with the input of a thousand muckamucks whether or not Muncaster will push the green button in the room marked ROOF CONTROL CENTRE. "This is all it usually comes down to," says Muncaster, finger just above the button.

Today, however, Muncaster will give the green light to an assistant from just beneath the roof, via walkie-talkie. As we near our position, he informs me that I will not be allowed to "ride a panel" as the roof pulls open 31 stories above the artificial turf. I feign disappointment.

Now is the time. Muncaster gives the order. The Guy Who Opens the Roof and I are crouching on a catwalk. The first roof panel silently sweeps open at SkyDome, tousling my hair as it goes by. Sunlight is suddenly being sucked into every corner of the empty ballpark. Handel's *Hallelujah Chorus* is playing in my head. Muncaster, yawning, doesn't seem to hear it.

My
Baseball

♦

BY WILLIAM SAROYAN

WE CLOSE WITH THIS ESSAY BY NOVELIST WILLIAM SAROYAN,
WRITTEN FOR SPORTS ILLUSTRATED ON THE OCCASION OF THE
1956 WORLD SERIES. WE THINK IT CONTINUES TO EXPRESS THE
ESSENCE OF THE GAME.

Baseball is caring. Player and fan alike must care, or there is no
game. If there's no game, there's no pennant race and no
World Series. And for all any of us know there might soon be
no nation at all.

The caring is whole and constant, whether warranted or
hopeless, tender or angry, ribald or reverent. From the first
pitch to the last out the caring continues. With a score of 6–0,
two outs, two strikes, nobody on, only an average batter at
bat, it is still possible, and sometimes necessary, to believe
something can still happen—for the simple reason that it *has*
happened before, and very probably will again. And when it
does, won't that be the day? Isn't that alone almost enough to
live for, assuming there might just be little else? To witness so
pure a demonstration of the unaccountable way by which the
human spirit achieves stunning, unbelievable grandeur?

If the caring isn't for a team (because a team won't come

through, or can't), then for the game itself, the annual ritual, moving with time and the world, the carefully planned and slowly accelerated approach to the great reward—the outcome, the answer, the revelation of the best, the winner.

It is good to care—in any dimension. More Americans put their spare (and purest?) caring into baseball than into anything else I can think of—and most of them put at least a *little* of it there. Most of them know the game is going on all the time, like the tides, and suspect there's a reason, or at least wonder about it. What *is* all the fuss about the whole year, and all the excitement every October? *Is* this a nation of kids, or what? Why not existentialism instead of baseball, for instance? Well, for one thing, you've got to be tired to care for old existentialism, and Americans just aren't ready to be that tired yet. For another, baseball can be trusted, as great art can, and bad art can't, especially as it comes from Hollywood, where sharp dealing is an accepted principle of profit-making. And it doesn't matter that baseball is very, very big business—quite the contrary. That only makes its truth all the more touching and magnificent. It doesn't matter, either, that the great players don't think of baseball as I do, for instance. Why should they? It's enough for them to go after being great and then to *be* great—and then to be no longer able, as time goes by.

I'm devoted to the game, to all of the teams in both leagues and to the World Series, because I don't know of anything better of its kind to be devoted to—and it's always out there with that anonymous crowd of the hungry and faithful, watching and waiting, in the stadium—their eyes on the geometric design of the fresh diamond, all set for the unfolding of another episode in the great drama, which cannot be put anywhere else—not into movies, not onto the stage, not even onto the television screen (although that's pretty good when you're held captive somewhere 3,000 miles away from the great place and the grand moment), not into books, and not even into statistics, although the game has grown on them.

It's a game—the biggest and best and most decent yet. The idea is to win the most games in the American or the National League, and then to go on and win the World Series: to establish a statistic, and tie it forever to the rag-tag experience of a whole people for a whole year.

I happen to be sorry Cincinnati didn't have the pitching, but they look awfully good for next year. It was great, too, the way Pittsburgh took off early in the season and then came back for a moment near the end and very nearly took the soul out of the Dodgers—but didn't, and that's the important thing as far as the Bums are concerned. I'm sorry, too, that Milwaukee got slugged by St. Louis, but you've got to like the Cardinals, too. You've got to like the game. No team is ever willing to stop caring. The fact is they *can't,* and there is the secret of the game's importance and appeal.

It is a tradition that the President throw out the first ball of the season, but somewhere in the bleachers the poets are around, too.

I don't think you'd get Casey Stengel in any arena of human activity other than baseball, and not getting him would be a national disaster, unbeknownst as it might be. Alston, too— another kind entirely. Bragan. Tebbetts. All of them. Fighting it out with their players and their fans, their friends and enemies, umpires and newspapermen but, most of all, facts and figures—statistics. You don't get Sandy Amoros, either, running in from left field as fast as he can go after an inning in which he dropped one he *had* caught—knowing it might cost the team the pennant. Knowing and waiting, and then hitting and saving the damned pennant, and then fielding and saving it, and then hitting and saving it again—knowing, saying nothing, on the theory (some say) that he doesn't speak much English. That could be it, all right, but there could be another theory, too, and the kids know it, and the old men and the old women know it, and the cab drivers and the cops and people in hospitals and penitentiaries and other lonely places. They don't know Sandy—but what he did, they know *that.* And it's a good thing to know. You wouldn't get Robinson, either—from the beginning. Or Williams, twice back from the wars, or the heroic return of Sal Maglie, and all the others, each made great and more deeply human than ever by the game.

Well, is it a game? Is that all it is? So the Dodgers win it again in 1956. So the Yanks win. So what? What good does *that* do the nation? What good does that do the world?

A little good. *Quite* a little.

And there's always next year, too.